Oratory
in action

❊

Published in our
centenary year
～ 2004 ～
MANCHESTER
UNIVERSITY
PRESS

Oratory
in action

edited by

MICHAEL EDWARDS
& CHRISTOPHER REID

❀

Manchester University Press
Manchester & New York

*distributed exclusively in the USA
by Palgrave*

Published by Manchester University Press
Oxford Road, Manchester M13 9NR, UK
and Room 400, 175 Fifth Avenue,
New York, NY 10010, USA
www.manchesteruniversitypress.co.uk

Distributed exclusively in the USA by
Palgrave, 175 Fifth Avenue, New York,
NY 10010, USA

Distributed exclusively in Canada by
UBC Press, University of British Columbia,
2029 West Mall, Vancouver, BC,
Canada V6T 1Z2

*British Library Cataloguing-in-Publication
Data* A catalogue record for this book is
available from the British Library

*Library of Congress Cataloging-in-
Publication Data applied for*

ISBN 0 7190 6280 2 *hardback*
     0 7190 6281 0 *paperback*

First published 2004

11 10 09 08 07 06 05 04   10 9 8 7 6 5 4 3 2 1

Designed in Fournier and Frutiger
by Max Nettleton FCSD
Typeset by Carnegie Publishing Ltd,
Lancaster
Printed in Great Britain
by CPI, Bath

Contents

✳

List of contributors

ALASTAIR BLANSHARD
is Lecturer in Classics, University of Reading

MICHAEL EDWARDS
is Reader in Classics, Queen Mary, University of London

AIDEEN HARTNEY
was a teaching fellow at the University of Bristol

MALCOLM HEATH
is Professor of Greek Language and Literature, University of Leeds

LYNETTE HUNTER
is Professor of the History of Rhetoric, University of Leeds

CHRISTOPHER REID
is Senior Lecturer in English, Queen Mary, University of London

PAUL ROBERTSHAW
is Senior Lecturer in Law, University of Wales Cardiff

MICHAEL SIMPSON
is Lecturer in English, Goldsmiths College, University of London

CHRISTOPHER SMITH
is Senior Fellow, University of East Anglia, Norwich

STEPHEN USHER
was Senior Lecturer in Classics, Royal Holloway, University of London

ELENI VOLONAKI
is Associate Lecturer, Open University

Preface and acknowledgements

✳

The editors would like to thank the staff of the School of English and Drama, Queen Mary, University of London, and of Manchester University Press for their encouragement, patience, and helpful advice during the preparation of this volume.

The editors wish to thank Palgrave for permission to publish a revised version of Michael Simpson's essay, which first appeared in T. Fulford (ed.), *Romanticism and Millenarianism* (2002).

The introductions to Chapters 2–11 were written by the editors.

1

Introduction

MICHAEL EDWARDS
& CHRISTOPHER REID

✳

It has become commonplace today to lament the loss of the arts of eloquence. In our electronic age, it is said, the conditions which once allowed oratory to flourish have all but disappeared. Speech communities have been fractured; the ambitions of political oratory have been trivialised, its passions and arguments reduced to mere sound bites; and the sites of public debate have been privatised and rededicated to the gods of a consumer culture. Striking examples of public speech, such as the Earl Spencer's eulogy on Princess Diana, are greeted with surprise as the last gasps of a dying art rather than as proof of the vitality of the tradition. Where are the eminent speakers who once commanded the platform, roused the noble passions of their audiences, and engaged them in serious debate? Where are the audiences capable of inspiring speakers to such acts of eloquence?

This feeling that oratory is in a state of steep (and perhaps irreversible) decline is a recurrent theme in western rhetoric.[1] Leading historians and rhetoricians of the first century AD – the elder Seneca, Tacitus, Quintilian, 'Longinus' – were united in their belief that oratory had lost its former glories, though they gave different reasons to account for that decline.[2] Some feared that in an age of empire Roman tastes had become so enfeebled by luxury that the language itself had been contaminated and could no longer sustain the manly arts of eloquence. Some blamed the impoverished instruction which aspiring orators received. Where once they had been tested in real conditions, facing 'opponents and rivals fighting with swords of steel, not of wood', they were now content to practise schoolyard declamations, grand-sounding but vacuous, safe from the heat of actual debate.[3] At the heart of many of these first-century explanations of decline (though voiced with cautious indirection) is a political argument which associates the flourishing of eloquence with the cultures and institutions of free states. 'What need of long speeches in the senate?', asks a speaker in Tacitus' *Dialogue on Orators*. 'Our great men swiftly reach agreement. What need of constant harangues to the people? The deliberations of state are not left to the ignorant many – they are the duty of one man, the wisest.'[4] Eloquence, it is implied, is a republican virtue which takes root in the clash of opinion and competitive free speech found in conditions of political liberty. In democracies, says a speaker in 'Longinus'' treatise, 'the availability of political reward sharpens and polishes up orators' talents by giving them exercise; they shine forth, free in a free world'.[5] But in imperial Rome (as earlier in Greece after the Macedonian conquest) these conditions no longer obtained.

Closer to our own time the decline of eloquence was explained in somewhat different terms by the philosopher David Hume. In his essay *Of Eloquence*, first published in 1742, Hume contrasts the transcendent achievements of ancient oratory with the mediocrity of contemporary public speech. Where Demosthenes and Cicero had once mobilised a sublime and impassioned oratory in service of the republic, what passes for eloquence in the modern age is little more, Hume suggests, than 'good sense, delivered in proper expression'.[6] In Hume's view, the British Parliament miserably fails the test of ancient eloquence: it has produced no orator of pre-eminent genius and its rational and argumentative discourse lacks elevation and persuasive force. Politeness and civility, the benefits enjoyed by a modern commercial people, had not come cost-free. What we had lost was the grandeur of the ancient orators, their fertility of invention, and their striking figures of speech: in short, a power of eloquence which not only reminded but in some sense made a nation what it was.

'The ideal of eloquence always refers back to the virtuous eloquence of a former age', concludes an astute commentator on Hume's essay.[7] Not that these narratives of decline are simply nostalgic. What unites them is the belief that the state of eloquence is an index of the present health of the body politic. They return to the ancient examples but they do so in order to speak to the particular concerns of their own time: in imperial Rome, the loss of a republican spirit; in Hume's Britain, a feeling that economic improvement may bring with it a cultural loss; today, perhaps, a growing sense of disconnection from political institutions and a crisis of public accountability. Yet there is undeniably something mythic about the idea of eloquence against which they measure the deficiencies of their own age. The image of the (invariably male) orator who, for good or ill, and by force of words alone, transfixes his audience in a moment of unmediated publicness has long haunted western culture. That image is perhaps most famously celebrated by Cicero near the beginning of his dialogue *De oratore*, when his spokesman, Crassus, declares that

> there is to my mind no more excellent thing than the power, by means of oratory, to get a hold on assemblies of men, win their good will, direct their inclinations wherever the speaker wishes, or divert them from whatever he wishes. In every free nation, and most of all in communities which have attained the enjoyment of peace and tranquillity, this one art has always flourished above the rest and ever reigned supreme.[8]

Rhetoricians have tried to explain this power, and to teach their readers how to perfect the skills required to harness it. For some, however, the power of oratory at its most intense has always been beyond the rule of art and therefore also beyond representation other than by means of a vocabulary of divine ardour and irresistible natural force. 'Longinus' saw Demosthenes as the supreme embodiment of a sublime eloquence which leaped over the normal channels of persuasion and through sheer intensity of impression commanded assent. 'The crash of his thunder, the brilliance of his lightning make all other orators, of all ages, insignificant', 'Longinus' insists. 'It would be easier to open your eyes to an approaching

thunderbolt than to face up to his unremitting emotional blows.'[9] Later observers, struck by the heroic speakers of their day, were to write in similar terms. A Parliamentary witness reported how in the course of a debate in 1777 Edmund Burke attacked his opponent 'with repeated flashes of wit like the forked glare of lightning in a thunderstorm under the line. He was shrivelled under it like a blooming tree after a hurricane.'[10] The novelist Fanny Burney was an avowed supporter of Warren Hastings, Governor-General of Bengal. Nevertheless, during his trial for misgovernment in India, she confided in her diary that she had been almost overcome by the speech with which Burke had opened the case against him in 1789: 'at times I confess, with all that I felt, wished, and thought concerning Mr. Hastings, the whirlwind of [Burke's] eloquence nearly drew me into its vortex'.[11] As this last example suggests, the orator's power has often been experienced and feared as manipulative and coercive. Yet the narratives of decline point to a more positive valuing of eloquence as an integrative power of speech which binds speaker and audience together in a transcending moment of community. When Winston Churchill addressed a gathering of military leaders in France in 1940 his eloquence reportedly carried conviction even to those unfamiliar with his native tongue. According to one eyewitness:

> [Everyone] was deeply moved, carried away by the emotion that surged from Winston Churchill in great torrents. It was not necessary to understand his words

to seize his meaning. The interpreters were silent, it never occurred to them to translate the sentences as they poured from him, hot and passionately sincere. When they did translate, even the pale echo of the original words was formidable as is a great storm passing from sight and hearing beyond a mountain range.[12]

These anecdotes, embroidered though they may be, alert us to some of the powers and possibilities (but also abuses) of public speech which our title – *Oratory in Action* – seeks to capture and the essays in this book try in various ways to understand and illustrate. The studies which follow examine the practice of persuasive speech in a number of historical periods (from classical Athens to the present day) and in a range of locations and spaces: law-courts, pulpits, parliaments, conference halls, newspaper columns, poems, television screens. Underlying the volume, and raised explicitly in the closing chapter, is the question of how far this may still be considered a living tradition. With this in mind, we have chosen to arrange the chapters in roughly chronological order but they could also be read in a sequence governed by genre. Such an ordering would certainly make sense to those familiar with the rhetorical tradition. In the founding text of that tradition, Aristotle proposes that any situation of speech is comprised of three essential factors: the speaker, the subject of the speech, and the audience. On this basis he identifies three kinds of oratory, each of which is characterised by a specific audience function and by a particular reference to time. Thus in some situations, he observes, the audience performs the role of a judge, but in making its judgements it may be asked to look primarily either to the past or to the future. In judicial (or forensic) oratory the audience judges past events and the speaker's role is either to accuse or to defend. In political (or deliberative) oratory the audience judges the expediency of future (or proposed) events and the speaker's role is either to exhort – to urge an advantageous course of action – or to dissuade. In addition to these still very recognisable types, Aristotle describes a third variant of the speech situation where the audience is placed as a spectator rather than as a judge. He has in mind what has come to be known as the 'display' oratory staged on ceremonial occasions (funeral orations and triumphal processions, for example) when the audience is not primarily involved in taking a decision and the speaker's role is to praise (or, much less frequently, to blame). Aristotle called this kind of oratory epideictic (or demonstrative). While epideictic oratory often looks to the past, not least in order to praise the virtues of the departed, its real time is the present moment when those virtues must be renewed and realised rhetorically in the minds of the audience.[13]

Aristotle's scheme exerted a powerful influence over the subsequent development of rhetoric and oratory but like many schemes it is apt to appear overly schematic. It is easy to see, for instance, that both political and forensic oratory often employ the supposedly epideictic form of praise and blame in their speeches. Furthermore, it has often been observed that epideictic itself is less clearly defined than the two other kinds, and indeed historically it has evolved as what Kenneth Burke has described as a 'catch-all' category used to accommodate forms of public speech which fall outside the more strictly drawn limits of political and judicial oratory.[14] If in many ways the chapters in this volume confirm the enduring value of Aristotle's insights, they may also test their practical applicability. Three of the contributors examine examples of forensic oratory in action but they do so in quite different contexts. Eleni Volonaki looks in detail at techniques of persuasion employed by the celebrated Athenian speechwriter Lysias in speeches which sought to bring members of the former Athenian oligarchy to account for their deeds, and in so doing she shows how closely forensic oratory can be intertwined with political functions and themes. Lysias' renown eventually earned him a place in the classical canon of ten Attic orators. The orators with whom Malcolm Heath is concerned have a lesser claim to fame. In the provincial courts of the later Roman Empire, as in our own, speakers were not typically engaged in the prosecution of state criminals of high rank. Nor were the lessons of rhetorical theory necessarily uppermost in their minds when they spoke. Forensic oratory was an everyday business in which the sublimity of a Demosthenes would have been out of

place, and the records which Heath examines bring us unusually close to the cut and thrust of what he calls the 'practical advocacy' of empire. Forensic oratory in modern courts of law consists of a number of distinctive speech acts: the swearing in of the jury, counsels' opening addresses, the examination and cross-examination of witnesses, counsels' closing speeches, the judge's summing up, the jury's verdict. Paul Robertshaw's chapter on the oratory of sentencing pronouncements looks at the final act in this process in what in recent years has been a topical and grisly context – trials of medical murderers – and reminds us that even the apparently most formal language of judicial statement may carry a strong persuasive, ethical, and emotional force.

The familiar image of the judge presiding over the courtroom, and pronouncing sentence over the accused who stands opposite in the dock, alerts us to the importance of the spatial context of forensic oratory. This is the theme of the volume's opening chapter. Alastair Blanshard argues that in order to understand forensic oratory we need to reconstruct the physical environment in which it was delivered. But rhetorical space is not shaped by buildings alone. As Blanshard shows, it is also constructed by ceremony: by the rituals (including rituals of speech) through which the law-court is 'performed into being'. The same may be said of many political assemblies. The British Parliament, though associated historically with a particular set of buildings in

Westminster, can in theory be summoned to meet in almost any convenient place.[15] As its root meaning, 'the action of speaking', suggests, Parliament may be understood as a verbal performance as much as a site. The space of the Commons Chamber ('the little hole into which we are all crammed to make the laws by which this great kingdom is governed', as Cobbett memorably described it),[16] and the ancient rituals which govern its oratorical events, are at the centre of the chapters by Christopher Smith and Christopher Reid. Smith's chapter presents a close-up view of the celebrated maiden speech (a rhetorical ritual – indeed, rite of passage – if ever there was one) delivered by F. E. Smith (later the First Earl of Birkenhead) in 1906, showing how he marshalled his skills as an orator to overcome the challenge of an occasion which had been further complicated by the disadvantageous balance of political forces he found inside the House. When Smith made his Parliamentary debut there were no women members in the Commons. When Margaret Thatcher made hers, more than fifty years later, there were still only twenty-five. As Reid points out in his account of her speaking career, the Commons, like most other debating chambers, retained an indelibly masculine character, and it is against this background that he examines the Iron Lady's negotiations with gendered models of political speech and her creation of a distinctive *ethos* of empowered femininity (on *ethos* and other technical rhetorical terms see the Glossary).

The exclusion of women, both as speakers and auditors, from public address has been a topic of much recent discussion. One place where many women could witness oratory in action, centuries before they were granted political rights, was inside a church. The conduct and spiritual welfare of the women in the congregation, no less than the men, could be the object of the orator's address, as Aideen Hartney shows in her chapter on the celebrated early Christian preacher John Chrysostom. Chrysostom's preaching emerges from Hartney's account as an important example of a revivification of oratory, remaking it for new audiences and new purposes. Christian scholars, well versed in the teachings of classical rhetoric, saw preaching as an appropriation and adaptation of the pagan arts of eloquence, and on that basis classified it as a form of epideictic oratory. Although it may now seem surprising, rhetoricians often placed poetry in the same category, reflecting in part the important public and ceremonial role poetry has played historically. Poetry's decline as a public art is usually thought of as a development of the later eighteenth century. That is the historical moment of Coleridge's long political poem, 'Fears in Solitude', which he wrote in response to the invasion crisis of 1798. As Michael Simpson tells us, Coleridge described 'Fears in Solitude' as 'a sort of middle thing between Poetry and Oratory'. Picking through the poem's many contradictions, not least as a work which seeks to address the nation while signally lacking confidence in that project, Simpson shows how the poem can be read as an anxious meditation on the ethics of persuasion and on the very possibility of meaningful public address at a time of national crisis.

The severance between poetry and oratory which Coleridge's remark assumes was more starkly announced in W. H. Auden's famous statement in his elegy on Yeats that 'poetry makes nothing happen'.[17] In contrast, it might be said, oratory is nothing if it is not language that makes things happen. In the most obvious sense, it is judged by its success or failure in achieving definite legal, political, or broadly ideological outcomes: by securing conviction or acquittal in a court of law, by persuading an assembly to adopt a particular policy, or by strengthening national morale on a ceremonial occasion. One of the commonplaces of classical oratory, as Stephen Usher demonstrates, was *kairos*, which means 'The time for action is now'. Or rather, that is one of its meanings. For, as Usher also shows, *kairos* referred not only to the world of external actions and facts but to the action of the speech itself. Demosthenes, or Churchill, or Thatcher urge their audiences to seize the moment for action but they also need to be able to judge the opportune moment for making such appeals, and the opportune way of preventing them. When to speak and when to stay silent; when to rouse and when to reason; when to adorn and when to say it plain: these things have their proper moment in the temporal order and action of the speech itself. In that sense, as one historian of public debate has recently put it, a speech is more than 'a prelude to an act':[18] it is itself an action, event, or, to return to Auden's idea of poetry, 'a way of happening'. It has an unusually important and pronounced (if also unpredictable) 'perlocutionary' effect, to borrow a term used by speech act theorists to describe the impact of an utterance on the addressee, audience, or reader.

According to one view, a precondition for this perlocutionary power is the orator's capacity to be equally moved. 'I was myself overcome by compassion before I tried to excite it in others', recalls Antonius in Cicero's *De oratore*.[19] Indeed, it was a mark of true eloquence that the speaker should, perhaps involuntarily, be moved not merely by the occasion but by the language and process of the speech itself, 'for the very quality of the diction, employed to stir the feelings of others, stirs the speaker himself even more deeply than any of his hearers'.[20] Modern orators, whether consciously or not, often seem to work on the same assumptions. Think, for example, of Bill Clinton's striking declaration of faith in his address accepting the presidential nomination at the Democratic Convention in 1992: 'I still believe in a place called hope.' Hope (Arkansas) is a place in Clinton's past – his place of birth or at any rate a place conveniently nearby – but it is also a place in, or vision of, his and the nation's future. But hope is a place in another sense: a commonplace, or *topos*, of deliberative and, especially, of Christian epideictic oratory. Clinton, who rose from rural poverty in Arkansas to the steps of the White House, is a product of that place called Hope and living proof that in America hope – the hope that even the disadvantaged can make good – is not a delusory passion. As an argument, this tells us that the man who has not forgotten his roots, and thus embodies the spirit of hope, is a fit person to lead the nation. Although Clinton (or his speechwriter) employs a pun to make his point, this does not mean that it lacks emotion. Far from it: at this confessional moment he proclaims himself moved by his own belief and asks the audience to share that emotion and the values bound up with it. The speaker's emotion leaps the boundary between the platform and the hall, producing a prized moment of connection.

At its most intense, then, oratory may be more than a vehicle for arguments and emotions: it is a morally kinetic action which leaves both audience and speaker something other than they were before the moment of address. Orators are changed because, in effect, they are their own first audiences, the rhetorical creations of their own powers of speech. At the same time, they do not simply address an already existing public. Just as the orator's character is recreated each time he or she mounts the platform, so the public is constituted or summoned into being by the action of the speech itself. Yet, as the earliest commentators understood, constructing a unified public through speech may be a formidable task, not least because even in relatively simple rhetorical situations orators have to address audiences characterised by their diversity. In his dialogue *Phaedrus*, Plato stresses the need for the speaker to have a profound knowledge of his addressee: a knowledge, tantamount to love, of the soul of that person which can perhaps be achieved only in a relationship of one-to-one communication.[21] In his *Rhetoric*, Aristotle considers how orators may deal with the problem of diversity in the larger gatherings they were more likely to have to address. He identifies different kinds of (or different elements within) audiences – the young, the old, the well-born, the wealthy, and so on – and suggests that each of these groups has a general character which the orator must attend to when constructing his arguments.[22] If this diversity was a challenge to the orator in Athens in the fourth century BC, one might ask what hope there is for the orator in an era of mass communication, when the audience may number millions and when those millions are necessarily invisible and practically unknown to the speaker. This is one of the topics of our final chapter. Looking back to the example of Cicero, Lynette Hunter argues that, in its refusal to address the phenomenon of increasing diversity, political speech today limits the possibilities of political engagement and commitment on the part of its audiences. It tries to be all things to all of us, and consequently 'tends to gut the issues of any real debate, to offer to speak for us rather than to us'. In a sense, then, our final essay returns us to the theme of decline with which this introduction began. But, like the volume as a whole, Hunter's chapter shows us that looking back is also a way of looking forward, and that the lessons of oratory's past may allow us to imagine 'a new rhetor for our age'. For classical rhetoricians such as Cicero and Quintilian the skills of public speaking were not optional extras, to be reserved for specialists in speech or for the single-minded few who were preoccupied with cutting a figure on the political or legal stage. They were a fundamental part of the education of a citizen, for eloquence, skill in discourse, was what equipped a person for citizenship and the challenges of being both repsonsible and free. Rhetoric had no particular content; it was what Aristotle characterised as a *technê*, an art or method of thinking and speaking, realised practically in specific contexts, rather than a body of knowledge. For centuries rhetoric remained at the heart of humane learning and oratory, which embodied the lessons of rhetoric, had what might be called

anachronistically a 'cross-disciplinary' appeal. We hope that the chapters which follow, contributed by scholars working in a variety of fields, will help readers from different disciplines – classical studies, literature, history, law, performance studies – recover something of oratory's reach, along with its original sense of common purpose. To that end the volume is in both generic and historical terms deliberately wide-ranging. Each of the chapters focuses on a particular oratorical practice, practitioner, or issue. Since oratorical success depends crucially upon sensitivity to the occasion (and, above all, to the character of the audience), the conditions which shaped the speaker's performance are highlighted. The editors have contributed introductory prefaces to the chapters which draw together the themes of the volume as a whole. It is our view that the action of oratory remains central to human communication and community. We hope that the chapters which follow will inspire further investigation into this vital human activity.

NOTES

1 We use the term 'oratory' in the traditional sense of the *practice* of public speaking. By 'rhetoric' we mean the principles of persuasion described by theorists of public speech and promulgated by teachers in works of instruction.

2 See G. A. Kennedy, *A New History of Classical Rhetoric* (Princeton, 1994), pp. 186–92. The identity of the author of the treatise *On Sublimity* is unknown. For the sake of convenience the traditional attribution to 'Longinus' is retained here.

3 Tacitus, *Dialogue on Orators* 34, as translated in D. A. Russell and M. Winterbottom, *Ancient Literary Criticism* (Oxford, 1972), p. 454.

4 Tacitus, *Dialogue* 41, trans. Russell and Winterbottom, p. 458.

5 'Longinus', *On Sublimity* 44.3, trans. Russell and Winterbottom, p. 501.

6 David Hume, *Essays: Moral, Political, and Literary*, ed. E. F. Miller (Indianapolis, 1985), p. 104.

7 A. Potkay, *The Fate of Eloquence in the Age of Hume* (Ithaca and London, 1994), p. 31. Potkay's important study is of general relevance to the issues discussed in this introduction.

8 Cicero, *On the Orator* 1.8.30, as translated in E. W. Sutton and H. Rackham, *Cicero: De oratore*, 2 vols (Cambridge, Mass., and London, 1942), I.23.

9 'Longinus', *On Sublimity* 34.4, trans. Russell and Winterbottom, p. 494.

10 Cited by D. C. Bryant, 'The contemporary reception of Edmund Burke's speaking', in R. F. Howes (ed.), *Historical Studies in Rhetoric and Rhetoricians* (Ithaca, 1961), pp. 271–93 (p. 284).

11 Cited in G. Carnall and C. Nicholson (eds), *The Impeachment of Warren Hastings: Papers from a Bicentenary Commemoration* (Edinburgh, 1989), p. 11.

12 Brigadier-General Spears, cited in M. Gilbert, *Finest Hour: Winston S. Churchill 1939–41* (London, 1983), pp. 444–5.

13 Aristotle, *Rhetoric* 1.3. See the translation by G. A. Kennedy (New York and Oxford, 1991), pp. 47–51.

14 K. Burke, *A Rhetoric of Motives* (repr. Berkeley and Los Angeles, 1969), p. 70.

15 See A. Hawkyard, 'From Painted Chamber to St. Stephen's Chapel: the meeting places of the House of Commons at Westminster until 1603', in C. Jones and S. Kelsey (eds), *Housing Parliament: Dublin, Edinburgh and Westminster* (Edinburgh, 2002), pp. 62–84.

16 Cited by M. Hastings, *Parliament House: The Chambers of the House of Commons* (London, 1950), p. 115.

17 'In Memory of W. B. Yeats', in E. Mendelson (ed.), *The English Auden: Poems, Essays, & Dramatic Writings, 1927–1939* (London, 1977), pp. 241–3.

18 S. Coleman, *Stilled Tongues: From Soapbox to Soundbite* (London, 1997), p. 147.

19 *De oratore* 2.47.195, trans. Sutton and Rackham, I.339. For a later statement of this point of view see Winston Churchill, 'The scaffolding of rhetoric' (1897), in Randolph S. Churchill, *Winston S. Churchill*, Volume 1, Companion Part 2 (London, 1967), pp. 816–21.

20 *De oratore* 2.46.191, trans. Sutton and Rackham, I.335.

21 In effect, this leads Plato in the *Phaedrus* (269d–277a) to promote dialectic (i.e. argumentation on general issues developed through a pattern of questions and answers involving two interlocutors) over rhetoric. See Plato, *Phaedrus and Letters VII and VIII*, trans. W. Hamilton (Harmondsworth, 1973), pp. 88–99.

22 Aristotle, *Rhetoric* 2.12–17, trans. Kennedy, pp. 164–72.

2

The birth of the law-court: putting ancient and modern forensic rhetoric in its place

ALASTAIR BLANSHARD

✳

Alice had never been in a court of justice before, but she had read about them in books, and she was quite pleased to find that she knew the name of nearly everything there. 'That's the judge,' she said to herself, 'because of his great wig.'
Alice's Adventures in Wonderland

The Athenians of the fifth and fourth centuries BC had a deserved reputation for litigiousness. Only a relatively small number (about one hundred) of the speeches delivered in lawsuits during this period survive, but these cover a wide array of legal procedures. The settings for these trials were also varied. There were, for instance, five separate homicide courts, which heard cases of different kinds of killing. So, intentional homicide was tried in the court of the Areopagus (the 'Hill of Ares'), which met on a rock to the north-west of the Acropolis, whereas those who were already in exile for homicide and then prosecuted for a second killing were tried in a boat off the shore at Phreatto, because they were not permitted to set foot in Attica. Since a killer brought pollution on his community (as is perhaps best known from the plague afflicting Thebes in Sophocles' *Oedipus Tyrannus*), homicide trials were held in the open air. Roofed buildings, however, were used in other trials, again in a variety of locations, though most of the courts, which collectively were called 'dicasteries' (*dikastêria*), were located in the Agora (marketplace). Here, for example, the six junior magistrates, or archons, presided over various trials in the Heliaia (or more correctly Eliaia), a court which may have been in the north-east corner. Other buildings, such as the Stoa Poikile ('Painted Stoa'), did service in a legal capacity, and it was not so much the building itself that defined a courtroom but the rituals that took place within it, as Alastair Blanshard demonstrates in this chapter.

PERFORMANCE MATTERS

There is something dramatic about the law-court. It is a place that lends itself to narratives of good and evil.[1] Plot and motive are key. In criminal cases, prosecutors present us with society's demons – a cast of characters including vicious thugs, unruly youths, and predatory sex offenders. Figures who will inevitably be recast by defence lawyers as blameless innocents: the justifiably provoked; the victims of abuse and poverty; or hapless subjects of unhappy coincidence. Conviction and acquittal will ultimately depend on the ability to produce the more believable narrative of events. Physical evidence functions as a prop to propel the drama forward. Participants need to see the knife, the drugs, and the crime scene. Just like drama, realism can be created by exposing *some* of the dramatic techniques at play in the performance whilst concealing others.[2]

This relationship with drama should stimulate us to think of ways in which techniques for the analysis of drama can be applied to the study of forensic rhetoric. One obvious area is staging. Nobody would ever think of discussing a play as *just* a text. Instead, serious attention is paid to the environment in which the text is situated. All the circumstances of performance (lighting, scenery, seating, time of performance, acoustics, etc.) are subject to critical consideration. In contrast to this detailed analysis, the staging of forensic rhetoric has been a relatively neglected area. This is surprising as the study of forensic rhetoric can clearly benefit from such analysis. We know that environment makes a difference. Sermons heard in the hush of a church get a very different reaction from those blurted out on a street-corner by soap-box preachers to passing shoppers. Prime Ministers get a much better hearing in the House of Commons than they do on the steps of an underfunded hospital. Place legitimates the words of the speaker and controls the audience's reactions. It decides who hears the words, and how they hear them.

Staging is vital for the creation of 'forensic space' – a hallowed place separated off from society where special rules relating to language, argumentation, and conduct are applied in a belief that the application of these rules will produce justice. Here the environment cajoles the audience to be attentive and meditative. It reminds them of their purpose: the dispensation of justice. It supplies them with the criteria to judge the rhetoric that they will encounter. Tests will revolve around believability and proof (e.g. do statements prove facts? can these statements be believed? can we trust this witness?). This keyed-up, suspicious, highly-critical audience is far removed from audiences that we find for other rhetorical genres. No one questions too closely the platitudes of the funeral eulogy. Political invective is applauded for its cleverness, rather than its believability. Sermons demand belief without proof. The exhortation elevates its audience and induces warmth for the speaker.

This chapter attempts to construct a genealogy of forensic space. It is concerned with the practices that bring forensic space into being. It examines how various cultures and periods have constructed forensic space, with a general survey of different types of court buildings followed by a detailed discussion of the ancient Athenian law-courts. By illuminating some of the experience of the audience, it aims to raise issues and concerns that scholars may like to consider in their study of rhetorical texts and their reception. This chapter explores two different strategies for the formation of forensic space. *Monumentalisation* is the first one. Here forensic space is demarcated by edifices for the administration of justice. Huge scale, rich and elaborate fittings, and authoritarian detailing swamp and oppress the viewer. Spatial distinctions establish hierarchies and identify participants. The accused find themselves 'staged' before the prying eyes of the court. Authority resonates through every marble floor, plastered ceiling, and panelled hall.

Prior to the explosion of the practice of legal monumentalisation in the modern period, we find a world where forensic space is often established though *ritual*. It is through this second strategy that the ancient law-courts were set up. Here ritual and pageant serve to create a forensic atmosphere.[3] These rituals transform the environment and transport the participants and viewers to another place. For a short and glorious moment, the law-court comes into being, dispenses justice, and then disappears; only to reappear again at the next staging of the ritual.

Of course, one should not see these strategies as mutually exclusive. There is no strict division between a monumental legal landscape and a ritualised one. It is preferable to discuss the division as one based on predominant trends. Modern law-courts depend heavily on ritual, and are not exclusively housed in salubrious accommodation.[4] Ancient law-courts were not unknown to grand buildings.

PALACES OF JUSTICE

For lovers of Victorian Gothic architecture, the exhibition of designs for the New Royal Courts of Justice that opened on 8 February 1867 represents

1 View of Burges's entry for the London Law Courts Competition (1866). Courtesy of
RIBA Library Photographic Collection

a high-point (figure 1). Architecturally, it marked the stylistic domination
of Gothic over classicism with all competitors choosing to work in Gothic.
Visitors to the exhibition were treated to the castellated, whimsical, French
fantasy of Burges; the vast concourses and façadelike interiors of Water-
house; the traceried towers and massive central hall, two hundred feet high,
of Brandon; the excessively ecclesiastical design, with its dry symmetry
and balanced façade, of Lockwood; the classically tempered Gothic of
Gilbert Scott ornamented with a dome encrusted in Byzantine mosaics; and
the long façades, terminal climaxes, perfect roofline and imposing record
tower of the eventual winner and architect, G. E. Street.[5] However, in their
'plans ten times more intricate and incomprehensible than the Labyrinth
of Greece',[6] these buildings are not only 'the last great, contradiction-ridden
monument of the High Victorian Gothic'.[7] They also represent the climax
in the process of the monumentalisation of the law-court.[8]

The gradual consolidation of the law-courts into monumental spaces
designed exclusively for judicial use had been occurring throughout the
eighteenth and nineteenth centuries.[9] The competition itself was the result
of a Commission that recommended the amalgamation of eighteen separate
courts and twenty-two legal offices and chambers.[10] In choosing to work
in such a grand style, Street's Royal Courts of Justice is the logical extension

of a trend which had produced Dance's Old Bailey Session House (1778), Sloane's extension to Westminster Hall (1826), Elmes's Liverpool Assizes (1840), Barry's proposal for new Courts of Chancery (1840–41), and Gilbert Scott's design for Chancery Courts at Lincoln's Inn (1859).[11] A similar trend can be noticed in France with the Premier Grand Prix designs for law-courts by Bernard (1782), Blouet (1821), and Labrouste (1824) forming precursors to renovation of the Palais de Justice (1852–59) by Louis Duc.[12] Given such momentum, it is easy to understand the rallying-cry that 'Justice is entitled to be lodged in a palace' which ushered in the proposal for new law-courts.[13] The momentousness (and novelty) of the opening of the Royal Courts of Justice was not lost on *The Times*:

> The occasion ... is more than the simple opening of a building ... *It is the opening of a new era in the history of English Justice* ... for the first time since the rule of the Plantagenets, or rather the Angevins, the country will see consolidated in living and visible unity the heterogeneous mass of judicial bodies, each of which for so many centuries has had its own divergent history.[14]

Nor did the trend stop with the Royal Courts. In 1907, the 'New' Old Bailey opened. It is characterised by similar sumptuous design: facing of Portland stone with Cornish granite base; monumental staircase; Austrian oak panelling for the law-courts; all floors and corridors laid with Sicilian marble; a 67-foot dome adorned with lunettes showing allegorical paintings (Labour, Art, Wisdom, Truth); the pendentives of the dome incorporating sculpted reliefs; and – crowning the structure – the famous 12-foot high 'Lady of Justice', gilded with 87,000 sq. in. of gold leaf, which requires regilding every five years.[15]

A similar pattern occurred in the United States. Throughout the country, temporary, multi-function structures were replaced with purpose-built (often neoclassical) court-houses.[16] It is most strikingly observed in Washington. From 1810 onwards, the Supreme Court found itself in increasingly impressive surroundings. Latrobe's ambitiously vaulted court chamber (1819) was superseded by a move to the elegantly renovated Old Senate Chamber (1860).[17] However, none of these precursors can rival the court's final home – Cass Gilbert's neoclassical Supreme Court building (1935). This edifice built in the Beaux-Arts tradition combines monumental scale with extensive symbolism.[18] From the moment spectators approach the building, they are plunged into a complex world of allegory and didactic detailing. Guarding the entrance with their impassive gaze are James Earle

Fraser's super-life-size couple, *Contemplation of Justice* (woman resting her hand on a book of law whilst holding in the other a small figure of *Blind Justice*) and *Authority of Law* (man holding tablet of laws and sheathed sword). Above them rears the Corinthian portico of the court building. Each column is topped with an American eagle (as if the Corinthian order was not elaborate enough) and the structure is surmounted with Robert Ingersoll Aitkin's pedimental sculptural group, *Liberty Enthroned Guarded by Order and Authority*. Here Liberty flanked by Order and Authority (depicted respectively as a medieval knight and a lictor in military uniform carrying the fasces) gazes out to the distance while around her various figures representing aspects of Council and Research debate amongst themselves. In case the viewer is left in any doubt about what to make of this assemblage, the entablature spells out the guarantee, 'Equal Justice Under Law'. However, before access can be gained to such justice, petitioners have to suffer a history lesson. The entrance is comprised of two massive 6-ton bronze doors designed by Gilbert. Here, in eight panels, the evolution of the law is depicted. Beginning with the Shield of Achilles, the spectator travels through legal history and arrives at the crucial *Marbury* v. *Madison* opinion via the praetors of Rome, the codification of Justinian, and the signing of the Magna Carta. This same level of detailing is continued throughout the building. Portraits of Justinian keep a watchful eye in the library on modern law-makers. At every turn elements of legal symbolism can be found. Even the bronze elevator doors have their lintels adorned with the tablets of Moses. The viewer comes finally to the east pediment where Moses, Confucius, and Solon look approvingly down at the work of modern law-givers. Aesop, presumably too ugly to be allowed to mar the beauty of this tableau, has his wisdom acknowledged by the tortoise and hare in the right-hand corner – justice may be slow, but its course is sure.

The effect that this monumentalisation has produced on the conception of the court and the social practice surrounding courts should not be underestimated. The effect of the transition to a new neoclassical courthouse was observed by Judge Brietel, Chief Judge of the Court of Appeals:

Many years ago, grand juries of New York County used to hold their sessions in the old criminal court building ... They were old buildings. They were in disrepair. They were not too clean ... In the waiting rooms outside the grand jury rooms the witnesses from all walks of life, usually from the most humble levels, would assemble and wait ... While waiting the group would be noisy, engaging in voluble conversation, eating and drinking, and littering the room with the newspapers with which many of them sought to occupy their waiting time. Those waiting rooms were not places of dignity, let alone comfort.

In 1941, the new criminal court building ... was completed. It was ... a shining-clean, even immaculate, building. It was a great building ...

The thing that was remarkable ... was the strange change in the behavior of the witnesses ... Voices were subdued. Newspapers were read, but they did not become the ugly litter of an earlier day. Food and drink were not consumed by the waiting witnesses, because they feared to sully the quarters in which they were waiting.

No one told these people that they should keep their voices subdued. No one told them that they should abstain from food and drink while waiting. They just did so. [19]

Here architecture conditions the response of individuals. The gleaming marble and neoclassical façade function as means of oppressively disciplining individuals' actions and restricting their movements. We need to bear these considerations in mind when thinking about the rhetoric of the modern courtroom. The audience has already been given a series of important lessons even before a single word has been uttered. Dignity, authority, and power have already been impressed upon them. They have been reminded that history and the constitution are at stake in the proceedings. Justice may be blind, but all participants can feel her breath on the back of their necks.

LEGAL PAGEANTS

Modern courts are involved in a form of deceit. Their architecture bespeaks permanence and tradition. Yet, it is a tradition of recent invention. We should never forget the 'neo' which prefixes their architectural styles (classical, Gothic, etc.). Examination of legal practice prior to the era of the 'great courts' reveals a different picture. The legal topography prior to the construction of the Royal Courts of Justice in Cary Street was entirely dissimilar. In place of designated courts and clear, demarcated boundaries, we are presented with makeshift structures and a pattern of use characterised by overlapping of function.[20] There was little consistency in court size, design, or layout.[21] The court of the Vice-Chancellors was an adapted store-room.[22] The Equity courts met in temporary removable courtrooms in the Lincoln's Inn dining hall,[23] the same hall that functioned as a theatre for revels, masques and plays.[24] The Session House of the Old Bailey was available for rent by 'honest freemen' of the city.[25] Such arrangements were not without problems:

> Those who were unfortunate enough to have business in the Court of the Queen's Bench on June 14, must have been deeply scandalized at the manner in which the court was hustled from one place to another until it found rest for its weary foot in a little room in some out-of-the way part of the building.
>
> It had been announced that the Q. B. would hold its sittings in the Bail Court, a wretched enough place, but this court happened to be occupied by Mr. Justice Mellor as a second court of *Nisi Prius*; consequently the Q. B. had to find some other place of sitting, and the only available room was a mere shed occasionally used by one of the Vice-Chancellors, where, though the learned Judges were in the shade, the Bar and those in the body of the room were scorched by the heat of the sun.[26]

We find a similar pattern of use in the United States, with courts being held in town halls, private homes, taverns, schoolhouses, government offices, and sharing premises with agricultural fairs and travelling picture exhibitions.[27] Nor is this pattern entirely anachronistic. A recent survey of Magistrates' and County courts (the courts that perform the vast bulk of legal work) in England and Wales concluded that most courts were difficult to find, and not well signposted. The majority of County courts are housed in buildings that are described as either 'insignificant' or 'non-descript'. Overwhelmingly, the courts are not single-purpose buildings, but are housed in multi-purpose spaces.[28]

The evidence suggests that the model of the court as an institution that is topographically fixed and has exclusive spatial jurisdiction is a recent historical construction. For large stretches of history, courts were institutions that occupied temporary and variable spaces. This does not mean that they were without significance. It is a modern misconception that only permanence and grandeur guarantee authority. Despite the fact that they were held in hired rooms and covered places and were only annual events, the great criminal trials at the Old Bailey of the thirteenth and fourteenth centuries were spectacles of authority and power attracting large crowds.[29]

This authority and power derived not from architecture but from performance. Courts were physically 'performed into being'. Court ceremony assisted by various props demarcated spatial divisions, identified participants, and conditioned speech.[30] An example of such performance is found in the travelling Assizes – the periodic sessions of the High Court held in each county of England and Wales. The (actual?) court business was preceded by a procession composed of trumpeters, the sheriff and his bailiff, local officers and gentry, pikemen, and liverymen specially clothed for the occasion. This procession was accompanied by bells, music, and a Latin oration. The robed judge would process, accompanied by the sheriff, into the local church for a special Assizes sermon delivered by the sheriff's chaplain. The judge would then process to the court-house, in which the various officers of the court would arrange themselves in rank of seniority. At this point, the crier would enjoin silence. The 'Commission of the Court' issued by the Crown was read and, in a performance of the symbolic order, the calendar of all county officials was called (mayors, justices of the peace, coroners, stewards, constables, bailiffs, etc.). This was followed by the swearing in of the 'grand' jury. The performance climaxed in the judge reading the 'solemn charge' – a panegyric to law, justice, and the supremacy of the Crown peppered with classical, literary, historical, and political allusions.[31] These elaborate preliminaries to these sessions served to transform (suspend disbelief in) the often shabby, cramped, insufficient, conditions of most courts.[32] Indeed, such elaborate ceremony was often at odds with the legal work which needed to be conducted:

> [We are often treated to] the spectacle of a highly trained and paid judge of the High Court making a stately progress through these counties accompanied by all the paraphernalia of sheriffs, chaplains, marshals, associates, clerks, trumpeters, javelin-men; grand juries are assembled; special and common juries are selected and summoned; and after all this preparation, the only cases to be tried are a few paltry larcenies or misdemeanors ... and either no civil business at all, or a few trumpery cases.[33]

However, it must be remembered that practical legal work was only partially the concern of these courts. They fulfilled important symbolic functions and, as representatives of the Crown, the power of the State was (re)inscribed every time they came into being.[34]

CLASSICAL RITUAL

It is this ritualistic strategy for the creation of forensic space that predominates at the birth of forensic rhetoric in Greece. One of the striking features of forensic rhetoric is that, unlike every other type of public performance within Athens, it is impossible to locate it within a specific architectural environment. For every other type of performance, whether it is comedy, tragedy, dithyrambs, or even other types of rhetoric, we can describe, with a reasonable amount of consistency, its topographical location and the nature of its architectural environment.[35] Forensic rhetoric provides the exception. In Athens, this 'city of theatres', the law-court has no real place to lay its platform. Trying to define what constituted in architectural terms a *dikastêrion* (law-court) is a difficult problem.[36] Even if we separate out the highly individualistic homicide courts, it is impossible to generalise about the remaining jury courts.[37] As with the primitive courts of England, Wales, France, and America, two aspects are distinctive about the architecture of these sites – firstly the extraordinary range of sites and types of buildings used to house law-courts; and secondly the often multi-functional nature of these sites.

Our literary records detail at least eighteen different designations for law-courts. These designations follow a variety of patterns. We have courts named after people (Kallion, Metiocheion), places (Odeion, Painted Stoa, 'against the walls', 'First', 'Middle', 'near Lykos'), physical descriptions ('pushed-in', 'greater', 'triangle'), colours (Batrachioun (the Frog Court), Phoinikioun (the Crimson Court)), officials ('of the Eleven', 'of the Archon') and age ('new'). This complex nomenclature has been the subject of several generally inconclusive studies.[38] It is not clear how many courts were operational, as a number of names may refer to the same court. Recent studies have tended to favour a relatively minimalist position of five or fewer actual buildings being used as courts.[39]

However, this minimal position is far from certain. For example, even the two sites most commonly rejected from our literary record, the Ardettos Hill and the Theseion, cannot be ruled out entirely.[40] The Ardettos Hill, while recorded as a law-court only in an oddly phrased passage in the second-century AD writer Pollux, has strong juridical connections as the site for the administration of the so-called heliastic oath taken annually by jurors.[41] Additionally, it is near the site of the homicide court at the sanctuary of Pallas Athena and Zeus.[42] Similarly, the description of a court at the Theseion occurs only in late sources: the ninth-century AD lexicon of Photios and *Etymologicum magnum*. However, we know of parallel cases of courts near or in shrines: most obviously the Palladion and the Delphinion. It was clearly an important civic building, being decorated with noteworthy images of Athenians fighting Amazons, the battle of Lapiths and Centaurs and other scenes from the life of Theseus.[43] We can trace with certainty its use as a council and assembly chamber.[44] It was used as the site for the allocation of magistracies to the Thesmothetai.[45] Moreover, it seems to be associated with the Shrine of the Erinyes as a place of sanctuary, especially for slaves.[46] It may be the case that it was used as a law-court only to judge cases involving slaves who sought sanctuary there.[47] Even a cursory survey of the known and possible sites indicates the problems with generalisation.

In his recent study, *The Lawcourts at Athens*, Boegehold identifies a number of buildings dotted throughout Athens which were used as law-courts. Literary and epigraphic sources identify the Odeion of Pericles, the Painted Stoa, and the Stoa of Zeus as all having judicial associations, while another site, the *poros* (limestone) benches on the side of the Kolonos Agoraios, is possibly alluded to as a court in a comedy by Aristophanes.[48] Archaeological excavation has provided strong evidence that the buildings under the Stoa of Attalos (Buildings A–D) were extensively used as law-courts in the fourth century BC, the period that produced most of our surviving examples of Greek forensic oratory.

There are two striking facts about the identified sites for law-courts. Firstly they are often characterised by a pattern of use where one sole function fails to predominate. They are self-consciously multi-functional buildings. Secondly there is a complete lack of uniformity in design. They vary tremendously in size, shape, and floor plan. The Odeion, Stoa Poikile, the Stoa of Zeus, and Buildings B and C were roofed. Building A and the *poros* benches were not. The Odeion and the Stoas were distinctive, important buildings that were defined in terms of different and specifically non-legal features – the Stoa by its paintings and the Odeion by its fabulous roof shaped in the form of a Persian tent.[49] Buildings A–D were plain, undecorated, and were a shoddy construction put together with second-hand materials (figure 2).[50] The picture becomes even more blurred once we include the *poros* benches, from which Hansen observes: 'it follows that the architectural setting of the Athenian *dikasteria* was indeed inconspicuous and as far removed from monumental architecture as anything can be'.[51]

It is hardly surprising that, when Athenians thought about law-courts, they rarely thought about places or buildings. Instead, law-courts to them were symbolised by legal equipment and procedure. Great emphasis was placed on the transformative power of court paraphernalia. They were the props that underpinned the performances that transformed stoa, odeion,

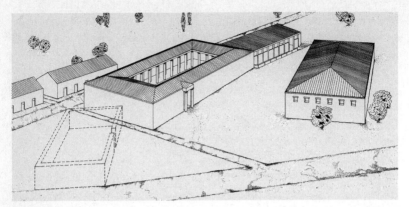

2 Reconstruction of buildings identified as fourth-century Athenian law-courts (published in R. F. Townsend, *Athenian Agora XXVII: The East Side of the Agora: The Remains beneath the Stoa of Attalus* (Princeton, 1995). Courtesy of American School of Classical Studies at Athens: Agora Excavations)

square peristyle or open-air bench into a law-court. Like the temporary screens and benches of the Courts of Chancery in Lincoln's Inn, the travelling Assizes, the provincial *parlements* of France, or the rural court sessions of the United States, the Athenian court is demarcated by a series of temporary and movable fences (*truphaktoi*) and lattice-work gates (*kinklides*). These served to demarcate the court from the outside world and subdivide the jury from the officials and speakers.[52] They were flimsy structures whose strength lay not in their structural soundness but in their role as social markers.[53]

Within this space, the presence of the court was further signified by the large amount of court equipment (water-clocks, hoppers, urns, trays, staves, painted boards, etc.). In his lexicon of rhetorical terms, Pollux lists numerous separate items that are found in law-courts.[54] Comics played with the peculiarity of the material. In a fragment of *Olbia* by Eubulus (Frag. 74 *Poetae comici graeci*), the poet jokes that in Athens different types of legal equipment are as plentiful and varied as the fresh produce in its market. The significance of this equipment is demonstrated by Aristophanes in the 'court scene' in the *Wasps* (805–1008). The scene begins farcically with much humour derived from the comic substitution of domestic goods for various features of the law-court (819–62). Bdelycleon turns a slave into the hero Lykos, wooden boards into noticeboards, a pig-pen into barriers and screens, and ladling jugs into voting urns. Even Philocleon joins into the spirit of the scene, transforming his chamber-pot into a water-clock. It is only when all this has occurred that Philocleon will recognise the place as a court and the trial can begin. On one level, this scene plays humorously with the idea of the collapse of public and private spaces.[55] However, like much humour, these jokes are based on unease. Part of this unease comes not just from the distinctions between public and private spaces but from the ease with which these boundaries can be elided. The scene is a comment on the portability of the court and its lack of permanence. The joke is not just that the court should not easily or readily be in a private house, it is also that it *can* easily or readily be in a house. This point is emphasised to the audience by Philocleon's exclamation at Bdelycleon's ingenuity: 'You've come up with a good and very local solution' (859). Here 'local' (*epichôriôs*) brings it home to the audience that this is a particularly Athenian problem.

However, it was not just props and lattice fences which created the law-court. Its *real* presence came not through physical objects but through the elaborate ceremonies which performed it into existence. The most complete and elaborate description of these ceremonies is contained in the pseudo-Aristotelian *Athenaion politeia*.[56] The performance it describes represents the culmination in a trend towards greater complexity that had been building since the inception of the court.[57]

The performance began early on the day of the court sessions. From the common store officials removed the equipment needed for court business and processed to the various tribal meeting points around the law-courts.[58] Water was fetched from a special fountain adorned with a bronze statue of a lion.[59] Each piece of equipment was marked with the name of the tribe to which it belonged.[60] This division of men and equipment by tribe is the first sign (although the motif is often repeated throughout the performance) that this is an event where every element of the citizen body will be represented. The next step was the designation of buildings as courts and the allotment of a letter to them as an administrative device. This procedure of 'naming the courts' was conducted by the Thesmothetai, who balloted out to each location a letter from lambda onwards depending on the number of courts required. With due ceremony, a large, public representation of this letter was borne by an attendant to each location.[61]

Meanwhile, at ten separate locations, potential jurors and court officials had gathered, according to tribe, to conduct the procedure for the selection of their tribal contribution to the jury panel. This procedure, described in

Ath. pol. 63–6, became intelligible only with Dow's (1939) reconstruction of the sorting machine.[62] With its elaborate ceremony, complex equipment (twenty sorting machines, twenty urns [*hydriai*], over one hundred boxes, thousands of coloured staves and inscribed tokens),[63] and constant reliance on the ever-so-democratic procedure of allotment,[64] the performance goes far beyond the practical requirements for the prevention of jury-stacking. The selection procedure created a sense of occasion that was stoked by the juror's tensions about potential selection or rejection.

The first step in the procedure involves the jurors placing their allotment token, according to the letter stamped on it, into one of the ten boxes (*Ath. pol.* 64.1). The symbolic relationship between a juror and his allotment token should not be underplayed. It was a public symbol of his status in the city. This long thin strip of metal designated his name, identified his father and deme, and indicated that he was over thirty, and enjoyed full political and economic freedom, neither being in debt to the Treasury nor suffering loss of citizenship (*Ath. pol.* 63.3). The stamped seals demonstrated the city's endorsement of his right to act as a juror or magistrate.[65] This strong relationship between a man's identity and his allotment token is indicated by Mantitheus's complaint that to allow his half-brother to use his name is the equivalent of giving him the use of his token (Dem. 39.10–12). This relationship continued even after death, with many Athenians taking the extraordinary (and illegal) step of being buried with their allotment tokens. Such an act has obvious ideological implications, as Kroll notes: 'it is hard to think of a more appropriate symbol of an Athenian's nearly professional involvement in democratic government. In heroic times the Greek aristocrat was buried with his bronze sword and armor; in the quieter, democratic fourth century an Athenian might be buried with his bronze allotment plate.'[66]

The charged and important nature of these objects was reflected in the allotment procedure. After the potential jurors had placed their allotment tokens in the correct box, the Thesmothetes would select one from each container. These men, as representatives of their tribal jury division, were charged with loading the sorting machines with the allotment tokens of the other members of their division (*Ath. pol.* 64.2). These hundred men (ten per tribe) were automatically selected as jurors (*Ath. pol.* 64.3). Once the sorting machine was loaded, the Thesmothetes would pour black and white balls into a funnel connected to a tube from which he would draw them out at the bottom.[67] The colour of each ball determined whether a row of allotment tokens was accepted or rejected (white for acceptance, black for rejection). The result of each successful selection was announced by a herald (*Ath. pol.* 64.3).[68] As it seems that only the names of those successfully chosen were announced, and because once the allotment tokens were loaded into the sorting machine it was impossible to see any individual's name, potential jurors were left in suspense about their chances of selection until the final drawing. This selection of jurors was followed by an equally complicated procedure involving sorting machines for assigning magistrates to various courts (*Ath. pol.* 66.1).

After his selection, the juror passed through a lattice-gate and received his staff of office and a token (lit. 'acorn') that indicated the court to which he had been assigned. This assignation was also indicated by the colour of his staff that mirrored the various colours of the painted lintels on the doorways of the courts (*Ath. pol.* 65.2). These staves served to signify the office of juror. Moreover, the redundant colouring served to tie that office to a specific place.[69] The symbolic function of the staff is signified by the fact that if the jurors, after delivering a vote of 'guilty', had to listen to speeches about the severity of their penalty, they reclaimed their staff in order to process into the courtroom (*Ath. pol.* 69.2). Without their staves, they were not properly jurors. Demosthenes reminds the juror of the consequences of receiving his staff: 'Whenever you come to judge public cases, you must ponder that each of you receives the pride of Athens, when you take up your staff and badge' (Dem. 18.210).

Once he had processed to the courtroom, the juror's token was checked and he was assigned a seat.[70] This random seat-allocation was the culmination of a procedure of isolating the juror. After initially assembling in his tribal group, he found himself increasingly removed from his compatriots and normal 'networks of social association'. After the court was full, the magistrates selected (again by lot) ten jurors: one to be in charge of the water-clock (as a sign of which the juror received a symbolic hammer), four to be in charge of the voting, and five to handle the return of allotment tokens,[71] and the distribution of jury pay; this dispersal occurring by tribe (*Ath. pol.* 66.2–3). At this point, some sort of visual signal was given,[72] the herald announced the case, and the litigants and their supporters processed in and took up their position by their respective platforms. The law-court was now properly constituted and could begin business.

Throughout this account, I have tried to stress the highly elaborate, performative nature of these preliminaries. They go far beyond any practical purpose. Instead, I propose that they served to inscribe the court into the Attic topography. Given the temporary, and variable, nature of the built environment of the law-courts, this inscription was otherwise impossible to achieve. Ritual builds a law-court as strong and clearly defined as one of marble or Portland stone.

FINAL SUBMISSIONS

Law-courts are not neutral spaces. They prime their audiences and feed their expectations. If we wish to understand the dynamics of forensic rhetoric, we need to be attuned to the implications of such activities. When assessing courtroom rhetoric, scholars should consider the entire judicial atmosphere. Audiences will have been through a number of rituals and exposed to a variety of different experiences. All participants in the court utilise and respond to their environment. Space can be manipulated and coloured. Architecture induces ideas. The distance between jury and accused can highlight the abnormality of alleged criminals or exaggerate their isolation and defencelessness. Juries, guided by advocates, decide whether they want to bridge that gap or extend it. Scales and images of *Blind Justice* remind the jury that the weight of every word needs to be weighed. The judge is excluded from this process. The authority of the judge's words is guaranteed by his position: seated on his bench, the words come literally from 'on high'.

Similarly the performance of rhetoric in the premodern period was coloured by the rituals which had preceded it. The fanfare that accompanied the travelling Assizes reminded communities that they were part of a much larger network of authority, rule, and privilege. They provided an opportunity for the centre to speak to the periphery. The rulings of the court form part of a dense weave of other speech acts – oaths, sermons, and panegyrics. A full range of rhetorical exempla was paraded before an admiring audience. Forensic rhetoric did not stand alone, but was incorporated within a number of other genres. This blending results in a product that is firmly embedded in a particular time and place. It needs to be appreciated in its surroundings. To do otherwise would mean losing verbal and thematic echoes, added depth, and potential contradictory messages and moments of audience resistance.

A similar consideration confronts the reader of ancient forensic rhetoric. To understand this material, readers need to embed themselves in the jurors' experience – see through their eyes, hear through their ears. The juror listened to speeches in a packed courtroom crammed on benches with a number of his fellow citizens. To get there he had undergone a number of elaborate rituals. Fate has singled out the juror and chosen him to perform this civic duty. He formed part of a tribal delegation sent to administer justice. He felt his authority and the burdens he carried with it as he processed with his staff through the marketplace of Athens. The interest of the city has been shown by the busy activities of the Thesmothetai. As he arrived at his destination, he often found himself in a place with a variety of theatrical, philosophic, or administrative associations. Each of these jostled with the duty he now had to perform. A duty upon which, every ritual and speaker constantly reminded him, hung the future of the state. He was steeled for drama, not light entertainment.

NOTES

1 On the role of narrative, drama, and story-telling in the modern law-court see P. Brooks and P. Gewirtz (eds), *Law's Stories: Narrative and Rhetoric in the Law* (New Haven and London, 1996). For ancient parallels see E. Hall, 'Lawcourt dramas: the power of performance in Greek forensic oratory', *Bulletin of the Institute of Classical Studies*, 40 (1995), 39–58.

2 For an example of the advantages an advocate can gain from exposing the 'dramatic' conventions of the court-room see A. M. Dershowitz, 'Life is not a dramatic narrative', in Brooks and Gewirtz (eds), *Law's Stories*, pp. 99–105.

3 The role of public ceremonies in defining and creating civic space and identity has been explored recently in Roman imperial Ephesus by G. M. Rogers, *The Sacred Identity of Ephesos: Foundation Myths of a Roman City* (London, 1991), pp. 80–126. Similar studies have been attempted for different periods and places: see E. Muir, *Civic Ritual in Renaissance Venice* (Princeton, 1981), pp. 185–211; N. Davis, 'The sacred and the body social in sixteenth-century Lyon', *Past & Present*, 90 (1981), 40–70; R. Trexler, 'Ritual behaviour in Renaissance Florence: the setting', *Medievalia et Humanistica*, new series 4 (1973), 125–44; and R. Darnton, *The Great Cat Massacre and Other Episodes in French Cultural History* (New York, 1984), pp. 107–43.

4 The obvious exceptions in the UK are Magistrates' Courts (see discussion below). These perform the bulk of legal business and yet are often housed in unprepossessing buildings. However, even these courts are not without aspirations for greater things – see the guidelines laid out in the Magistrates' Courts design guide published by the Home Office (Central Building Services – Design Research and Advisory Unit) in 1991.

5 For an account of the competition and the entries see D. B. Brownlee, *The Law Courts: The Architecture of George Edmund Street* (New York, 1984), pp. 104–50. Further discussion is provided in J. Kinnard, 'G. E. Street, the Law-Courts and the "seventies"',

in P. Ferriday (ed.), *Victorian Architecture* (London, 1963), pp. 221–34; M. H. Port, 'The new law courts competition, 1866–67', *Architectural History*, 11 (1968), 75–93; and J. Summerson, 'A Victorian competition: the Royal Courts of Justice', in *Victorian Architecture: Four Studies in Evaluation* (New York, 1970), pp. 77–117.

6 *The Times* (19 November 1867), p. 6.

7 Brownlee, *The Law Courts*, p. 102.

8 Cf. the judgement of B. Abel-Smith and R. Stevens, *Lawyers and the Courts: A Sociological Study of the English Legal System, 1750–1965* (London, 1967), p. 80: 'A design intended more to enhance the status of the judges than to suit the convenience of litigants'. They quote Baron Huddleston (p. 80 n. 3): 'Among its beauties three might be singled out: the courts were constructed so that counsel could not hear the judges, the judge could not hear the witness, and the jury could hear neither.'

9 This trend mimics the gradual consolidation of power toward the courts of Common Law with the decline (through rationalisation and centralisation) of the courts of Equity, Admiralty, and the Ecclesiastical Courts. For an account of this trend see W. S. Holdsworth, *History of English Law*, rev. edn, ed. A. L. Goodhart and H. G. Hanbury, 16 vols (London, 1964), I. 633–50. The new Royal Law Courts are symbols of that triumph. On the nineteenth century as the period which sees the greatest sustained attack on legal pluralism see H. W. Arthurs, 'Special courts, special law: legal pluralism in nineteenth century England', in G. R. Rubin and D. Sugarman (eds), *Law, Economy and Society, 1750–1914: Essays in the History of English Law* (Abingdon, 1984), pp. 380–411, who records that prior to the reforms of the nineteenth century 'apart from arbitrators, domestic tribunals, administrative tribunals and justices of the peace, over 300 local courts actively exercised [effectively independent] jurisdiction as late as 1830' (pp. 380–1).

10 'Report of the Commissioners Appointed to Inquire into the Expediency of Bringing together into One Place or Neighbourhood All the Superior Courts of Law and Equity, the Probate and Divorce Courts, and the High Court of the Admiralty, and the Various Offices Belonging to the Same; and into the Means which Exist or May Be Supplied for Providing a Site or Sites, and for Erecting Suitable Buildings, for Carrying out this Object', *British Parliamentary Papers*, vol. 31 (1860).

11 This trend is traced in Brownlee, *The Law Courts*, pp. 37–83.

12 For the Premier Grand Prix designs see L.-P. Baltard and A.-L.-T. Vaudoyer, *Grand Prix d'architecture couronnés par l'Académie Royale des Beaux-Arts de France* (Paris, 1834).

13 'The law and lawyers', *Law Times* (29 January 1859), p. 217.

14 *The Times* (2 December 1882), p. 6 (my emphasis).

15 For specifications see S. Jackson, *The Old Bailey* (London, 1978), pp. 119–20.

16 For example see the studies of H. A. Johnson and R. K. Andrist, *Historic Courthouses of New York State* (New York, 1977); G. Waddell, *Robert Mills's Courthouses and Jails* (New York, 1981).

17 On the early court buildings see R. P. Reeder, 'The first homes of the Supreme Court of the United States', *Proceedings of the American Philosophical Society*, 76 (1936), 543–96.

18 For discussions of the history, architecture, and detailing of the Supreme Court building see the studies by L. Friedman, *The Supreme Court* (Edgemont, 1987); R. Kennedy,

Greek Revival America (New York, 1989); B. Schwartz, *A History of the Supreme Court* (New York, 1993); and E. Witt, *Guide to the U. S. Supreme Court* (Washington, 1979).

19 Johnson and Andrist, *Historic Courthouses*, pp. 11–12.

20 It should be noted that the summary fails to give a complete legal topography. For example, it ignores the vast majority of Inns of which 'a definitive and exhaustive list seems scarcely possible'. Over thirty famous legal Inns are known. Again variation and lack of specificity are the defining features. We have a number of cases with one Inn sharing three names and three Inns sharing one name. The nineteenth century sees the decline in the diversity of Inns as well as of the courts, with the majority of closures occurring in two waves (1884–92; 1900–3). For an account of the Inns, see R. Megarry, *Inns Ancient and Modern: A Topographical and Historical Introduction to the Inns of Court, Inns of Chancery, and the Serjeants' Inn* (London, 1972). The most comprehensive study of the London legal topography is E. William, *Early Holborn and the Legal Quarter of London* (London, 1927).

21 For example compare the hierarchy of height and the horizontal division of space on a plan of the Chancellor's Court in Lincoln's Inn with the curved graduations of space and the lack of distinction in height between pleader and judge in the Court of Doctors' Commons, as illustrated in G. D. Squibb, *Doctors' Commons: A History of the College of Advocates and Doctors of Law* (Oxford, 1977).

22 Brownlee, *The Law Courts*, p. 50.

23 This prompted one correspondent in his plea for reform to thunder 'The Lord Chancellor of England now sits, by sufferance, in a dining hall!!' – *Law Times* (16 November 1844), quoted in Brownlee, *The Law Courts*, p. 52. The opening of Dickens's *Bleak House* is set during the Court of Chancery's session in Lincoln's Inn Old Hall. For a discussion of Dickens's portrayal of this session see G. Hurst, *Lincoln's Inn Essays* (London, 1949), pp. 109–20. Studies of engravings of the period reveal a court defined by a series of moveable desks, benches, and partitions which barely serve to exclude the milling crowds on the court's periphery. See, for example, the engravings of Pugin and Rowlandson (1808) in Hurst, *Lincoln's Inn*, facing p. 109, and Shepherd (1841) in Megarry, *Inns Ancient and Modern*, frontispiece.

24 On the Inns of Court as sites for theatrical events see W. C. Richardson, *A History of the Inns of Court: With Special Reference to the Renaissance* (Baton Rouge, 1975), pp. 211–44.

25 B. O'Donnell, *The Old Bailey and its Trials* (London, 1950), p. 37.

26 *Law Times* (18 June 1864), p. 367.

27 For examples of multiple use in connection with court-houses see the survey in Johnson and Andrist, *Historic Courthouses*, pp. 19, 22 (town halls); 20, 68, 163 (private homes); 31, 40, 103, 136 (taverns); 34, 68 (schoolhouses); 90, 96, 142, 161 (offices).

28 National Federation of Consumer Groups, *Court Facilities in England and Wales: A Consumer Survey* (Newcastle, 1984), pp. 8, 13 (ease of finding and signage); 34 (appearance of County Courts); 10, 29 (building function).

29 For a discussion of these trials see O'Donnell, *The Old Bailey*, pp. 31–7.

30 The effect of such ceremony is not lost in the modern legal world. The difference is that such performance is now specifically framed within an architecture that of itself makes us receptive to acts of power.

31 For an account of the preliminaries see J. S. Cockburn, *History of the English Assizes, 1558–1714* (Cambridge, 1972), pp. 65–9.

32 For a description of the deplorable conditions of most courts see Cockburn, *History of the English Assizes*, p. 53.

33 *Law Journal* (7 November 1903) quoted in Abel-Smith and Stevens, *Lawyers and the Courts*, p. 88.

34 Ancient historians may ponder the similarity with Pisistratus' institution of travelling judges (*Ath. pol.* 16.5). This move presumably concentrated regional power at the centre at the expense of local nobilities. For discussion see P. J. Rhodes, *A Commentary on the Aristotelian Athenaion Politeia* (Oxford, 1981), pp. 215–16.

35 It is hard not to get the added edge of Cleon's comments that the Athenians have become 'spectators' (*theatai*) of speeches (Thucydides 3.38.4) given the structural similarities between the Pnyx and the theatre of Dionysus.

36 It is precisely the lack of identifying clues that has made the identification of the court of the *Heliaia* in the Agora so notoriously difficult. Identification is done entirely on site-finds, not architectural features. See H. Hommel, *Heliaia: Untersuchung – zur Verfassung und Prozeßordnung des athenischen Volksgerichts, insbesondere zum Schlußteil der* Ἀθηναίων Πολιτεία *des Aristoteles* (Philologus Suppl. 19, Leipzig, 1927); M. H. Hansen, 'The Athenian Heliaia from Solon to Aristotle', *Classica et Mediaevalia*, 33 (1982), 9–47, reprinted with addenda in Hansen, *The Athenian Ecclesia II: A Collection of Articles 1983–89* (Copenhagen, 1989), pp. 219–62.

37 On the individualistic nature of the homicide courts see the conclusion of A. L. Boegehold, *The Athenian Agora: Vol. XXVIII. The Lawcourts at Athens: Sites, Buildings, Equipment, Procedure, and Testimonia* (Princeton, 1995), p. 44 – 'no obvious pattern of disposition emerges nor any easy way to account for the differing physical situation of each court'.

38 For example see the discussion in G. F. Schoemann, 'Appendix de dicasteriis', *Opuscula academica* (Berlin, 1856), I.220–48; Th. Thalheim, 'Δικαστήρια', in A. F. von Pauly, G. Wissowa, et al. *Real-Encyclopädie der classischen Altertumswissenschaft* (Stuttgart, 1903), V, cols 571–4; J. H. Lipsius, *Das attische Recht und Rechtsverfahren, unter Benutzung des attischen Prozesses von M. H. E. Meier und G. F. Schömann* (Leipzig, 1915), pp. 167–75; R. J. Bonner and G. Smith, *The Administration of Justice from Homer to Aristotle*, 2 vols (Chicago, 1930–38), I.234; G. Busolt and H. Swoboda, *Griechische Staatskunde*, 2 vols (Munich, 1920–26), II.1154ff.; F. Jacoby, *Die Fragmente der griechischen Historiker* (Leiden, 1923–), 324 Androtion F59, pp. 164–7 (commentary), 146–53 (notes); D. M. MacDowell, *Aristophanes: Wasps* (Oxford, 1971), pp. 273–5; P. Harding, *Androtion and the Atthis* (Oxford, 1994), pp. 185–6; Boegehold, *The Lawcourts at Athens*, pp. 3–9.

39 Boegehold, *The Lawcourts at Athens*, p. 9.

40 Scholarship has almost universally followed Lipsius, *Das attische Recht*, I.171 n. 21 in rejecting these as sites for law-courts.

41 For testimonia see Boegehold, *The Lawcourts at Athens*, pp. 186–7.

42 For the Palladion near the Ardettos Hill see Plutarch, *Theseus* 27.3–5; cf. D. M. MacDowell, *Athenian Homicide Law in the Age of the Orators* (Manchester, 1963), p. 58. On the unsuitability of the structure identified as the Palladion by J. Travlos, *Pictorial*

Dictionary of Athens (London, 1971), pp. 412–22, see Boegehold, *The Lawcourts at Athens*, p. 48.

43 See the description in Pausanias 1.17.2–6.

44 See, for example, *Ath. pol.* 15.4; *IG* Π² 1039.2–3.

45 Aeschines 3.13; cf. *Ath. pol.* 62.1.

46 For example see Aristophanes, *Knights* 1311–12.

47 For this practice see K. A. Christensen, 'The Theseion: a slave refuge', *American Journal of Ancient History*, 9 (1984), 23–32.

48 For the argument see A. L. Boegehold, 'Philokleon's court', *Hesperia*, 36 (1967), 111–20.

49 For examples see Pausanias 1.15.1–16.1 (paintings) and Plutarch, *Pericles* 13.9–11 (roof).

50 H. A. Thompson and R. E. Wycherley, *The Athenian Agora: Vol. XIV. The Agora of Athens, The History, Shape and Uses of an Ancient City Center* (Princeton, 1972), p. 59.

51 M. H. Hansen and T. Fischer-Hansen, 'Monumental political architecture in archaic and classical Greek poleis: evidence and historical significance', in D. Whitehead (ed.), *From Political Architecture to Stephanus Byzantius* (Stuttgart, 1994), pp. 23–90 (p. 77).

52 For a discussion of the terms see F. Salviat, 'Dédicace d' un τρύφακτος par les Hermaïstes Déliens', *Bulletin de Correspondance Hellénique*, 87 (1963), 252–64 (p. 260); S. Dow, 'Aristotle, the kleroteria and the courts', *Harvard Studies in Classical Philology*, 50 (1939), 1–34 (pp. 20–2); G. Roux, 'Aristophane, Xénophon, le pseudo-Démosthène et l'architecture du bouleuterion d'Athènes', *Bulletin de Correspondance Hellénique*, 100 (1976), 475–83; P. J. Rhodes, *The Athenian Boule* (Oxford, 1972), pp. 33–44. The various options and positions are summarised in Boegehold, *The Lawcourts at Athens*, pp. 195–6.

53 Cf. Demosthenes 25.23 where the speaker boasts that, despite the frailty of the *kinklis* in the bouleuterion, it is more than sufficient to keep the counsels of the Boule secret.

54 Pollux 8.16–18. For the collection of testimonia relating to the minor moveable court equipment see Boegehold, *The Lawcourts at Athens*, pp. 208–41.

55 On public and private space as one of the central themes in the *Wasps* (e.g. the transition from public law-court to private symposium) see G. Crane, 'Oikos and agora: mapping the polis in Aristophanes' *Wasps*', in G. W. Dobrov (ed.), *The City as Comedy: Society and Representation in Athenian Drama* (Chapel Hill, 1998), pp. 198–229.

56 The elaborateness of the description in the *Ath. pol.* has been striking to many critics. For bibliography see Rhodes, *Commentary*, p. 697. Rhodes's description of it as 'disproportionately lengthy' is typical. However, it is within the context of Athenian 'performance culture' that we can begin to see why such elaboration is necessary. For my interpretation of these notoriously difficult passages in the *Ath. pol.* I have tended to follow Boegehold, *The Lawcourts at Athens*.

57 For a description of this trend see Rhodes, *Commentary*, p. 697; A. L. Boegehold, 'Three court days', in *Symposion 1990: Vorträge zur griechischen und hellenistischen Rechtsgeschichte* (Cologne, 1995), pp. 165–82; Boegehold, *The Lawcourts at Athens*, pp. 21–42.

58 For the suggestion of a common store see Boegehold, *The Lawcourts at Athens*, p. 84. The common store may be near the find-spot of the water-clock by the Tholos, a place identified with the storage of official measures; see M. Lang and M. Crosby, *The Athenian Agora: Vol. X. Weights, Measures and Tokens* (Princeton, 1964), p. 41. This site has been the location of a large number of small finds associated with the law-courts. For a map displaying dispersal of finds and interpretation see R. F. Townsend, *The Athenian*

Agora: Vol. XXVII. The East Side of the Agora: The Remains beneath the Stoa of Attalos (Princeton, 1995), p. 41.

59 Pollux 8.113. For the archaeological evidence in support of such a fountain see Boegehold, *The Lawcourts at Athens*, p. 75 n. 21.

60 For example see the water-clock inscribed with the designation *Antiochidos*. For a discussion of this inscription and its implications for possible non-dikastic use see S. Young, 'An Athenian clepsydra', *Hesperia*, 8 (1939), 274–84 (pp. 282–4).

61 For a description of the designation ceremony and this procession see *Ath. pol.* 63.5.

62 For subsequent discussion of the use of the sorting machine see J. D. Bishop, 'The cleroterium', *Journal of Hellenic Studies*, 90 (1970), 1–14; Rhodes, *Commentary*, pp. 706–9; A. L. Boegehold, 'Many letters: Aristophanes *Plutus* 1166–1167', in K. J. Rigsby (ed.), *Studies Presented to Sterling Dow on His Eightieth Birthday* (Durham: NC, 1984), pp. 23–9; Boegehold, *The Lawcourts at Athens*, pp. 230–1; E. S. Staveley, *Greek and Roman Voting and Elections* (London, 1972), pp. 62–7.

63 Significantly, the account of the selection procedure begins with an inventory of all the required equipment. See *Ath. pol.* 63.2.

64 On sortition as a fundamentally democratic procedure see R. K. Sinclair, *Democracy and Participation in Athens* (Cambridge, 1988), pp. 17–18.

65 On the meaning of these primary seals see J. H. Kroll, *Athenian Bronze Allotment Plates* (Cambridge, Mass., 1972), pp. 51–6.

66 Kroll, *Athenian Bronze Allotment Plates*, p. 9.

67 For a full description of the mechanics of the procedure see Dow, 'Aristotle, the kleroteria and the courts'.

68 Assuming the most credible reconstruction of the text. For discussion on this point see Rhodes, *Commentary*, p. 709.

69 On the redundancy of the colouring and the extra potential for confusion it caused, see Rhodes, *Commentary*, p. 711.

70 On the allotment of seating in the courtroom see Boegehold, 'Many letters'.

71 The assumption that it was these jurors who handled the return of the allotment tokens is based on Kenyon's supplement to the text at 65.4. For this addition, see Rhodes, *Commentary*, pp. 713–14.

72 See MacDowell, *Aristophanes: Wasps*, p. 226 on *Wasps* 690.

3

Creating responsibility: assigning blame for the Thirty[1]

ELENI VOLONAKI

❋

So far the setting of the Athenian legal process. We now turn to some examples of Athenian oratory and law in action, in the speeches of Lysias (possibly 459/8 to c. 380 BC). Lawsuits in Athens were of two types: private suits (*dikai idiai*), which affected only the individuals concerned, and public suits (*dikai dêmosiai*), mostly called *graphai*, which affected the State as a whole. The latter could be initiated by 'anyone who wishes' (*ho boulomenos*) among the adult male citizen body, so long as the prosecutor was not suffering from a loss of citizen rights (*atimia*). In either type of suit the litigants on both sides were expected to deliver their own cases, giving one or two set speeches depending on the procedure involved. Help was at hand for those whose rhetorical powers were limited, in the form of professional speech writers, or *logographoi*. One of the most successful logographers was Lysias, who was born in Athens into a wealthy family (his father Cephalus was on friendly terms with Pericles and his house in Piraeus is the setting of Plato's *Republic*) but of Sicilian parentage. This made him a resident alien (metic), not a citizen, a status which restricted his involvement in the legal system, but he made full use of his rhetorical powers in helping others. His career took off, however, as a result of his own prosecution of Eratosthenes, a member of the short-lived, infamous regime of the Thirty Tyrants, whom he accused of causing the death of his brother Polemarchus. The legal procedure he used to do this is unclear, but was possibly connected with the audit (*euthunai*) that members of the Thirty were obliged to undergo after the restoration of the democracy if they wished to remain in Athens. Lysias was also involved in other cases concerning the tyrants and those connected with them, which took place even though the Athenians had sworn an oath of amnesty to let bygones be bygones, as Eleni Volonaki demonstrates in her chapter.

✳

INTRODUCTION: THE RHETORICAL FIGURE OF *DEINOSIS*

A common rhetorical figure with wide applicability to public and private life in every society is to exaggerate responsibility for the actions of a person or a group of people for various purposes. For example, it is used by political figures to win the people's vote, by the media to increase popularity, and by individuals to make personal profit or establish their own position against others.

Ancient rhetoricians called the rhetorical means to exaggerate responsibility *deinosis*, defining it as 'the emotional *amplificatio* which aims to "appal"'.[2] According to Aristotle, *deinosis* is a rhetorical *topos* common to all kinds of rhetoric, 'for all men employ extenuation or amplification whether deliberating, praising or blaming, accusing or defending'.[3] As such, this rhetorical means of persuasion appears to have had a great appeal to the Athenians in the fifth and fourth centuries BC. Particularly in forensic oratory the amplification of crimes or guilt with reference to the past was often applied and effectively used for character assassination. On certain occasions, it was also employed in the presentation of the facts and arguments. This chapter examines the rhetorical technique of exaggerating the degree of individual responsibility in order to secure conviction, as an example of *deinosis* used in forensic oratory. In particular, it deals with one aspect of the exploitation of anti-oligarchic hostility in the years after the overthrow of the regime of the Thirty tyrants, as presented in the orations preserved to us from that period.

After the defeat of the Athenians in the battle at Aegospotami in 404, a peace was made between them and the Spartans on the following conditions: the return of the exiled oligarchs (participants in the oligarchic revolution of 411 and others) to Athens, the destruction of the Long Walls and the fortifications of the Piraeus, and the surrender of Athens's maritime power. The returning exiles with Spartan support set up the regime of the Thirty (404/3).[4] Within a short period of time, conflicts arose between their members (especially Critias, the leader of the extreme oligarchs, and Theramenes, the leader of the moderates) owing to cruelties committed against Athenian citizens and resident aliens (metics).[5] A revolution was organised by Thrasybulus in Phyle, which led to the overthrow of the oligarchy of the Thirty and the restoration of the democracy. The reconciliation took place in 403/2, when all Athenians swore an oath never to recall the past misdeeds of anyone except the Thirty (and those involved in their regime), and not even of those if they successfully submitted to an examination.[6] Allegedly, after the oath of the Amnesty had been sworn, the two parties henceforth lived together as fellow-citizens and all the people abided by this oath.[7]

However, as will be shown, speeches delivered in trials after the reconciliation agreement had been made down to the middle of the fourth century reveal a violation of the spirit of the Amnesty in their use of the rhetorical means to exaggerate individual responsibility for the crimes of the Thirty. This rhetorical technique is found in prosecution speeches in public cases, where the prosecution will exaggerate responsibility for crimes and disasters in order to represent defendants as 'monsters', who have purposely acted against the security of the state or the democratic constitution. Extant speeches of this kind, however, are few.[8]

The focus of this paper will be on the rhetorical technique to assign 'sole' individual responsibility not merely for the crimes of the Thirty but also for the whole oligarchic constitution. For this purpose, three prosecution speeches – the only ones preserved to us that employ this particular technique – composed by Lysias a few years after the restoration of the democracy will be examined. Firstly, however, we will briefly discuss the use of the same rhetorical technique to exploit 'partial' responsibility for the actions of the Thirty, as found in prosecution speeches dated from the first decade until the middle of the fourth century.

'PARTIAL' INDIVIDUAL RESPONSIBILITY

Arguments from comparison constitute a commonplace for character assassination. Litigants often attempt to blacken the character of their opponent either by emphatically contrasting his misbehaviour with the integrity of well-known political figures or by drawing a parallel with the dishonesty of other notorious criminals from the past. The Thirty tyrants, their motivation and conduct, offer an example from the latter category. The representation of criminals as similar to or even potentially worse than the Thirty tyrants appears to be an effective rhetorical means to prejudice the jury against the opposing party, and thus secure their conviction. This type of rhetorical device is mainly used as an argument from *ethos* in prosecution speeches, delivered after the Amnesty agreement of 403, to portray defendants as threatening the interests of the whole Athenian people (*dêmos*).

Lysias' speech *Against Hippotherses* (P. Oxy. 1606; Frag. 1 in the Budé edition[9]), which was delivered shortly after the restoration of the democracy, involves a dispute over property confiscated from Lysias by the Thirty. Hippotherses prosecuted Lysias concerning most likely a claim over a slave girl.[10] The speaker, who delivers the speech on Lysias' behalf, attacks all those who bought possessions that had been illegally confiscated by the Thirty in order to imply that Hippotherses' claim over Lysias' property is unjust (lines 118ff.):

> And yet you would have every right to be angry at those who purchased your property during such misfortunes: for in the first place, the Thirty would not have sold it if purchasers had not existed.[11]

This passage elevates the collusion of the buyers (a result of the depredations of the Thirty) almost to the level of cause or motive, and emphasises the culpability of those who bought confiscated property.

Another speech by Lysias, *Against Alcibiades* (speech 14), was delivered in a prosecution brought against Alcibiades, the son of the famous Alcibiades,[12] for dereliction of military duty,[13] probably in 395 (at the beginning of the Corinthian War). The speaker attacks the whole family of Alcibiades for their anti-democratic *ethos*; the emphasis is placed upon the role of the father Alcibiades, who is charged with all the disasters that befell the Athenians after their defeat in the Peloponnesian War, including the establishment of the regime of the Thirty (§39):

> So if any of you pities those who died in the sea battle, or feels shame for those enslaved by the enemy, or is angry about the destruction of the walls, or hates the Spartans, or detests the Thirty – for all these things you must regard the defendant's father as responsible. You must remember that your ancestors twice

ostracized both the defendant's great-grandfather Alcibiades, and Megacles his father's maternal grandfather, and that the older ones among you condemned the defendant's father to death.

The association of the elder Alcibiades with the Thirty, whose establishment was a direct result of the loss of the Peloponnesian War, is cleverly manipulated here by Lysias in order to associate the younger Alcibiades with the current enemy.[14] The implication is that the defendant should be considered an enemy of the city of Athens, as his father was. Since his father had set up the regime of the Thirty with Spartan help, the defendant would share the same pro-Spartan feelings, now that Athens was involved in a war against the Spartans in Boeotia. It is obvious that the speaker draws on the hostility the Athenians still felt toward the Thirty to exaggerate the elder Alcibiades' responsibility for the whole of the regime and so prejudice the jurors against his son.[15]

Within the first decade of the fourth century a speech by Isocrates, *Against Lochites* (speech 20), was delivered in a suit for heavy damages against a rich young citizen, Lochites, who had allegedly struck the prosecutor.[16] The speaker, being himself 'a poor man and one of the people' (20.19), appeals to the necessity of restraining and punishing violence, especially under the democracy, and thus to the conviction of the defendant. To emphasise this appeal, he identifies Lochites' insolence with the spirit and attitude of those oligarchs who twice overthrew the democracy, the Four Hundred and the Thirty (§§10–11):

> For we ourselves have twice seen the democracy overthrown and twice we have been deprived of freedom, not by those who were guilty of other crimes, but by persons who contemned the laws and were willing to be slaves of the enemy while wantonly outraging their fellow-citizens. Lochites is one of these persons. For even though he was too young to have belonged to the oligarchy established at that time, yet his character at any rate is in harmony with their régime. For it was men of like disposition who betrayed our power to the enemy, razed the walls of the fatherland, and put to death without a trial fifteen hundred citizens.[17]

Lochites, obviously, could not have been associated with the oligarchy of the Thirty since he was very young when it was established. However, the identification of his conduct with the brutality shown by the Thirty is an effective rhetorical device used for character assassination. Isocrates excites animosity against the oligarchs to isolate the defendant from the citizen group as a monstrous criminal and an enemy of the democratic constitution.

A similar example of exaggerating a litigant's 'indirect' association with the Thirty is found in Demosthenes' speech *Against Androtion* (speech 22), delivered at a *graphê paranomôn* (prosecution for an illegal proposal) in 355. In this case Euctemon prosecutes Androtion for proposing the gift of a crown to the retiring councillors of the year 356/5 without the formality of a preliminary decree of the Council, and even though the Council could not afford such expenses. With reference to the public service of Androtion, the prosecutor strongly criticises him and charges him with responsibility for the incident of the melting of the crowns. To emphasise this accusation Demosthenes portrays the defendant as a public man more disgraceful even than the Thirty (§52):

> I shall not, then, trouble to show that the defendant has proved himself more brutal than any oligarchy anywhere in the world. But here, in our own city, at what period were the most outrageous things done? You will all say, 'Under the Thirty Tyrants'. Now under the Thirty, as we are informed, no man forfeited the power to save his life who could hide himself at home; what we denounce the Thirty for is that they arrested men illegally in the market-place. This man displayed a brutality so far in excess of theirs that he, a public man under a democracy, turned every man's private house into a gaol by conducting the Eleven into your homes.[18]

In this passage, the speaker exploits the ultimate degree of brutality and immorality as shown by the Thirty to demonstrate how Androtion, a public figure of a democratic constitution, has even surpassed this kind of behaviour. The depiction of the defendant as 'the most dangerous enemy of the democracy' aims to contrast him with the speaker himself, who claims an honest democratic *ethos*, so that the jury may sympathise with the prosecution side. Furthermore, it effectively stimulates the hostility of the jurors toward all oligarchs, but particularly toward Androtion, whom they are enticed into convicting for personal damage.[19]

It has been shown that the rhetorical technique of exaggerating the opposing side's indirect association with the regime of the Thirty – their establishment with Spartan support, motivation, spirit and attitude, brutality and immorality – is a common means of persuasion; it is used mainly for character assassination in forensic speeches, delivered under the restored democracy of 403 until the middle of the fourth century. As such, the rhetorical abuse of the Thirty reflects the immense degree of hostility still felt by the Athenians toward the oligarchic constitution.

'SOLE' INDIVIDUAL RESPONSIBILITY

With reference to crimes committed in the last decade of the fifth century, Lysias' technique focuses on the connection of the opponent's action with the crimes of the Thirty, appealing thereby to the audience's prejudice against the oligarchic constitution. Even when dealing with minor figures, Lysias tends to attribute sole responsibility for the whole of the regime. He further involves the hearers personally in the sufferings of the Athenians at the hands of the tyrants to isolate the defendant from the jurors and represent him as an enemy of the democracy, and converts a politically disparate audience retrospectively into stalwart partisans of democracy. In order to illustrate the rhetorical technique Lysias employs to create sole individual responsibility for the whole of the Thirty, a few examples will be discussed selected from Lysias' speeches *Against Eratosthenes* (speech 12), *Against Agoratus* (speech 13), and *Against Nicomachus* (speech 30).

In the speech *Against Agoratus*, the speaker accuses Agoratus of being responsible for the murder of his brother-in-law, Dionysodorus. The political background of the events narrated in the speech relates to the year 404/3, when rapid changes occurred at Athens. After the defeat of the Athenian fleet at the end of the Peloponnesian War, peace was made between Sparta and Athens, which imposed unfavourable terms on the Athenians (see above). Lysias' account focuses on the activity of individual political figures during the period of the peace negotiations between Sparta and Athens, when the ground was prepared for the oligarchic revolution and the subversion of democracy. Theramenes, the Athenian ambassador in charge of peace negotiations who soon became a prominent political figure as one of the Thirty, was conspiring together with a group of oligarchs against the constitution (§§8–17). Their conspiracy had further support from the Council of the year before the Thirty. When political figures who supported the Athenian *dêmos* – demagogues, generals, and taxiarchs – showed resistance to the peace terms proposed by Theramenes, the oligarchs felt threatened and planned to destroy them. Firstly, they set up a trial against Cleophon on the excuse of a military offence and condemned him to death (§§7–12). Subsequently, a conspiracy was hatched to eliminate Strombichides (a general), Dionysodorus (a taxiarch), and many other democrats. The conspirators used Theocritus and Agoratus as *mênutai* (informers) to lay information, and according to the speaker they wished to make the denunciations seem voluntary (§§18–22). The Council first interrogated Theocritus, and then decreed the arrest of Agoratus.

However, Nicias and Nicomenes presented themselves as sureties for Agoratus, and after giving bail undertook to produce him before the Council later. According to the speaker, Agoratus' sureties, being concerned with the safety of the city, attempted to persuade him to escape (§§23–8). Agoratus refused and, after a second decree of the Council, he was finally arrested at the altar of Artemis' temple in Munychia. He made two depositions, the first before the Council against the taxiarchs and generals, and the second one before the Assembly at the theatre of Munychia, where further names were given (§§30–2). The accused were arrested and the Athenian *dêmos* decided that they be tried in court by a jury of two thousand citizens (§35). When the Thirty came to power, they cancelled the appointed trial and replaced it by an unconstitutional procedure in the Council, where the defendants were all condemned to death, with the exception of Agoratus, who was allegedly acquitted on the ground that he had given true information.

In order to establish the charge of responsibility for murder, the prosecution needs to convince the jury that Agoratus deliberately denounced the victims. The claim that Agoratus was party to the oligarchic conspiracy against the democrats is stressed throughout the speech. In support of this argument, the speaker repeatedly points out that Agoratus rejected the chance he was given by his sureties to rescue his life and avoid giving any names. More specifically, in §§24–6, the prosecution claims the following:

> The guarantors and the others decided that they should get Agoratus away as soon as possible. They brought two boats to anchor nearby, and pleaded with him to flee Athens by any means possible. They said they would sail with him, until the situation became stable, and they pointed out that if he were brought in front of the Council, he would perhaps be compelled under torture to reveal the names of such Athenians as might be suggested by people wanting to cause trouble in the city.
>
> That was what they pleaded. They had prepared the boats and were themselves ready to sail with him, but Agoratus here refused to follow their advice. And yet, Agoratus, unless you were in the plot and knew that you would suffer no harm, why you did not leave, given that the boats had been prepared and your guarantors were ready to sail with you? You still could have done this, given that the Council had not yet got you into its power.

The implication here is that Agoratus must have been part of the oligarchic plot and, knowing that he was protected by the oligarchs, he therefore refused to leave Athens.[20]

Lysias attempts to draw firm boundaries between the two groups of 'oligarchs' and 'democrats' in order to emphasise the conflict and convince the jurors of Agoratus' anti-democratic activity. According to the speaker, Agoratus was used as the tool of the oligarchs for being a suitable informer and was not party to the generals' and taxiarchs' activity, nor was he connected with them in any other way (§§18, 61). In view of the speaker's attempt to stimulate existing political rivalries that involved individual political leaders, Lysias' approach to the personalities of Theramenes and Cleophon, two political leaders who were controversial during their life and remained so even after their death, appears to strengthen the argument that Agoratus' conduct was consistent with the oligarchic plans. The speaker's aim is to associate Agoratus with Theramenes and the other oligarchs who plotted the death of the democrats. Therefore, Cleophon is praised as a 'martyr' whereas Theramenes is strongly attacked as a 'traitor' for establishing the oligarchy of the Thirty.

To make the homicide charge more plausible, Lysias attempts to connect Agoratus with the Thirty, who actually put the democrats to death through illegal means. The speaker illustrates in detail the suspension of democratic institutions with reference to the voting process and the presidency of the Thirty at the trial of the democrats (§§36–8). The emphasis that is placed upon the injustice practised against the defendants by the Thirty is used to put the blame on Agoratus, since he was the one who had made the deposition. The point stressed by the speaker is that Agoratus' denunciations caused the arrest of the victims, and this in turn led to the establishment of the oligarchy. It is to be noted that Agoratus was not the only one arrested; also, Hippias from Thasos and Xenophon from Courion were summoned together with Agoratus by the Council (§54). Lysias focuses solely on Agoratus and deliberately isolates him from a group of *mênutai* to charge him with the entire responsibility for the denunciations, and consequently the death of all the victims. In §34, Agoratus is further charged with all the events of the period following his denunciations:

> When his victims had been arrested and imprisoned, at that moment Lysander sailed into your harbors, your ships were handed over to the Spartans, the walls were pulled down, the Thirty were appointed, and all possible evils fell on the city.

The speaker is further associating Agoratus with the Thirty by representing him as a benefactor of the oligarchic constitution for providing information they could use for their purposes, and who in consequence was the only one released (§38).[21] The exaggerated contrast between the conviction of all the other defendants and Agoratus' acquittal distracts the jurors' attention from the fact that the democrats were killed by the Thirty and emphasises Agoratus' responsibility for the action of the tyrants. This is further underlined by the idea that, if Agoratus had not made the denunciation, his victims would not have been subsequently put to death by the Thirty (§§35–6).

Agoratus' association with the regime of the Thirty and their crimes is strengthened by the speaker's hints at Agoratus' ulterior motives for refusing to follow his sureties' plan to escape from Athens (§§18, 52–3). Particularly in §61, the speaker explicitly states that Agoratus' motive related to his possible active participation in the oligarchic constitution:

> You, on the other hand, knew nothing that would discredit your victims. You were won over by the promise that if they were destroyed, you would have a share in the constitution that was being established at the time. And so you denounced and murdered many good Athenians.

The speaker bases his refutation of the defence claim that Agoratus was granted some citizen privileges as a reward for killing Phrynichus, a prominent member of the regime of the Four Hundred, partly on the same idea that Agoratus' action was related to the oligarchic constitution. Among other points, the speaker stresses that Agoratus could not have been a killer of Phrynichus since otherwise the Thirty would have avenged Phrynichus' murder and killed him (§§74–6).[22] Lysias' fallacy here is to treat the oligarchs as a single cohesive group who formed both regimes, the Four Hundred and the Thirty. Hence, the fact that Agoratus was allowed to live by the Thirty is manipulated to demonstrate that Agoratus was a person of oligarchic affiliations, who must have done great harm to the Athenian *dêmos*. However, Athenian political parties were not officially formed or stable,[23] and not even all the members of a single regime shared the same views.

Agoratus' guilt of homicide is rhetorically emphasised by presenting him as responsible for all the miseries which befell the city of Athens, on both a public and a personal level, during the regime of the Thirty. Firstly he is charged with the deaths of three hundred citizens of Eleusis and also three hundred citizens of Salamis at the hands of the Thirty, when they wished to establish their base at Eleusis and have these places as safe havens

(§44; cf. 12.52). Secondly he is accused of causing the deaths of many innocent Athenian citizens, owing to which old parents, unmarried sisters, and young children were left unprotected (§45). Thirdly he is presented as responsible for the unfavourable peace-terms of 404, which caused the crisis of the Athenian empire in terms of both financial power and prestige (§46). Finally he is associated with the exile of the Athenian democrats and the confiscation of their properties by the Thirty (§47). The speaker exaggerates Agoratus' responsibility for all these misfortunes, and argues that the oligarchic revolution would have been prevented if Agoratus had not denounced the democrats (§§47–8):

> Those good men recognised this and refused to allow the peace to be made. But you, Agoratus, killed them, when they wanted to do something good for the city. You denounced them for plotting against the city, and you were the cause of all the disasters that happened to the city. So each of you, gentlemen, should remember both your private sufferings and those that were common to the city, and take vengeance on the man who caused them.

The personal involvement of the jurors in the misfortunes allegedly caused to each one of them by Agoratus succeeds in arousing hostility against the defendant and isolating him from the citizen group as their enemy. On account of their sufferings, the vengeance on Agoratus becomes a personal matter for the jurors, who are thus invited to convict him for his oligarchic activity. This kind of appeal is expanded further in the epilogue of the speech, where the jurors are implicated in an imaginary trial of the dead and are asked to prove their friendship toward them by convicting the defendant (§§94–6). The present trial is depicted as a retrial where the jurors are asked to acquit those whom the Thirty condemned to death and condemn to death those whom the Thirty acquitted. The outcome of these syllogisms is that Agoratus is to be convicted given that the Thirty, at the trial of the democrats, had acquitted him.

Lysias constructs Agoratus' persona to suit a murderer, and, as has become clear, he employs an oligarchic *ethos* to convince the audience of his guilt. Emphasis is placed upon Agoratus' alleged collusion with the oligarchs before the establishment of the Thirty; the accusation that Agoratus voluntarily made the deposition is solely based upon the assertion that his action was made in exchange for some profit or power to be gained within the rising oligarchic constitution. Agoratus is further associated with the oligarchic regime of the Thirty, and connected with their verdict against his victims, as well as all the misfortunes caused by them to the Athenians. The arguments concerning Agoratus' oligarchic affiliations and compliance with the actions of the tyrants are stressed throughout the speech not only to attack the defendant's character but more importantly to establish the fundamental question of intentionality in the factual case of homicide. It is to be noted that the prosecution case appears to be a weak one since it fails to prove that Agoratus voluntarily laid the information against the democrats. Nevertheless, the establishment of the charge for murder upon the exaggerated responsibility attributed to him for the crimes of the Thirty seems an effective rhetorical means of persuasion to be used in 399, a few years after the Amnesty agreement.

In the speech *Against Nicomachus*, Lysias uses the same technique of character assassination and represents the defendant as a person of oligarchic affiliations, who complied with the regime of the Thirty. Nicomachus was appointed an *anagrapheus* [24] of the secular and sacred laws and was elected to this office for two periods of time, 410–404 and 403–399. He was engaged with the publication of the Athenian laws in use at the end of the fifth century. Although the case involves the alleged misconduct of the defendant during the second term, when he was working on the publication of a systematic calendar of sacrifices, the prosecutor aims to convince the jury that Nicomachus was continuously abusing his authority for a long period of time. According to the speaker, Nicomachus received bribes during both terms of office (§§2, 11, 23, 25, 27), and inscribed whichever laws he wanted or was told to, whilst he omitted others (§3).

As an example of such behaviour, Nicomachus is accused of having presented a law in court the day of Cleophon's trial that allowed the members of the Council before the Thirty to be judges together with the jurors (§§10–14). The implication is that it was a fabrication, and Nicomachus having complied with the oligarchs, who were conspiring at the time against the constitution, made a fictitious law to eliminate Cleophon. The speaker's purpose here is double, firstly to demonstrate Nicomachus' collusion with the oligarchs and secondly to establish the accusation of abusing legal authority (§11):

> The Council wanted to destroy Cleophon and were afraid that they would not be able to get him executed there. So they persuaded Nicomachus to produce a law which said that the Council should judge the case together with the *dikastai* (jurors). And this fellow, the greatest of criminals, was so blatantly part of the plot that he produced this law on the day the trial was held.

The speaker as far as possible avoids making any direct reference to Cleophon's personality to arouse the sympathy of all members of the jury, and focuses on the victimisation of Cleophon by the oligarchs to make Nicomachus responsible both for judicial murder and for the overthrow of democracy. Furthermore, the representation of Nicomachus' act as agreeable to the Thirty demonstrates his willing collusion with the oligarchs and strengthens the argument on responsibility (§14):

> And if he tries to defend himself against these charges, you should remember that he produced the law in question at a moment of crisis when the constitution was being overthrown, that he did this to curry favor with those who overthrew the democracy, and that he gave judicial authority to the same Council in which Satyrus and Chremon held the dominant power and under which Strombichides and Calliades and many other excellent citizens perished.

The evidence concerning Cleophon's execution is essential to the anticipation of Nicomachus' claims of democratic *ethos*, and as such is connected with another argument about Nicomachus' exile during the regime of the Thirty. Lysias correlates arguments normally used of democratic *ethos*, such as the exile under the Thirty and the execution by the Thirty, with those oligarchs who suffered this kind of misfortune. He appeals to the existence of ambiguous behaviour within the oligarchic regime and includes Nicomachus among those oligarchs who were rejected by the Thirty. In contrast to the case of Agoratus, here Lysias recognises that the oligarchs were not a cohesive group. The difference is that the factual case in speech 13 is solely based upon Agoratus' alleged collusion with the oligarchs that motivated him to make the deposition against the democrats, and therefore Lysias needs to present firmly the conflict between the groups of the democrats (victims) and the oligarchs (murderers). In the case of Nicomachus, however, his alleged conspiracy with the oligarchs is used for character assassination rather than to establish the main charge concerning the abuse of legal authority. Hence, it is adequate for the speaker to show that Nicomachus fell a victim of the oligarchs and was sent into exile, even though he had been bribed and used by them for Cleophon's execution, in order to refute any claim of democratic behaviour.

The degree of Nicomachus' responsibility is expanded to the financial crisis in the Athenian economy after the end of the Peloponnesian War, and also to all forms of internal maladministration during the oligarchic revolution. Nicomachus is attacked for ignoring the losses of the city in favour of his own profit (§§21–2):

> But this is the man who in two years has already spent twelve talents more than necessary, and has tried to defraud the city of six talents per year, even though he could see that the city needed money, that the Spartans were making threats whenever we did not send them payments, that the Boeotians were resorting to raids because we were unable to repay two talents, and that the shipsheds and the city walls were in ruins. He also knew that whenever the Council in a given year has enough money for its administration, it does no harm, but whenever it is reduced to desperation, it is forced to accept impeachments (*eisangeliai*), to confiscate the property of the citizens, and to allow itself to be persuaded by those of the orators whose advice is most corrupt.

According to the speaker, the city of Athens was drained of its money because of Nicomachus' maladministration, and was consequently prevented from repaying its debts and improving its fortifications for defence. Nicomachus is also depicted as forcing the Council to practise the illegal activity of using law-courts as a source of revenue for the city. By implication, Nicomachus appears to have supported the authoritative role of the Council before the Thirty in conspiring against the constitution. Moreover, the depiction of the jurors as representing all the Athenians who had suffered from the disasters allegedly caused by Nicomachus is effectively used to urge them to take revenge.

It has become clear that Nicomachus is attacked not only as a corrupt official but also as an enemy of democracy, who was responsible for the execution of Cleophon and many other democrats, such as Strombichides and Calliades, and subsequently for the establishment of the oligarchic constitution. The character assassination is further based on his responsibility for the crisis of the city of Athens and the illegal activity of the Council at the time of the oligarchic revolution. In effect, his alleged collusion with the oligarchs strengthens the charge against Nicomachus that he abused his authority as *anagrapheus* of the Athenian laws, aiming not at the interests of the city and the democratic institutions but at his own benefit.

Lysias' speeches 13 and 30 are chronologically close; on the basis of internal evidence of the speeches, 30 was delivered late in 399 — the last year of Nicomachus' second term of office[25] – and 13 a few months later in 399/8.[26] What is interesting about these two speeches is that, while memories of the terror are so fresh, the attribution of exaggerated responsibility can be made even against minor figures. Both Nicomachus and

Agoratus are attacked for their servile origin and are therefore isolated from the citizen group by Lysias in order to arouse the contempt and prejudice of the jurors. Agoratus was in fact a privileged metic with the right of owning land and a house in Attica (see above), granted to him as an award by the Athenian *dêmos* for the killing of Phrynichus.[27] Nicomachus evidently was more important than Agoratus; despite his servile background, he was an Athenian citizen, appointed to the public office of *anagrapheus* for a long period of ten years. He must have had important links with the political figures after the restoration of the democracy, since, according to the speaker, he was supported at the trial not only by his friends but also by men of political power. But even though he played a prominent role in the process of publication of the Athenian laws in the last decade of the fifth century, he nevertheless was not a major political figure but simply an expert in legal matters.

In contrast to the cases of Agoratus and Nicomachus, Eratosthenes who is accused of being responsible for the murder of Polemarchus, Lysias' brother, was a major political figure, as one of the Thirty. In the speech *Against Eratosthenes* Lysias applies the same device concerning the opponent's responsibility to establish his charge. He dissociates Eratosthenes' action from the crimes committed by the rest of the Thirty and presents him as solely responsible for the murder. He manipulates the power of Eratosthenes and depicts his act as independent from the decisions of the Thirty.

On the basis of the defence claim that Eratosthenes had opposed the decision of the Thirty to kill Polemarchus as unjust, Lysias argues that he should not subsequently have arrested him (§26):

> That you spoke against those who wanted to kill us when the majority of your colleagues were in control of our fate, but that when it was in your hands alone to rescue Polemarchus or not, you summarily dragged him off to prison? [28]

Furthermore, Lysias expands the degree of Eratosthenes' responsibility by exaggerating rhetorically the possibilities he had to avoid arresting Polemarchus (§§30–1):

> What is more, Eratosthenes seized and arrested him not at home but in the street, where he could have left both Polemarchus and the Thirty's instructions unviolated. You are angry against all the Thirty, because they invaded your houses and carried out searches for you or any of your families. But if you must pardon those who killed others to save themselves, then it would be more

legitimate to pardon those who conducted house arrests, for it was dangerous for them not to go or to deny it once they had carried out the arrest. Eratosthenes, on the other hand, could have said he did not meet Polemarchus or that he never saw him: there was no means of verifying this, and so it could not be disproved if his enemies had wanted to.[29]

In order to strengthen the accusation about Eratosthenes' responsibility for Polemarchus' murder and refute the defence claim that his action was dictated by the orders of the Thirty, Lysias portrays Eratosthenes as one of the most powerful members of the tyranny, who caused all the miseries following the defeat of Athens at the battle of Aegospotami. Eratosthenes and Critias together are described as the initiators of the oligarchic conspiracy during the period of peace negotiations between Athens and Sparta (§§43–4). Eratosthenes is accused of putting to death three hundred citizens in Salamis and in Eleusis, during the oligarchy of the Thirty (§52). It is worth noting that the same accusation is used against Agoratus, and apparently the death of those people was such a great loss that it can be used by Lysias to appeal to the Athenians' sympathy for the victims. Eratosthenes is also charged with the crisis in the city of Athens at the time of reconciliation between the party from Piraeus and the party from the city, when Eratosthenes borrowed a hundred talents from Sparta and asked Lysander to hire auxiliaries with a view to the city's destruction (§§53–61). Finally the strong attack on Theramenes is meant to disprove Eratosthenes' claim to have supported a moderate policy as a Theramenist, while amplifying the degree of his own responsibility for sharing in Theramenes' betrayal of the Athenian demos (§§62–78).

On balance, Lysias creates here exaggerated responsibility in two opposite forms for the same rhetorical purpose, to prove that Eratosthenes was responsible for Polemarchus' murder; firstly he isolates Eratosthenes' crime from those committed by the rest of the tyrants to demonstrate his guilt, and secondly he associates him with the most prominent members of the Thirty to show that he had the power to prevent the killing. By these means the charge of intentionality is rhetorically established and appears persuasive.

CONCLUSION

Most of the speeches presented in this chapter were delivered a few years after the restoration of the democracy in 403. The rhetorical exaggeration of the opponent's responsibility for the actions attributed to the Thirty is effectively used by orators to persuade the audience in this manner to convict the defendant.

The attempt to arouse the anger of the jurors against the defendants as enemies of democracy is based upon the common belief in the superiority of the democratic institutions, despite the fact that, especially at a time when the political situation might not yet have been stabilised, not all the members of the jury necessarily shared the values of the democratic constitution. It has been shown that in particular Lysias applies emphatically and extensively the rhetorical *topos* of pro-oligarchic conduct in relation to the regime of the Thirty, not only to attack the character of the opponents but also to establish the main charges as presented in the last three speeches. With reference to the Athenians' attitude toward the reconciliation agreement as formulated in 403, it can be assumed that, even though they were legally bound by the oath of the Amnesty not to take revenge on the past deeds of the tyrants, in practice they were willing to break the spirit of the Amnesty and exact revenge upon crimes allegedly relating to any kind of oligarchic activity.

NOTES

1 This chapter develops ideas originally presented at a conference on 'Oratory in Action' in the School of English and Drama, Queen Mary, University of London. I would like to express my appreciation to the editors, Michael Edwards and Christopher Reid, for their invitation to contribute to the present volume.

2 H. Lausberg, *Handbook of Literary Rhetoric: A Foundation for Literary Study*, ed. D. E. Orton and R. D. Anderson (Leiden, 1998), §257.3.c; cf. §438: *deinosis* is 'the inflaming of the audience's emotions in order to bring them to take sides against the opposing party'.

3 Aristotle, *Rhetoric* 2.18.4.

4 Xenophon, *Hellenica* 2.3.11–14; *Ath. pol.* 34.2–35; see P. Krentz, *The Thirty at Athens* (Ithaca, 1982).

5 Xen. *Hell.* 2.3.15–56; *Ath. pol.* 36.

6 *Ath. pol.* 39.6; see T. C. Loening, *The Reconciliation Agreement of 403/402 BC in Athens: Its Content and Application* (Hermes Einzelschriften 53, Stuttgart, 1987).

7 Xen. *Hell.* 2.4.43.

8 For the purposes of the present chapter, defence speeches which include refutations of one's connection with the Thirty are not included. For an example of such a defence speech see Lysias, *On Overthrowing the Democracy* (speech 25), where the speaker attempts to reject any collusion with the Thirty, even though he had remained in the city under their oligarchy.

9 L. Gernet and M. Bizos, *Lysias: Discours*, 2 vols (Paris, 1924–26).

10 Further on the charges in this speech see S. C. Todd, *Lysias* (Austin, 2000), pp. 367–8.

11 The translations of all texts by Lysias cited in this chapter are from Todd, *Lysias*.

12 For the career of Alcibiades the general see J. K. Davies, *Athenian Propertied Families* (Oxford, 1971), pp. 17–21, and for the son, the defendant here, pp. 21–2.

13 Further on the charge see C. Carey, *Lysias: Selected Speeches* (Cambridge, 1989), pp. 144–6; Todd, *Lsyias*, pp. 161–2.

14 See Carey, *Lysias*, p. 175.

15 It is to be noted that the speaker misrepresents the role of the elder Alcibiades who was a threat to the Thirty rather than their associate; see Carey, *Lysias*, pp. 165–70.

16 The date of the speech is not certain but from internal evidence it can be assumed that it was delivered several years after the oligarchy of the Thirty and before the walls of Athens were rebuilt in 393 (cf. §11).

17 Trans. L. Van Hook, *Isocrates III* (Cambridge, Mass., 1945).

18 Trans. J. H. Vince, *Demosthenes III* (Cambridge, Mass., 1935).

19 For the same line of argumentation (with the same phrasing) see Demosthenes, *Against Timocrates* (24.164).

20 The details of the incident that occurred at the altar of Artemis' temple at Munychia are plausibly presented but not substantiated. That no proof is offered raises some doubts over the reliability of the speaker's allegations concerning the intention of the sureties to accompany Agoratus and the preparation of two vessels for the expedition. Further, Lysias may be deliberately distorting the facts in his assertion that, if Agoratus fled from Athens, he would suffer no loss or harm on the ground that he was not an Athenian citizen. In fact, Agoratus may have had good reasons for not wishing to escape from Athens; he was a privileged metic granted the right of *enktesis* (to own land and property in Attica) and he may have had a family, run a business, or owned property. Moreover, it is not certain whether Agoratus' safety was guaranteed by the democrats, and it is possible that he put faith in the oligarchs who were at the time rising in power. It is even possible that he actually accepted bribes to act in accordance with the oligarchic plans. Nevertheless, his refusal to leave, if true, does not prove that he voluntarily made the deposition.

21 The speaker suppresses the point that Agoratus was tried together with his victims as a defendant and also that before the Thirty he had laid the information under compulsion which he did not resist, in contrast to other persons such as Aristophanes of Cholleidai, who preferred to die rather than give names (§§60–1).

22 The argument from probability that the Thirty could be expected to avenge Phrynichus' murder since it marked the fall of the oligarchy of the Four Hundred with the exile of most of its members is logically plausible but weak in practice. Not all the enemies of the Four Hundred would necessarily be punished by the Thirty; Theramenes, for example, was accepted by the Thirty and was executed only when he quarrelled with Critias.

23 Cf. Lysias 25.9: 'Consider how often the supporters of each of the two types of constitution changed their allegiances, gentlemen of the jury. Did not Phrynichus, Peisander, and their friends the demagogues establish the first oligarchy because they were afraid of punishment for the many crimes they had committed against you? Did not many of the Four Hundred return from exile together with those from Piraeus?

Did not some of those who had driven the Four Hundred into exile subsequently become members of the Thirty? Among those who had registered their names for Eleusis, there were some who marched out with you and besieged those on their own side.'

24 The title of the commissioners appointed to codify and publish the Athenian laws in the last decade of the fifth century.

25 According to the speaker, Nicomachus retained the second office for four years (§4). The speaker's statement in §29, 'you have elected Nicomachus for the publication of our ancestral rites', suggests that the Athenian Assembly appointed Nicomachus as *anagrapheus* of the sacred laws, and such an action can by implication be dated only after the restoration of the democracy in 403. Thus, Nicomachus' second office lasted from 403 until 399.

26 From the speaker's arguments concerning the *topos* of time in 13.83, it can be inferred that the period elapsed from the time of Agoratus' alleged crime until the date of trial is five years; given that Agoratus' alleged victims were put to death under the oligarchy of the Thirty (404/3), the trial must have taken place in 399/8.

27 From the evidence of the inscription (second rider: *Inscriptiones Graecae* I² 110: 14–38), it is clear that the Council decided to record on the Acropolis the name of Agoratus and other conspirators as benefactors of the Athenians, and give them the right of *enktesis*, the privilege of being placed under the protection of the Council and the Prytaneis (i.e. 'presidents', the fifty members of a tribe who directed the Council for one-tenth of the year, each of the ten tribes serving in turn), and the option of further benefits in the future if the Council so decided. The possibility that Agoratus was granted Athenian citizenship at a later stage than the other benefits cannot be excluded, but it remains conjectural owing to the corrupt text of the preserved inscription.

28 Lysias here implies that Eratosthenes was in a position of authority. But the question is whether Eratosthenes was unaccompanied or not. As S. Usher, *Greek Orators I: Antiphon and Lysias* (Warminster, 1985), p. 241 states, 'even if the Thirty had ordered only a house-search, his companions would be witnesses to an escape, wherever it took place'.

29 Again here the problem is that Eratosthenes might have been not alone but accompanied by his companions (see note 28).

4

Kairos in fourth-century Greek oratory

STEPHEN USHER

✳

As was noted in the Introduction, Aristotle (*Rhetoric* 1.3) divided rhetoric into three forms: forensic (legal), deliberative (political), and the catch-all epideictic (display). Although Aristotle's scheme regularly serves as the basis for categorisation of speeches ancient and modern, its limitations are already evident in Lysias' speech *Against Eratosthenes*, where to all intents and purposes forensic rhetoric gives way to epideictic in §41. Another form of categorisation was undertaken from the third century BC in the great libraries of Alexandria and Pergamum, where ancient scholars began the mammoth task of editing Greek texts as far back as the epics of Homer and allocating them to their proper genres; and the next stage was to select the authors considered to be the best representatives of these genres and so establish literary canons. The canon of the best ten Attic orators included Lysias and his contemporary Isocrates, who in the late 390s or early 380s set up a school of rhetoric in Athens. This school rivalled Plato's Academy, offering potential politicians a more practical curriculum in politics and rhetoric, and set the standards for the Graeco-Roman educational system for centuries to come. Isocrates' students, who were not only Athenians but came from across the Greek world, studied great writers from the past, such as the historian Thucydides, and also political tracts composed by their master himself. Like Lysias' *Against Eratosthenes*, these discourses, such as the famous *Panegyricus*, in which Isocrates promotes the concept of a Panhellenic expedition against the Persian empire under Athenian leadership, defy simple classification under Aristotle's scheme, with elements of epideictic rhetoric blended into the overall deliberative structure. A recurrent theme in the discourses, as Stephen Usher discusses, is the concept of seizing the right moment to do something (*kairos*), a lesson which was well understood by Demosthenes himself, the greatest of the Greek orators, even though he was not a pupil of Isocrates (traditionally, he could not afford the fees after his estate was plundered by his guardians). If, then, Isocrates' works were composed to be read rather than spoken, they nevertheless make an important contribution to oratory in action in the politics of fourth-century Athens and indeed Greece as a whole.

✳

The implied challenge in Vollgraff's remark[1] that *kairos* deserves a monograph to itself has not yet been taken up in a comprehensive form. But recently there have been valuable semantic studies, such as that of J. R. Wilson;[2] and M. Valozza and N. O'Sullivan have renewed interest in the function of *kairos* in fifth- and fourth-century rhetoric and criticism.[3] As a guiding principle or concept in literary composition, 'the right or appropriate measure', 'the right moment to employ particular rhetorical devices or effects', *kairos* determines the writer's decisions as to length, emphasis, content, and good taste in general. In this chapter, I fall short of meeting Vollgraff's challenge, but at least widen the discussion to include the oratorical role of *kairos* as a deliberative and epideictic *topos*. While conceding that many examples of this *kairos topos* convey an uncomplicated message to an audience that the time for action is now, I shall try to show how the practical and theoretical concepts merge in the minds of those writers who were conscious of the complete range of the word's critical and rhetorical applications.

Examples of the simple *kairos topos* are to be found wherever a speaker is urging his audience to act. The Ionian (i.e. eastern) Greeks are addressed in Herodotus (6.11) by Dionysius of Phocaea when they are still vacillating about war against the Persians: 'Our affairs are upon a razor's edge between being free men and slaves.' The word *kairos* is not actually used, but the imagery of the old saying (it appears in Homer, *Iliad* 10.173) was incorporated by the fourth-century BC sculptor Lysippus into his allegorical statue of the divine Kairos, whose other features include winged feet, representing his fleeting, transient, evanescent nature; and especially his half-shaven head – having a forelock to be grasped ('Grasp time by the forelock' – Sir Philip Sidney) as he approaches, but baldness, nothing to hold on to, as he departs. Herodotus elsewhere uses *kairos* in its temporal senses, only approaching conceptual force in the expression *es kairon*, which in the contexts where it occurs also contains the added idea of 'to good purpose' (1.206, 4.139, 7.144, 9.87). Thucydides has some dramatic examples of purely temporal *kairos*, as when Pericles utters the generalisation that 'the opportunities of war will not brook delay' (1.142.1); but more interesting is the link with the *topos* of expediency (*sumpheron*) introduced by the Corcyrean ambassadors to Athens (1.36), when they say that 'the greatest opportunities' would be gained or lost by accepting or rejecting alliance with their state; and they go on to specify Corcyra's geographical position and the size of its fleet. A psychological twist, characteristic of Thucydides, gives *kairos* added power when the Corinthians, urging the Athenians to reject alliance with Corcyra, say that this rejection, by being well-timed (*kairon echousa*), could even dispel Corinthian suspicions about other perceived Athenian acts of hostility (1.42.3). This touches upon the *topos* of justice, and the tensions between that *topos* and that of expediency are a major subject of scholarly debate when these speeches are discussed.[4] These examples, and others (2.34.8, 43.2, 3.13.3 (related to expediency), 4.27.4, 54.4 (time and place), 59.2, 90.2 (time and place), 7.11.1), while illustrating mainly the purely temporal or occasional connotation of *kairos*, do to a limited extent include its other associations.

When we turn to writers who have a foot in two camps, that of practical writing in one of the creative literary genres, such as oratory and history, and that of literary theory and didacticism, we encounter *kairos* as a unifying concept. An orator must not only use it as a theme or *topos* but observe it in his own act of composition. For a start, he must know when to speak and when to be silent:

> There are two kinds of occasion on which you should speak – when you know the subject clearly, and when necessity compels you. These are the only occasions when speech is better than silence: on all others it is better to be silent than to speak. (Isocrates 1, *To Demonicus* 41)[5]

and, having decided to speak, when to do so at length, and when to do so briefly:

and when he has also learnt the right occasions for speaking and remaining silent, and has come to recognise the right and wrong time for brevity, pathos, indignation, and the other modes of speech he has studied, then and not till then has he perfected his art. (Plato, *Phaedrus* 272a)[6]

The *Phaedrus* passage is especially important, because it follows a longer, though summary, account of contemporary rhetorical theory (266c–269c), the original sources of which we do not have. A little earlier (271d), Plato has identified a related requirement for successful oratory. This may be called 'know your audience', or perhaps, aping the imagery of the turf, 'horses for discourses'. Plato says that a certain type of audience will be persuaded to take such-and-such a course of action for such-and-such a reason, while another will be hard to persuade with the same argument. The introduction of the concept of *kairos* here as a criterion of when to apply different rhetorical styles or techniques establishes it firmly in the compositional process.

Knowing when to speak, our orator or statesman will also know when to recommend action, thus converting *kairos* from a guiding principle to, in some circumstances, a call to arms. Just as politicians must grasp opportunities at their zenith (Isocrates 2, *To Nicocles* 33),[7] and act upon them, so will they counsel their audiences to follow them. The 'occasion' of a speech confers upon it an immediacy of interest (Isocrates 5, *To Philip* 26): the speaker is making it at that particular time because there is an urgent matter to be decided and acted upon, and he must impress this urgency on his audience.

It is wholly predictable to find Isocrates a unifying authority for both our aspects of *kairos*. He wrote discourses such as the *Panegyricus* and the *Archidamus*, which purported to be, or were models of, deliberative oratory; and, as a teacher, he was interested in rhetorical theory. In the *proemium* of the *Panegyricus* the two aspects come together:

> The opportunity [for a successful expedition against Persia] has not yet passed, and the only time we should cease talking about it is when either events have reached a conclusion and there is no further need to make plans about them, or it is seen that discussion has been exhausted and there is no way left for further speakers to improve upon it. (Isocrates 4, *Panegyricus* 5)

Here deliberative *kairos* and literary-critical *kairos* appear side-by-side. One should speak while, as a counsellor, one has not yet been overtaken by events, and while, as an orator, one has not yet been anticipated by one's fellow speakers, and can still contribute arguments relevant to the debate. The best example of Isocrates' use of *kairos* purely and straightforwardly as a *topos* is also in the *Panegyricus*. After devoting most of the discourse to justification of the expedition and Athenian leadership of it, in section 160 (out of a total of 189) he says:

> Therefore it seems to me that the incentives for us to start a war against them [the Persians] are very numerous, but none is plainer than the present opportunity (*ho parôn kairos*), which we must not let slip; for it is shameful to neglect a chance when it is to hand and remember it only when it has passed.

Here the 'opportunity' arises from the perceived present weakness of the Great King's empire. But Isocrates emphasises that this may be only temporary, so the Greeks must strike now. From the structural standpoint, it is to be noted that the *kairos topos* forms a dramatic coda to a more general section on the theme of possibility (*dunaton*). When it is remembered that the *Panegyricus* took ten years to compose, and was read at leisure long after the events, it becomes natural to think that readers would become more and more preoccupied with these literary-critical considerations. Literary-critical *kairos* is operational in passages where Isocrates is discussing proportional representation of subject matter (13, *Against the Sophists* 16, and 9, *Euagoras* 34). In both these passages he is concerned with the compositional process, a subject of continual interest in his educational system (*paideia*). When he says that due attention should be paid to the *kairoi*, he is referring to the proper proportion in the deployment of different items of subject matter. In *Against the Sophists* 16, this *kairos* is one of the agents of composition, the others being arrangement or interplay, arresting ideas, and stylistic ornamentation.

Hence it is no surprise to find elsewhere in Isocrates that the literary and rhetorical associations of *kairos* receive most attention; and most modern scholars follow his lead. On the subject in general, Isocrates inherits his cast of mind from the older sophists. We read in Diogenes Laertius (9.52) that Protagoras 'explained the power of *kairos*', and, while it is difficult to draw anything precise from biographical snippets such as that offered by an author writing at anything up to fifth hand, it could certainly include speaking at the right time and in the right terms to the right audience, using correct grammar and etymology, the study of which by Protagoras is attested by several sources.[8] But there is more. A central tenet of the sophists is relativism, which includes in particular the belief in the impossibility of absolute knowledge and in the primary importance of individual viewpoints and opinions. This shifting, subjective nature of knowledge may be extended to time: just as individual men's perceptions are peculiar to and valid for themselves, so different opportunities and occasions serve to diversify further these perceptions and the thoughts, words, and actions that arise from them. It is partly against this background that we may approach a more specific statement which brings into the picture another, perhaps more influential, sophist, Gorgias of Leontini. The Augustan critic Dionysius of Halicarnassus states:

> But on the subject of timeliness (good taste) no rhetorician or philosopher has produced a definitive treatise up to the present time. Even the first man who set his hand to writing about it, Gorgias of Leontini, succeeded in writing nothing that was worth mentioning. Indeed, the nature of the subject is not such that it can be covered by an all-embracing, technical method of treatment, nor can timeliness be pursued successfully by science, but only by judgement. (*On Literary Composition* 12)

This failure may be partly explained by the slippery nature of the subject and its associations outlined above, which Dionysius recognises; but other matters associated with Gorgias serve to explain more clearly his position. The first of these is his accomplishment as an impromptu speaker. In common with other sophists, and especially Hippias of Elis, Gorgias claimed to be able to speak off the cuff on any subject proposed by his audience (Philostratus, *Lives of the Sophists*, *Proemium* 482), comprehending the circumstances of the moment and taking them as his inspiration. But such an ability, to be practically effective, required not merely verbal conjury or wizardry (a word – *goêteia* – which occurs frequently in connection with Gorgias), but rational persuasive powers which can be acquired only through understanding of the time, place, and audience he is a addressing. Vollgraff is right to find reference to this in the words 'ability to speak, to be silent or to act, as the situation requires', an otherwise obscure phrase embedded in a fragment of Gorgias' Funeral Speech, where it is preceded by the speaker's claim that he can do so (in the catchy phrase 'I have the ability to say what I wish, and would wish to say what the situation demands'). We need not doubt Gorgias' realisation of the importance of *kairos* and his ability to exploit it, if we can believe that his presence and performance on the Leontinian embassy to Athens in 427 swung the Ecclesia in favour of the Athenian involvement in Sicilian politics which ultimately led to the disastrous Sicilian Expedition.[9] This may excite our admiration, but in considering Gorgias there is always a lingering unease about the moral angle. He readily acknowledges, even delights in, the power of the *logos* (speech) to induce 'deceit' (*apatê*; *Helen* 10). So whose *kairos* is uppermost in his scheme of things? His own – the speaker bamboozling his audience? Or does his conception of *kairos* have ethical foundations?[10] Too little is known about Gorgias to answer that question; but it is one that should be asked nevertheless. For Isocrates the dilemma was practical rather than moral, since the morality of the speaker (himself) is taken for granted, and hence the issue was practical rather than ethical. Since certain knowledge of what is good is impossible, one's guide to *kairos* is *doxa* ('opinion', 'subjective judgement').[11]

Returning to our search for connections between topical and critical *kairos*, we may note briefly a contribution from Thucydides, who wrote of his speeches that they contained or selected *ta deonta* ('what was required of the occasion', 1.22.1). This is the first *kairos* manifesto; but its meaning has been the subject of endless debate. The possible alternatives hinge upon a whole range of applications of the *kairos* concept. 'What was required' could include choice of subject matter, character of audience, the occasion itself, the degree of rhetorical resource called for, including emotional appeal; also 'taste' in a more general sense, which could include both what an audience could have been expected to have received favourably at the time and what a future readership would find both instructive and aesthetically satisfying.

Demosthenes, as a career politician, faced that challenge more directly. Throughout his public life, he was confronting situations which called for action (or in some cases the advocation of inaction). *Kairos* makes frequent appearances as a *topos*, with varying degrees of urgency, in the *Olynthiacs* and *Philippics*. Lysippus' statue comes to mind again as Kairos is personified in 1, *First Olynthiac* 2, where it 'almost gives voice and speaks out'. Indeed, the *First Olynthiac*, like the *First Philippic*, is all about *kairos*, and it takes two forms: Philip's threat to Olynthus creates both a crisis (1.2, 20) and a moment of god-sent opportunity (1.10; cf. 2.1–2; 9, *Third Philippic* 38, 'fortune provides the opportunity') – the latter because answering the Olynthians' call for help would automatically give the Athenians new allies and a foothold on a strategic spot from which Philip could be attacked, or at worst repelled. Demosthenes also suggests (1, *First Olynthiac* 24) that Philip's uneasy relations with his neighbours make him vulnerable – 'think of his difficulties as your opportunity'. Alongside this straightforward deployment of *kairos* as a deliberative *topos*, we find briefly the other rhetorical or literary *kairos* when (2, *Second Olynthiac* 4) he refers paraleiptically to a subject which is to recur frequently in later speeches – that of the alleged partisans of Philip in the Athenian midst. Here he says, 'I perceive that now is not the occasion (*kairos*) to speak about these men.' Now this is a personal angle on *kairos* which had a practical bearing on any speaker to an Athenian audience, when it is borne in mind that a politician could be held to account and punished for his failed policies. This fear is behind the argument in 3, *Third Olynthiac* 10–13, where he says, if I may summarise, that it is pointless to expect a statesman to advocate necessary but controversial policies if he is to be ruined (*apolesthai*) for his pains. In these dangerous conditions, the *kairos* will not find the man to explain it or exploit it. Earlier in his career, Demosthenes has stayed on safer ground, counselling quiet financial reorganisation rather than overt warlike preparations in the speech *On the Symmories*. In the meantime, in speeches such as *For the Liberty of the Rhodians* and *For the Megalopolitans*, the absence of a *kairos* call may seem surprising, but will seem less so if the texts we have are versions of the originals which were published as political tracts.

The two *kairoi* may be seen to interact or their roles may merge as we look at Demosthenes' encounters with his arch-rival Aeschines. In the proemium of his speech *On the False Embassy* (19.3), Demosthenes complains that the passing of the *kairoi* of the events in question – the Athenian embassies to the court of Philip II of Macedon in 346 (the present trial was in 343) – dictates the handling of his side of the case. Because only the ambassadors involved and a few of their attendants knew what actually happened, Demosthenes spends a good deal of time on general arguments, for example on the duties of ambassadors (§§4–7), and on the arousal of emotion against his opponent on the evidence of actions which he cannot now prove and which his opponent flatly denies. The two antagonists select their own preferred events and put exactly opposite interpretations on those which they both record. (They are thus the true prototypes of our modern spin-doctors.) For his part, Aeschines devotes much of his time to Demosthenes' behaviour on the embassies. This is partly concerned with literary-critical *kairos*, but in its negative sense: his misuse of his oratorical talents ('malicious antitheses', 2, *On the Embassy* 4); misdirected emotional appeal (§10); strange vocabulary (he said (§21) that he would 'sew up

Philip's mouth with an unsoaked reed (or rush)'); his use (§40) of vulgar terms such as the untranslatable *paipalema* and *palimbolon*; and perhaps we should add, as an extreme if unlucky example of *akairia* (picking the wrong moment), his breaking down in a bout of stage-fright when it came to his turn to address Philip (§§34–5). Aeschines must have really enjoyed telling that story! At any rate, those criticisms of Demosthenes' taste, or lack of sense of propriety (*to prepon*) correspond with *kairos* as understood and applied by Dionysius and other critics.

Demosthenes had the opportunity to vindicate his policies and his political career in his greatest speech, *On the Crown*. Amid several references to crises and opportunities seized or lost, and to limitations imposed on action by *kairoi* (§239), there is one which crystallises the duality of the concept: 'Just consider; for though the time for action has passed, the time for understanding these events is always present for men of good sense' (§48). Whereas for his impermanent role of statesman and counsellor, on occasions such as Philip's seizure of the strategically vital town of Elatea, *kairos* served to proclaim 'cometh the hour, cometh the man' (§172), for his much more lasting gift of political teaching to posterity, *kairos* this time in its achronous sense has a permanent place, like that which Thucydides wanted for his history, 'a possession for ever'. This achronous *kairos*, the ever-present opportunity to learn, in a sense bridges the gap between the other two *kairoi*: 'men of good sense' are susceptible to both, as both are educative, the *topos* on a practical, the critical concept on an aesthetic level.

Kairos in the sense of 'good taste', which includes particularly sense of proportion and propriety, lies behind many of the discussions conducted by literary critics such as Philodemus, Demetrius, and Dionysius. They lie outside my present brief, but one is worth mentioning. Dionysius finds Dinarchus, the last of the Attic Orators, inferior to his model Demosthenes in 'sense of proportion, of occasion and propriety' (*On Dinarchus* 8). This provides a fitting counterblast to Dinarchus' criticism of Demosthenes (1.31), purely on the topical side of *kairos*, when he says that Demosthenes has made use of many personal opportunities in his speeches (that is, to forward his own career, both political and literary) but had missed all those *kairoi* that could have benefited his fellow citizens. It is always salutary to be reminded of the opposition to Demosthenes and his policies, as has become fashionable in the last thirty years or so; but I think he retains his central position quite comfortably, certainly in literature, and as a patriotic figure in history. He certainly identified *kairos* in both its senses.

So *kairos*, paradoxically, can be always present, when it heralds sound advice or connotes good literary taste. What I have tried to do is to track the interplay between its different nuances, to suggest that authors such as Isocrates and Demosthenes were thinking of a broad range of its meanings when they were apparently using it in a narrower sense; and finally to show how the concept pervades rhetorical practice and literary theory, enriching and animating both.

NOTES

1 W. Vollgraff, *L'Oraison funèbre de Gorgias* (Leiden, 1952), p. 22.
2 J. R. Wilson, 'KAIROS as "due measure"', *Glotta*, 58 (1980), 177–204; 'Kairos as "Profit"', *Classical Quarterly*, 31 (1981), 418–20.
3 M. Vallozza, 'Καιρός nella teoria retorica di Alcidamante e di Isocrate, overro nell' oratoria orale e scritta', *Quaderni Urbinati di Cultura Classica*, 50 (1985), 119–23; N. O'-Sullivan, *Alcidamas, Aristophanes and the Beginnings of Greek Stylistic Theory* (Hermes Einzelschriften 60, Stuttgart, 1992).
4 See M. Heath, 'Justice in Thucydides' Athenian speeches', *Historia*, 39 (1990), 385–400.
5 Cf. Anaxarchus, *On Kingship* (Frag. 72 Diels).
6 Cf. Isocrates 4, *Panegyricus* 9.
7 Cf. 'opportunity is fleeting' (Demetrius, *On Style* 4).
8 For example, Plato, *Phaedrus* 267c; Hermias in L. Radermacher (ed.), *Artium Scriptores: Reste der voraristotelischen Rhetorik* (Vienna, 1951), p. 36.
9 Diodorus Siculus (12.53.5), or rather his probable source Timaeus, is very clear, saying that 'in the end he won the Athenians over to an alliance with the Leontinians'; and the more contemporary Plato (*Hippias Major* 282b) says 'he was judged by the Assembly to have given the best speech' (presumably on either side of the argument, hence carrying the day).
10 M. Untersteiner, *The Sophists*, trans. K. Freeman (London, 1957), p. 108, argues that *apatê* is ethically neutral, being concerned with the creative aspect of deception. The deceiver engages in his concealment of the truth for reasons which may be good or bad.
11 Isocrates 13, *Against the Sophists* 17–18; 15, *Antidosis* 18; 12, *Panathenaicus* 30: 'judgement which seizes moments of opportunity'.

5

Practical advocacy in Roman Egypt

MALCOLM HEATH

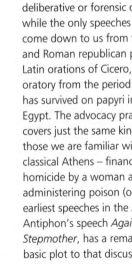

It is easy to think of Greek oratory as declining in the wake of the Macedonian conquest by Philip II and his son Alexander, as the *poleis* lost their independence and the *bêma* its central role in debate and decision-making. Any lingering hopes of a return to political freedom after Alexander's death were quickly dashed by the victory of his general Antipater at Crannon in 322; and Macedonian rule would, in due course, be replaced by the even tighter control of Rome. The age of great political speakers such as Demosthenes and Aeschines was gone for good, and rhetorical activity turned its attention to the sphere of theory, though unfortunately its products are almost entirely lost to us until the early Roman works of the first century BC (the *Rhetorica ad Herennium* and Cicero's *De inventione*). But, as Malcolm Heath rightly observes, loss of political freedom did not mean the end of deliberative or forensic oratory; and while the only speeches that have come down to us from the Hellenistic and Roman republican periods are the Latin orations of Cicero, some Greek oratory from the period of the Empire has survived on papyri in the sands of Egypt. The advocacy practised there covers just the same kinds of topics as those we are familiar with from classical Athens – financial chicanery, homicide by a woman allegedly administering poison (one of the earliest speeches in the Attic corpus, Antiphon's speech *Against the Stepmother*, has a remarkably similar basic plot to that discussed below), a dispute over land – even if the judicial procedure is in many ways different. But these court records have a far greater claim to immediacy and authenticity than the literary products of the Attic corpus, as Heath demonstrates – they are excellent examples of forensic oratory in action.

❋

The Roman Empire has left us no forensic speeches comparable to the masterworks of classical Athens or late republican Rome: no Demosthenes or Lysias, no Cicero. But we do have access to proceedings in the Empire's courts. Among the masses of documentary papyri recovered in modern times from the Egyptian desert are transcripts of court proceedings, written up from the shorthand record taken during trials.[1] These transcripts arguably give us more direct access to the courts than do the works of the classical orators: the speeches they preserve are not literary texts revised and embellished at leisure after the event, but as near as possible[2] oratory *in action*.

The most systematic study of this material, in Crook's *Legal Advocacy in the Roman World*, aims primarily to elucidate the role of advocates within the court system.[3] By contrast, my focus will be on the advocates' rhetorical technique, and specifically on their techniques of *argument*. Rhetoric is often associated with style and presentation, and it is true that at the highest levels of rhetorical training in antiquity intense effort was devoted to the cultivation of stylistic excellence. But the groundwork of rhetorical training gave systematic attention to the analysis of rhetorical problems and the development of appropriate argumentative strategies to deal with them – that is, in the terminology of ancient rhetoricians, to *invention*. My main point of reference in analysing the arguments used in the papyri will be the techniques of invention set out in rhetorical treatises written in Greek (the language used by the advocates we shall be observing) in the second, third and fourth centuries AD (the period to which the papyri themselves date).[4]

The goal of my investigation is a better understanding of the relationship between oratory in action and contemporary rhetorical theory and teaching.[5] Various features of late ancient rhetoric are widely thought to distance it from real oratory. The theoretical systems are formidably complex, a sign (some would say) of arid pedantry. Declamation, the standard training exercise set to students, required the composition of mock-speeches in which fictitious laws were applied to hypothetical scenarios that were often conventionalised and unrealistic, replete with cruel tyrants, wicked step-mothers and such like. Sophists (teachers of rhetoric at the highest level of the profession) could win immense prestige by virtuoso displays in declamations that flaunted the extreme artifice of their conception and expression.[6] It is sometimes supposed that the taste for display and extreme artifice, the retreat from reality and the academic preoccupation with over-elaborated theory reflect a corruption of rhetoric inevitable in a world in which imperial despotism had put an end to free political and legal processes, making 'real' oratory impossible. And yet there were still political and legal processes. Throughout the Empire courts and local and regional councils took decisions about matters which, if not epoch-making in world-historical terms, were of the utmost importance to those involved. These institutions depended on the existence of a social elite in which the ability to speak competently in public was widely disseminated – that is, a rhetorically trained elite. It is possible that rhetoric was taught in sophistic schools in a way that failed to connect with the practical demands of contemporary courts and councils. But there is ancient evidence to the contrary. For example, when enemies of the distinguished fourth-century sophist Libanius wanted to undermine his professional standing, they claimed that his pupils were failing to make the grade as advocates and administrators; this criticism makes sense only if what a sophist taught his pupils was expected to be applicable in those contexts.[7]

The papyri offer a chance to test the connection between theory and practice. We should not expect to find textbook examples of sophistic oratory in the papyri. Rhetorical training was not intended to produce orators who would adhere rigidly to a set framework; rather, it used a set framework to impart a repertoire of skills and techniques meant to be applied flexibly according to the needs of each concrete situation. Moreover, the papyri do not come from the main centres of culture, and are concerned with affairs at a relatively humble social level, at which we should expect to find less elaborate and sophisticated advocacy. So in comparing what was taught by sophists and academic theorists with what advocates did in ordinary courts we should look not for identity but for a degree of continuity sufficient for the two bodies of material to prove mutually illuminating.

DEMETRIUS' DEPOSIT

Demetrius, a freedman, claims to have deposited 2000 drachmas with Geminus, a wealthy man who had formerly employed him as household steward; Geminus has died, and Demetrius is seeking to recover the deposit from his brother Paulinus. The preamble to the court record describes Paulinus as a former gymnasiarch. The gymnasiarch was responsible for supplying at his own expense oil and other consumables for the gymnasium, a central and distinctive feature of Greek civic culture. So this was a 'liturgy' in the original Greek sense: a public service in which personal expense incurred on behalf of the community was rewarded with enhanced status. Tenure of this office marks Paulinus out as a member of the wealthiest stratum of local society. He faces the ex-slave and former employee Demetrius across a wide social gulf.

This case was heard in AD 127 by the *stratêgos* of Arsinoe.[8] Demetrius' advocate Ammonius opens proceedings with a short speech, his only contribution to the trial:

> In the petition which my client presented he stated two grounds of complaint against our opponent: one concerning the mortgage of some houses, the other concerning 2000 drachmas which he deposited with Geminus, the brother of Paulinus. The complaint concerning the houses he passes over for the present; but as for the 2000 drachmas, now that Geminus is dead, he claims the right to get them back from Paulinus, as having care of his estate. I will explain how Geminus got the money. My client, who was a member of his household, and indeed at one time his steward, deposited 2000 drachmas with him, and had the note of the deposit made out in the name of a friend of his, Atrenus. So he claims the right, on production of Geminus' note to Atrenus, to get the money back.

This statement, seemingly clear and straightforward, is in fact deeply flawed, and Paulinus' advocate Palamedes proceeds to take it apart: 'My client could avoid the complaint concerning the 2000 drachmas completely: for he is not the guardian of his brother's sons ...' The legal grounds on which Paulinus denies responsibility for his nephews' inherited liabilities are left vague – probably with good reason. If he had a legally compelling case against being cited, there was a procedural recourse (*paragraphê*) which could have been used at the start of the hearing to get the case thrown out (as we shall see in later examples). The fact that Palamedes did not attempt this suggests that he knows it would not have worked. But the use of an argument that falls short of being legally compelling as a preliminary skirmishing tactic to make the other side look bad is a textbook device (technically, a *paragraphikon* – something like a *paragraphê*).[9] At once we have a point of contact between Palamedes' advocacy and academic rhetorical theory.

Both sides have used a counterfactual prejudicially: Demetrius *could have* pressed another complaint against his opponent (who is really even more villainous than he appears) but magnanimously refrains; Paulinus *could have* avoided the plaintiff's main complaint (which is really invalid) but disdains to rely on a technicality. Palamedes next proclaims the strength of his client's position by showing that he can refute both complaints – the one that has not been pressed, as well as the one that he did not really need to answer:

> But to give you a full picture of our opponent's malpractice, he is willing to reply to both of the complaints made in the petition. The first complaint, as he himself stated it, is as follows: under the previous *stratêgos*, Claudius Dionysius, he complains that a judgement was given against Paulinus in connection with the mortgage of some houses, and adds that the judgement was that Paulinus should restore the mortgage to him. But now he wants to leave aside the judgement concerning these matters, because he knows that he will be found out. For Paulinus maintains very strongly that no judgement was made against him under Dionysius concerning the mortgage of the houses; it was made against other parties.

Demetrius protests ('I don't want to discuss that now'), but Palamedes is insistent, and when the magistrate demands an answer Demetrius has to concede that the judgement was not made against Paulinus ('But as I said before, I am not talking about that now: I claim the right to have my money back'). Thus the prejudicial reference to another dispute has backfired: since Demetrius' credibility is crucial to this case, the admission that his petition misrepresented the facts is damaging.[10]

Palamedes now turns to the main case:

> Already in this first point Demetrius has admitted that he misled His Excellency the governor; but in the matter concerning the money, you will find him still more at fault. I have to begin by saying a little about the persons involved. Geminus was a man of the highest standing, while our opponent is poor, and cannot show any good reason why he should have had the money. His admission that he was a member of Geminus' household, and at one time his steward, is extremely pertinent to the present enquiry: it is this that refutes him – the fact that he took paid employment because he was short of the basic necessities.

Here, too, Palamedes' argument corresponds to theoretical precept. In terms of the theory of issues (about which I shall have more to say below), the case is technically one of 'conjecture': that is, the point at issue is a disputed question of fact – did Demetrius deposit the money with Geminus or not? One important line of argument in such cases is an analysis of the agents involved in the alleged events, designed to establish motive and capacity.[11] It is through these two standard heads of argument that Palamedes first approaches the question of Demetrius' deposit. Emphasising that Geminus was a respectable and prosperous citizen, and Demetrius poor, carries an obvious implication: which is more likely to try to defraud the other of a substantial sum of money? Indeed, how could Demetrius have had so much cash to deposit?[12] The very fact that he took paid employment shows that he was short of funds.

Demetrius' employment next acquires an additional significance:

> And there must be a suspicion that during the time he spent in our house he stole the receipt – which he did not produce while the man himself was alive, and in a position to explain more exactly what happened; but as soon as he was dead, he came after the money.

In standard theory, the plaintiff (or prosecutor) in a conjectural case contends that certain acknowledged facts are signs that the disputed claim is true (in this case, for example, that the existence of a receipt is a sign of the disputed deposit); this has to be countered by reinterpreting the signs in a way that is favourable to the defence. In technical language, these two heads of argument are known respectively as the 'sequence of events' and 'transposition of the cause' or, more perspicuously, 'gloss' (the defendant is putting a favourable gloss on the apparently incriminating facts).[13] Palamedes here reinterprets the situation as theft and attempted fraud on Demetrius' part, thus turning the whole case round: the defence is an allegation against the plaintiff. Hence there is a second conjectural question: in response to the question whether Demetrius made the deposit, Palamedes poses the question whether Demetrius is engaged in a fraud. Technically speaking, this makes the case a 'conjunct' conjecture, of the kind known as 'incident'.[14] The precise definition of incident conjecture was at the heart of a heated third- and fourth-century academic controversy about the interpretation of Demosthenes' *False Embassy*.[15] It is interesting to find a link between this complex and seemingly arcane bit of rhetorical theory and a real case.

Within the second question, Palamedes has established that Demetrius had both a motive for the alleged fraud (poverty) and the capacity (his position in the household gave him the opportunity to steal the receipt); and he has added a construction of events which, he suggests, provides a sign of the defendant's guilt – the suspicious circumstance that Demetrius did not claim repayment while Geminus was alive. This last step is not compelling: Demetrius could reasonably say that he did not anticipate Geminus' death. Theorists taught that weak arguments should be surrounded, or at least followed, by stronger ones that will overshadow them and distract from their weakness. Palamedes accordingly hastens on to what he hopes will be a decisive point:

> I add a further point, of the utmost importance, that corroborates the exposure of Demetrius' fraud. I state that he does not even know Atrenus, in whose name he says the receipt is made out, and cannot tell us who he is or where he comes from.

At this point Demetrius interjects a correction ('It isn't Atrenus, but Deius son of Atrenus, a friend of mine, in whose name I had the receipt made out'), but Palamedes is undeterred, and proceeds to his knockout blow:

> He doesn't know who Deius is either, or where he is from. But it is not enough to produce Geminus' note; he should also produce a note from Deius acknowledging that he gave him the money mentioned in the receipt.

Palamedes has seized on a crucial flaw in the plaintiff's case. Ammonius' reference to a note of the deposit 'made out in the name of a friend of his' left a huge gap in the evidence. A document showing that Geminus received 2000 drachmas from (as we now know him to be) Deius son of Atrenus does not show that the 2000 drachmas were a deposit made by Demetrius. Palamedes' insistence on this point corresponds to the standard head of argument in conjecture known as 'demand for evidence', which draws attention to the inadequacy of your opponent's non-technical proofs (evidence, such as documents or witness statements, that exists independently of the advocate's rhetorical technique).[16] In the textbooks this argument is deployed near the beginning of one's speech, after the initial skirmishing (the *paragraphikon*) but before motive and capacity. But the textbooks also recognise that the default (or 'natural') order of the heads of argument can be varied according to the needs of a particular case. Here, reserving a seemingly decisive point to a climactic position at the end of the speech seems well judged.[17]

In fact, things now go awry. When Palamedes stated confidently that Demetrius did not know the person named in the note, he must have been putting forward as a statement of fact what was only an inference (he apparently had no independent knowledge of the people involved, since he followed Ammonius' mistake about the name). This inference must have looked safe: the missing piece of evidence was so important that if it had been available to the plaintiff he was (surely) bound to produce it; his silence must therefore be significant. But at this point Demetrius produces a note from Deius, apparently completing the chain of evidence that connects him to the money which Geminus received.

The hearing is not yet over. The documents are read out, and the magistrate observes that the note from Deius is dated two years after the receipt from Geminus. Demetrius' explanation ('While Geminus was alive he promised to give the money back; but after his death my opponents were unreasonable, and I had to get a note from Deius too') is challenged by Paulinus, who points out that the note from Deius is dated before Geminus' death; moreover, it refers to a loan, not a deposit. The magistrate adjourns the case to give Demetrius a chance to produce Deius in person, so that the authenticity of the receipt can be tested. We do not know the eventual outcome.

How far was Ammonius to blame for the flaws in his opening statement? The error over Deius' name is a minor point (perhaps he misheard in a hasty pre-trial briefing), and we can hardly hold him responsible for his client's tendentious misrepresentation of his other dispute with Paulinus. But the failure to mention the note from Deius does appear to be negligent. The gap in the evidence is so obvious and so important that any competent advocate should have raised the matter with his client; had this been done, the note from Deius would have come to light. In fact, we cannot be completely confident that Ammonius was at fault in this. If Demetrius knew that there were irregularities in the documentation (and the later dispute about dates shows that it was at best open to question) he had good reason to leave his advocate in the dark, reserving the note for use only if necessity arose. Even on this reconstruction, however, Ammonius seems to be passively transmitting the client's briefing; he provides no added value.

Unsurprisingly, there is a correlation between the litigant's resources and the quality of the advocacy that he can secure, for Palamedes is clearly a far more accomplished advocate. Given his client's relative wealth, Palamedes was probably retained before the trial and had time to prepare at least part of his speech in advance. Demetrius' petition referred to the other dispute, enabling Palamedes to ascertain the facts and prepare his treatment of this point with confidence. The arguments from motive and capacity, depending solely on knowledge of the social status and past history of Demetrius and Geminus, could also have been prepared in advance. But Demetrius' petition apparently did not mention the receipt made out to Deius (since it is unlikely that the mistake about Deius' name originated with Demetrius). If that is right, then Palamedes must have improvised his exploitation of the gaps in the plaintiff's documentary evidence, and consequently also the overall structure of his speech. Though Demetrius' production of the missing document must have been an unpleasant surprise, the subsequent wrangle shows that Palamedes' judgement on this point was basically sound: the opposition's failure to mention the document *was* significant – of its irregularities, if not of its non-existence.

THE DEATH OF MNESITHEUS

The melodramatic scenarios characteristic of declamation included female poisoners.[18] When a single text offers us an accusation of poisoning against a woman, with the counter-claim that this allegation was the last desperate act of a rejected lover's jealousy, and that his death was suicide, or even parricide, then it seems obvious that we are dealing with the lurid fantasies of declamation. But a declamation would not have encumbered these sensational themes with an obscure allegation of mortgage fraud involving the woman's daughter. Nor would the fictive characters of declamation have been given names – Hermione and her daughter Dionysia; the deceased Mnesitheus and his son Sarapion; Smaragdus, the slave who has absconded (the prosecution claims) with some crucial paperwork. This is a real case; another papyrus preserves related documents that allow us to follow its tortuous and inconclusive progress through the courts, in around AD 130.[19] The charges against Hermione and Dionysia were brought first to the regional court of the *epistratêgos*, who referred it to the prefect (provincial governor); Sarapion failed to attend as prosecutor; Hermione died; Dionysia petitioned the prefect for permission to return home; he referred her back to the *epistratêgos*. We do not know what happened after that.

This case, too, is one of conjecture (the disputed question is one of fact: did Hermione poison Mnesitheus?). As we saw in the case of Demetrius' deposit, one crucial requirement for the defence in conjectural cases is to show that the 'signs' (the facts that allegedly incriminate the accused) have an innocent explanation. Where the sign is something said or done by the person accused, the defence can reasonably be expected to state an explanation categorically (why *did* the defendant run away from the scene of the crime, if he was not the guilty party trying to evade capture?). But where the signs are things said or done by others (the textbook illustration is a war-hero accused of treason because the enemy erects a statue in his honour) the defence is under no obligation to state positively what the true explanation is; a variety of speculative explanations may be offered instead.[20] That is the situation here: the signs of the woman's guilt are the man's death in suspicious circumstances, and in particular his allegation against her. If we examine the circumstances (a technical term in rhetoric: who did what, where, when, why, and how?), we note the time and place of the accusation: he came out of his own house – not hers. So it is not that she poisoned him, and he at once exposed her. Would it not be more natural to suppose that the poisoning took place in his own house? If so, it might have been suicide (perhaps his business affairs were in crisis). Or it might have been something even more sinister – after all, the son (the accuser in the present case) as the man's heir was the one who stood to gain from his death. But why then did the dead man accuse the woman? It is easy to see how their business relationship might have given rise to grievances. Or perhaps the truth was quite the reverse: if he was in love with her, jealousy might have made him want to ensure that she did not outlive him.

That, at any rate, is the line of argument adopted in the papyrus:

> For it was from his house that he came out saying that he had been poisoned. When he came out of Hermione's house, he did not tell anyone that he had noticed anything or that he was suspicious of anything at all; but it was from his own house – and that of his son and prospective heir – that he came out saying he had been poisoned. He did indeed have reasons for administering the poison to himself which many others have had in preferring death to life. After all, he was ruined by creditors and at his wits' end. But if anyone did actually plot against him, his son is the likeliest.
>
> The reason why he brought the charge is clear in this way. It is possible that he had other annoyances during his time as steward; but the facts make clear that he was full of jealousy, though she did not know it, and he tried to call himself her husband; but when she denied him that title, he felt a lover's distress and did not want her to outlive him.

Hermione's premature death means that we cannot tell how well this defence would have worked in court. What is certain is that the person who conceived it thought and argued in ways that would not have been out of place in the rhetorical schools. It is not just the defence's sensationalism that is suggestive of the rhetorical schoolroom, but also its underlying logic: the route from theory to implementation is easily traced.

The editors describe this document as a speech. But prosecution arguments are cited conditionally ('if they should say …'), although the prosecution would have spoken before the defence. Perhaps, then, this is not the record of a speech actually made, but preparatory work. The compressed and confusing presentation of some of the material would also be easier to explain in a preliminary sketch. This might take the form of a draft speech, or a brief prepared for the advocate who will handle the case in court, sketching out the main line of argument with suggestions about how to meet various possible contingencies. That would make it a precursor of several fourth-century papyri in which the introductory formula 'You speak on behalf of …' reveals the nature of the document. Typically these later briefs have marginal annotations in a second hand. The client has (presumably) been interviewed and the case prepared by someone other than the advocate who will appear in court. That could be accounted for in a variety of ways; one possibility is that an experienced advocate is giving guidelines to less experienced colleagues.[21] Another form of collaboration between advocates will appear in the next example.

THE LAWS ARE ADMIRABLE, *BUT* …

The council of Arsinoe appointed villagers to civic liturgies. The villagers ignored the appointment, neither discharging the office nor formally appealing against it. They failed to answer a summons to the court of the *epistratêgos*, and judgement was given against them by default. Early in AD 250 the case came before the prefect.[22] Part of the hearing is concerned with a *paragraphê* (the kind of formal objection to the validity of the suit at which Palamedes' *paragraphikon* hinted) advanced on behalf of the villagers. So they must be the defendants; the case is a continuation of the council's attempt at legal coercion rather than a counter-move by the villagers. But the details are unclear: the first part of the papyrus is lost, and what survives is extensively damaged, making it difficult to reconstruct the proceedings in detail. To make matters worse, many documents are cited but not transcribed in full (only the opening words are given, with a cross-reference to an appended dossier, now lost). Moreover, the discussion is at places highly confusing, since the prefect is highly interventionist and there are unusually many participants: there are three speakers on the side of the villagers, while the council fields five – the president of the council and four advocates.

Of the council's four advocates, Lucius does no more (to judge from the extant portion) than read out documents. Ischyrion makes only a single, and singularly ill-judged, intervention. The villagers' *paragraphê* claims that the council meeting at which the appointments were made was not validly convened; the appointments would thus be invalid and the case against them void. When the prefect asks who convened the council, Ischyrion replies: 'The president only convenes the council nominally and to outward appearance, since the convenor is the law.' The prefect's response to this evasion displays commendable restraint: 'The law using some instrument. Some president was the convenor. *Which* president convened the council?' It is Philip, the advocate who speaks most in the extant portions of the papyrus, who gives the correct answer (or, at any rate, an answer which protects the legal position of the current president), and continues the exposition of the council's case. But according to the record the prefect twice addresses himself specifically to the council's fourth advocate, Serenus, whose interventions are few and for the most part laconic. Serenus, perhaps, is the most senior member of the team, overseeing the performance of assistants with varying levels of experience and competence. The extent of Philip's contribution suggests that he is the one most trusted.

Once the prefect is satisfied that the council meeting was validly convened, attention turns to the substantive case. The villagers cite a decision of the Emperor Severus that explicitly exempts villagers from civic liturgies, and the prefect challenges Serenus to match it ('You read me a law too'). But it is Philip who responds, countering the apparent illegality of the nomination by appealing from the letter of the law to its intent. This kind of argument aims to establish that the law in question is subject to a tacit restriction by showing that the underlying purpose of the legislation would be defeated were that restriction not applied.[23] Here, it is taken as evident that the laws exist to sustain civic life; so a tacit restriction of the law must be understood when application of its letter would be detrimental to the cities:

> The laws are indeed admirable and to be held in reverence; but in giving judgement you should observe how the prefects have been influenced by the needs of the cities; and it is the city's need with regard to which the law has

force. This is why prefects, on the many occasions when such laws have been put to them, have decided ... By law you are passing judgement on the Arsinoites, who in times past were populous, but now are ruined.

The prefect ignores Philip and challenges Serenus again: 'What do you say to the law of Severus and the judgements?' Serenus first repeats his colleague's point about the decline in civic prosperity (which the prefect dismisses: 'The argument from prosperity, or from the decline in prosperity, is the same for the villages as for the cities'), and then points to changes in administrative arrangements since the time of Severus. The suggestion in each case is that the application of Severus' decision is implicitly restricted by its presuppositions – the economic conditions and administrative structures that it took for granted; changed circumstances require a different ruling. This may be the best that could have been done, but the argument was unsuccessful: the prefect finds for the villagers on the basis of Severus' law. If the case is weak, skilled advocacy is no guarantee of victory.

THE HEIRS OF ATISIS

An argument about property rights in which both parties deny ownership of the disputed land may seem paradoxical; the explanation lies in their reluctance to accept the associated tax liability. The sisters Herais and Taesis inherited land in the village of Karanis from their father but, unable to meet the tax liability, they absconded. In their absence other villagers were required to cultivate the land (so that the village could still meet the tax demand). When the sisters returned the villagers restored the land to them, with a payment for rent. But the sisters (acting through Herais' husband Nilus) claim that part of the land 'restored' to them is really the responsibility of the heirs of Atisis, the man in whose name the land is registered. Atisis' heirs deny this. The case was heard in AD 339.[24]

Not only is the disputed land registered in the name of Atisis, but the defence will acknowledge that there is no documentary record of any formal transfer of title. The plaintiffs' advocate Theodorus may therefore have thought he had a strong case. But things do not go to plan. After some initial formalities, Theodorus is barely able to complete a sentence ('It was not lightly or thoughtlessly that my clients presented their petition to His Excellency the Prefect ...') before Alexander, acting for the heirs of Atisis, interrupts with a *paragraphê* challenging the validity of the suit:

My clients could have wished to bring this case before the higher court, so as to have our opponents, after being exposed as malicious litigants, undergo punishment. For there is nothing but malice in the petition which they submitted to the Prefect.

And now I shall formally depose before this august court the exception which I have entered, in order to prove to your excellency that our opponents have set the courts in motion against us without grounds. I have come to this court relying on a divine and venerated law of our masters the eternal Augusti, which provides that if someone has enjoyed possession of property for forty years, his possession is in no way to be removed from him, nor is there to be enquiry into the date of its origin.

Now, the father of our opponents owned in the vicinity of Karanis fields which had been made over or ceded to him – we do not know which. He performed the cultivation of these fields, and he appropriated their produce to himself, and likewise paid to the sacred treasury the public taxes arising from them; and no dispute arose during the forty-five years for which he (I mean the father of our opponents) possessed them, with no complaint brought against him. But it seems, to be brief, that the father of our opponents died leaving as heirs his daughters – I mean, our opponents. They were unable to meet the taxes sought for these fields, and resorted to flight. What could the superintendent of the rural district do? Concerned for his own safety and at the same time for the public revenues, he came to the village and assigned these fields to the peasants to farm. One of our opponents married Nilus, who is present here in court, and made a claim for rent against the villagers, since they had farmed the plots during the previous year; she demanded it and appropriated it to herself, on the grounds that she was the owner of the land.

Since, then, they have misled the higher authority, I ask you to permit me to read the divine and venerated law of our masters the eternal Augusti which provides that if a period of forty years passes with someone in possession of property, no one is to proceed in any way against the property or put an end to the longstanding possession.

The magistrate tries to test the chronological claims, but the defence has no documentary evidence of a transfer of title, and Theodorus for his part gives answers vague enough to have struck some commentators as suspicious. It seems likely, however, that he simply does not know the answers. It is hardly surprising if he has not been briefed on the dates, for a better advocate than Theodorus could be forgiven for failing to anticipate Alexander's clever ambush. A law designed to protect the rights of possessors has been turned into a tool for pinning them to the corresponding responsibilities. This has been described as a trick, or – more sympathetically –

as a creative 'stretching' of the law.[25] In fact Alexander is taking the law at face value; it is the other side that needs to show why the application of the law should be subject to a tacit restriction – to argue from letter to intent, as in the previous example. But this is beyond Theodorus' powers. When the magistrate has finished his questions, he merely continues the interrupted opening speech; that is, he asserts his clients' original position without attempting to meet Alexander's argument. He concludes by calling the villagers as witnesses. Since it was the villagers who assigned the disputed land to the sisters, it is unclear what he hoped to gain from this. When the village headman unsurprisingly confirms that the plaintiffs own the land and accepted rent for it, Theodorus is left lamely calling him a liar.

Alexander then springs another ambush: as well as the land, the plaintiffs are in possession of a house in the town also registered in the name of Atisis – which, presumably, they are not disowning. Nilus at first denies all knowledge of this house, and then (when the magistrate asks who is receiving the rent from it) says that it is derelict. The inconsistency does not impress the magistrate. He finds against the plaintiffs, referring to the law which Alexander cited, the testimony of the village headman, and Nilus' effective acknowlededgment of possession of the house. Nilus announces his intention to appeal.

Theodorus lacks flexibility, fails to respond to his opponent's arguments, calls unfriendly witnesses, and is very imperfectly informed about the background to the case. As with Ammonius, this may be to a large extent because he was badly briefed by Nilus, who seems not to be very bright. Even so, Theodorus is manifestly on a different level from Alexander. The latter is fluent, lucid, well-prepared, and tactically very clever. He is no Demosthenes; but he is evidently good at his job.

CONCLUSION

There is a wide variation in the competence of the advocates whose performance we have been considering, and in the role they perform for their clients. Ammonius acted as a mere spokesman for his client, a role needing little if any formal training. Other advocates, such as Palamedes and Alexander, display a level of technical skill that is likely to have been acquired through formal study.[26] But that is perhaps not certain: if the arguments used by these more skilled advocates are those that any intelligent, articulate, and reasonably experienced person could have found in a similar situation, then formal training need not be inferred. Methodological caution suggests that we should draw no firm conclusions about the background of any individual.

Assuming *some* formal training in rhetoric would not, in any case, mean that any of the advocates in our sample studied with one of the leading sophists. It is very unlikely that they did: these men are not orators at the pinnacle of the profession. Even so, we have been able to observe a number of connections between their techniques of argument and those recommended in theoretical textbooks. This has two implications: firstly, that the highest levels of the profession were not separated from less exalted teachers and practitioners by a radical gulf – we should think rather of an extended professional continuum; secondly, that those who had undergone sophistic training would have acquired skills and techniques useful in practical advocacy. This is, as I noted in the introduction, what ancient evidence would lead us to expect.

Again, we must be cautious in drawing conclusions. All we have established is that arguments useful in the mock-forensic exercises of sophistic schools bear *some* resemblance to arguments useful in real forensic practice; it would be astonishing were that not the case. Just as we were unable to draw firm conclusions about the influence of formal rhetorical training on the advocates in our sample, so we have not yet found evidence that the conditions of practical advocacy influenced what was taught by academic rhetoricians. In view of the pervasive artificiality of academic rhetoric, this may seem an implausible idea. It is instructive to compare the Greek theorists with Quintilian. The Greeks invariably illustrate their points by showing how they can be applied to declamation themes; by contrast, Quintilian frequently refers to real cases by way of illustration and the details of his thinking are consistently closer to real forensic tactics. While study with Greek rhetoricians did impart practically applicable skills, the absence of this kind of concrete, court-related advice suggests that more would have been needed to turn the rhetor's student into a practising advocate. There is evidence in literary sources for young aspirants attaching themselves to a senior advocate while gaining practical experience.[27] The examples in the papyri of advocates sharing a case (such as the team representing the council in our third example), and of briefs prepared by one advocate for another, arguably reflect such tutelage in operation at a lower social level.[28]

The material surveyed here may, however, point to less obvious ways in which the conditions of practical advocacy did influence academic rhetoric. One important branch of rhetorical doctrine was the theory of issues. This tries to classify together cases which have the same logical structure. For example, our first two examples are superficially diverse, being concerned respectively with a financial transaction and a homicide, but what is at issue is in a deeper sense the same. The question to be decided in both is conjectural – one of fact: did X do Y? In other homicide cases the question might be one of definition (granted that her actions resulted in his death, is it right to say that she *killed* him?) or evaluation (granted that she killed him, was she justified in doing so?). Rhetoricians in the second century developed a theoretical system in which there were thirteen issues, but by the end of the century they had also incorporated a puzzling anomaly into it.[29] In the earliest attested version of the system the issue called 'objection' (*metalêpsis*) covered cases in which the defence claims that an allegedly criminal act is licensed by some explicit legal provision, and this defence is disputed on circumstantial grounds (the prosecution concedes that the action is legal *per se*, but maintains that it was not legal for that person to do it, or to do it then, or there, or in that way). Subsequently, however, objection was expanded to include cases in which the defence challenges the validity of the proceedings on the basis of some explicit legal provision (which may be procedural: for example, a statute of limitation, or the rule of double jeopardy), and the subsequent dispute turns on the interpretation of that law. Since issue theory classifies cases according to their logical structure, this is strange: cases turning on substantive points about the act and its circumstances are grouped with cases turning on legal interpretation that need a radically different pattern of argument. The latter might more logically be classed under the legal issues (such as letter and intent), which is how they were classed before they were added to objection. There seems to be no explanation for this development internal to issue theory, but there may be an external explanation. We have seen defence advocates trying to pre-empt the plaintiff's case by means of a *paragraphê*. The anomalous hybrid issue of objection brings under one heading the different possibilities for countering such a pre-emptive move. It is possible, therefore, that the inner logic of the system has been adapted to reflect court conditions. If so, rhetorical theory was not an isolated academic activity.

More fundamentally, the evolution of issue theory in the second century went together with a change in the structure of the rhetorical syllabus. Older rhetoricians explained the basics of issue theory in the prolegomena to invention, and then proceeded sequentially through the standard parts of a speech (prologue, narrative, proof, peroration); it was only in the section on proof that specific advice was offered on the arguments appropriate to each issue. In Quintilian, too, the student has to work through a long study of the parts of a speech before learning anything concrete about how to argue a case. Greek theorists in the second century produced much more detailed and systematic analyses of how to argue each issue, and they attached them directly to the prolegomena. In other words, the student now learned how to evolve an appropriate strategy of argument for any given case before learning how to organise a speech according to the standard structure. This development makes sense on internal grounds (one needs to know how the case is to be argued before even the prologue can be composed), but it also seems well-adapted to a jurisdiction (technically, *cognitio extra ordinem*) in which the conduct of a trial is very largely at the magistrate's discretion. An advocate who has a set of argumentative tools that he can apply as opportunity arises without being bound to a formal structure will be able to function even if interruptions by the magistrate or the opponent replace the traditional exchange of extended formal speeches with less structured forms of dialogue.[30] In this respect too, then, it is possible to detect a sensitivity to the conditions of practical advocacy in the development of academic rhetoric.

The change in the structure of the rhetorical syllabus laid academic rhetoric open to further outside influences. The more closely what is taught in the elementary stages of rhetorical study matches what is needed for practical advocacy, the less incentive there is to progress to the more advanced stages. If opportunities to deliver extended formal speeches in court are scarce,[31] there is little to be gained from learning how to elaborate such a speech according to the traditional structure, and still less from the cultivation of a virtuoso style. By the latter part of the fourth century Libanius was complaining about the consequent shrinkage of rhetorical studies. In particular, he was dismayed to find that many of his pupils were willing to forgo advanced courses in rhetoric in order to study other practical subjects – such as shorthand, Latin, and law – useful for entry into the imperial bureaucracy, with its attendant privileges with regard to taxation.[32] Oratory, it may have seemed, was no longer where the action was.[33]

NOTES

1 For a brief survey of the legal system see N. Lewis, *Life in Egypt Under Roman Rule* (Oxford, 1983), pp. 185–95. This book and R. S. Bagnall, *Egypt in Late Antiquity* (Princeton, 1993), provide excellent introductions to the social and economic history of Roman Egypt, and the contribution of papyri to our knowledge of it, and may be consulted for clarification of background detail that space has compelled me to omit.

2 We have no control over errors or omissions in the record. Some transcripts are explicitly selective ('after other things, so-and-so said ...'), but we cannot know how much tacit or accidental selection and compression there has been. Moreover, damage to the papyrus means that in many cases the text is incomplete or partially illegible.

3 J. A. Crook, *Legal Advocacy in the Roman World* (London, 1995); readers should consult Crook for details of papyrological publications cited briefly below, and for further bibliography. Note that we are concerned with advocates, not lawyers. Their function was not to give expert legal opinion but to find the most persuasive way to exploit the facts of the given case and any relevant legal instruments for their clients' advantage, and it was for this that they were trained; legal qualifications did not become compulsory for advocates until the fifth century.

4 For an overview see M. Heath, 'Invention', in S. E. Porter (ed.), *A Handbook of Classical Rhetoric in the Hellenistic Period 330 BC–AD 400* (Leiden, 1997), pp. 89–119. In what follows I cite the most important extant text, Hermogenes *On Issues* (late second to early third century AD); references are by page and line in the edition of H. Rabe (Leipzig, 1913). Translation and commentary: M. Heath, *Hermogenes On Issues: Strategies of Argument in Later Greek Rhetoric* (Oxford, 1995).

5 This paper is part of an ongoing research project on the nature of rhetoric in late antiquity. For an interim report see M. Heath, 'Rhetoric in mid-antiquity', in T. P. Wiseman (ed.), *Classics in Progress* (London, 2002), pp. 419–39.

6 On declamation see D. A. Russell, *Greek Declamation* (Cambridge, 1983); D. H. Berry and M. Heath, 'Oratory and declamation', in S. Porter (ed.), *A Handbook of Classical Rhetoric*, pp. 393–420.

7 This and other evidence for the career-relevance of rhetorical training is briefly discussed in Heath, 'Rhetoric in mid-antiquity'. On the general question of rhetorical training and practice see M. Winterbottom, 'Schoolroom and courtroom', in B. Vickers (ed.), *Rhetoric Revalued* (New York, 1982), pp. 59–70, and the balanced remarks of Crook, *Legal Advocacy*, pp. 163–7.

8 P. Mil. Vogl. 25, reprinted *SB* Beiheft 2 (1961), pp. 30–3; Crook, *Legal Advocacy*, pp. 75–7. *Stratêgos* is literally 'general', but the title refers to a civilian district administrator.

9 Hermogenes 44.1–20.

10 Crook, *Legal Advocacy*, p. 76, disapproves of the fact that 'the magistrate (shame!) forces the plaintiff to give an answer'. But it was the plaintiff who raised the matter in his petition, and it is not clear why he should get away unchallenged with a prejudicial insinuation. It is striking, however, that while Demetrius' attempt at manipulation makes him look unscrupulous, Palamedes' ('My client could avoid the complaint concerning the 2000 drachmas completely ...') makes him look technically proficient.

11 Hermogenes 46.8–47.7.

12 The figures given by Lewis, *Life in Egypt*, p. 208, suggest that 2000 drachmas might be equivalent to three years' wages for the plaintiff when he was employed as a steward or household manager.

13 Hermogenes 47.8–48.2, 49.8–50.19.

14 Hermogenes 56.21–57.11.

15 I discuss this controversy in Heath, 'Rhetoric in mid-antiquity'.

16 Hermogenes 45.1–46.7.

17 Later commentators on Hermogenes in fact provide theoretical warrant for the postponement: Syrianus 2.72.9–12 Rabe; a precedent in Demosthenes, *On the False Embassy*, is claimed by Marcellinus, *Rhetores Graeci* 4.336.7–13 Walz, and *Prolegomenon Sylloge* 300.15–301.1 Rabe.

18 E. g. Hermogenes 45.2–8, 56.15–17. On declamation see n. 6 above.

19 P. Oxy. 472 (with a full translation: my quotation below starts at the beginning of the preserved portion of the text, but omits the section concerned with the mortgage fraud), 486 (the related documents); Crook, *Legal Advocacy*, p. 77.

20 Hermogenes 52.2–11.

21 Thus Crook, *Legal Advocacy*, pp. 114–18; references to the original sources can be found in his discussion.

22 *SB* 7696; Crook, *Legal Advocacy*, pp. 98–9. See T. C. Skeat and E. P. Wegener, 'A trial before the Prefect of Egypt Appius Sabinus', *Journal of Egyptian Archaeology*, 21 (1935), 224–47.

23 Hermogenes 82.5–83.13.

24 P. Col. VII 175 (= *SB* 12692); Crook, *Legal Advocacy*, pp. 104–7. The new material published in B. Kramer and D. Hagedorn, 'Zum Verhandlungsprotokoll P. Columbia VII 175', *Zeitschrift für Papyrologie und Epigraphik*, 45 (1982), 229–41, significantly changes our understanding of the case – showing, crucially, that the heirs of Atisis (not, as previously supposed, the villagers) were the defendants (consequently I find the conjecture that the sisters' father was also named Atisis unnecessary and, if true, irrelevant to the case).

25 Crook, *Legal Advocacy*, p. 106.

26 Theodorus' opening flourish raises hopes that his subsequent failure to rise to Alexander's challenge disappoints. The reasons for this failure can only be guessed at: poor training and lack of talent are not the only possibilities. One might, for example, imagine a beginner hampered by inexperience and unnerved by a distinguished opponent's reputation.

27 In *Letters* 6.23 Pliny accepts a case on condition that the client agrees to his appearing with a younger colleague whose career he wishes to forward. The sharp contrast which Pliny (2.14.2), Quintilian (10.5.19f., 12.11.4–7), and Tacitus (*Dialogue* 34) draw between traditional and contemporary practice, though doubtless exaggerated, suggests a tendency on the part of ambitious young men in contemporary Rome to bypass this junior stage of an aspirant advocate's career.

28 Crook, *Legal Advocacy*, p. 129.

29 For what follows see Hermogenes 42.5–43.8, 79.17–82.3, with my commentary *ad loc*.

30 Indeed, texts such as Hermogenes *On Issues* set out their analyses of the strategy of

argument appropriate for each issue in a quasi-dialogical form, alternating argument and counter-argument.

31 Opportunities for extended speeches were probably more common at higher social and professional levels. The Dmeir inscription (*SEG* 17.759; cf. Crook, *Legal Advocacy*, pp. 91–5) records a hearing before the Emperor Caracalla in 216. The parties to a dispute about the priesthood of Zeus in a Syrian village came to Antioch to have the case heard by the governor, but on finding the Emperor in residence the plaintiff petitioned him to hear the case. Though the litigants are of lowly status, the advocates can be identified as two of the most distinguished orators in the Empire; they were presumably assigned out of the Emperor's entourage (fairness to the litigants required advocates who would not be overawed by the imperial presence). After a *paragraphê* (there is no right of appeal to the Emperor, since the case has not been heard by the governor: Caracalla acknowledges the technical validity of this, but can see no harm in his hearing the case) the plaintiff's advocate says that he will speak for half an hour, prudently providing reassurance that he will not speak too long, and checking that his plan is acceptable to the person presiding. Unfortunately, the rest of the inscription is lost, denying us the opportunity to observe top-rank orators in action.

32 For a brief discussion of Libanius and his pupils see Heath, 'Rhetoric in mid-antiquity'.

33 I am grateful to Dominic Berry and Roger Brock for helpful suggestions. The research for this paper was completed with the support of a British Academy Research Readership. I have developed the argument further, with additional observations on some of the cases discussed here, in M. Heath, *Menander: A Rhetor in Context* (Oxford, 2004).

6

Transformation of the city: John Chrysostom's oratory in the homiletic form [1]

AIDEEN HARTNEY

❀

A category of epideictic rhetoric that Aristotle of course could not have foreseen is that of the pulpit. John Chrysostom, who is not to be confused with his much earlier rival to the title of 'Golden Mouth', Dio Cocceianus Chrysostom, was aptly named, though his sublime rhetorical powers served only to cause his eventual banishment from Constantinople, where he was a reluctant bishop. Just as Isocrates won renown more for his rhetoric than for his philosophical ideas, so was John's preaching a greater testament to his rhetorical prowess than his theological insight. His already conservative interpretation of the Scriptures covered Genesis, the Gospels of Matthew and John, the Acts, and the Epistles of Paul; and, as Aideen Hartney shows, his congregation was clearly far more interested in his speaking as a form of entertainment than in the message it contained. The congregation, as noted in Hartney's introduction, comprised women as well as men; but even the predominantly male society of classical Athens would perhaps have recognised the importance of women hearing the epideictic message – in one of our earliest pieces of epideictic, Pericles' Funeral Speech in book 2 of the history of Thucydides, Pericles specifically addresses women on their duty in Athenian society, if only briefly (Thucydides 2.45.2). His message is the *topos* that a woman's greatest glory is to be least talked about by men, a pagan tradition but an antecedent of John's ideal of the Christian housewife. Aristotle for his part would very much have recognised the rhetorical efficacy of John's homilies, which in turn makes him a worthy subject for inclusion in any volume on oratory in action.

✳

The realm of Christian preaching has recently come under increased attention from scholars of late antiquity, recognising that in the many sermons which survive valuable information can be found regarding the lifestyles and preoccupations of this era of society. The work of Pauline Allen and Wendy Mayer in Australia is a particularly good example of this process, as they work to construct a database of social information gathered from sermons preached in Antioch in the fourth and fifth centuries.[2] This is in marked contrast to the view once expressed by A. H. M. Jones, who said that after extensive study he could find nothing in Christian sermons that shed any light on day-to-day life in the later Roman Empire.[3] Indeed we are now discovering how very rich a source such sermons can be for information on everything from contemporary fashions to the length of the average working day.

But church preaching also sheds light on the process which has come to be known as the Christianisation of discourse, whereby a Christian frame of reference came to overlie the traditional structures and philosophies of the Graeco-Roman world.[4] As a key part of this process, the inherited techniques of oratory and public speaking were employed by leading church preachers to propound and disseminate their new ideas throughout the community. John Chrysostom, born in AD 349, was one of the most prolific and skilled practitioners of this approach, with his name actually being a tribute to this fact, meaning as it does 'Golden Mouth'. It is generally agreed that Chrysostom was educated by the renowned Antiochene orator Libanius, a staunch pagan, who nevertheless recognised the great talent of his student, and was said to have murmured on his deathbed that John should have been his successor 'if only the Christians had not stolen him from us'.[5] John instead made a name for himself in the ecclesiastical arena, writing prolifically and achieving recognition as an accomplished speaker at a comparatively early stage in his church career. His skill in this field won him a large number of loyal fans from among the worldly Antiochenes, who regularly flocked to hear him preach, and was also a contributory factor to his subsequent promotion to the episcopacy of Constantinople. An examination of some of John's work is therefore rewarding in any discussion of the role of rhetoric and oratorical skill in the expansion and consolidation of the Christian church within the Roman Empire.

The power and influence that could be wielded by a church preacher over the minds and hearts of a lay congregation was by no means underestimated by ecclesiastical authorities. In some places, therefore, only bishops were entrusted with the task. (In Antioch, however, John preached regularly while still a priest, initially because of extenuating circumstances surrounding the Riot of the Statues in Antioch in AD 387.) By the same token, it was deemed vital by Christian authorities that those with responsibility for the preaching ministry should strive to acquire excellence in the techniques of oratory, so as best to lead and guide their spiritual charges. Those who could not speak effectively could not hope to influence a worldly congregation, or even instruct them in the mysteries of the Christian faith. Therefore church preachers were encouraged to acquire and use all the skills of speech and persuasion which were available to them, so that they might adequately perform their duties. Ironically this led to an embrace of the tropes and trappings of classical literature, rhetoric, and philosophy, of which Christians theoretically disapproved, in an effort to reach their congregations with a shared language:

> The power of eloquence – so very effective in convincing us of either wrong or right – lies open to all. Why then, do not the good zealously procure it that it may serve truth, if the wicked, in order to gain unjustifiable and groundless cases, apply it to the advantages of injustice and error? [6]

Failure to equip themselves with all the tools at their disposal could lead Church authorities open to the charge of neglecting their flock, and being held responsible on the Day of Judgement for any loss of souls which might have occurred as a result. John Chrysostom himself was very concerned about those Christians who might not have had sufficient guidance for their souls on account of inadequate rhetorical skills on the part of their pastor. How else could ordinary people be convinced of the message of God and of the theological soundness of the doctrines being propounded by the Church authorities?

> If anyone is without this skill [of good public speaking], the souls of those who are put under his care (I mean of the weaker and more meddlesome kind) are

no better off than ships which are continually storm tossed. So the Priest should do all that he is able, to acquire this means of strength.[7]

These high standards were not only demanded by Church authorities themselves, with their dedication to their pastoral duties, but were also expected by members of the laity. This can be seen in the very selection process of which homilies should be kept for posterity. Shorthand scribes would attend the churches in late antiquity and transcribe the sermons of those preachers who were considered skilled enough. As the church historian Socrates sorrowfully tells us of one bishop Atticus of Constantinople:

> Formerly, while a presbyter, he had been accustomed, after composing his sermons, to commit them to memory, and then recite them in the church; but by diligent application, he acquired confidence and made his instruction extemporaneous and eloquent. His discourses, however, were not such as to be received with much applause by his auditors or to deserve to be committed to writing.[8]

John Chrysostom, however, was a preacher who obviously met with the highest of contemporary approval, since an extraordinary number of his sermons have been preserved for us by these shorthand scribes. His style was rhetorically polished, therefore sometimes seeming quite complex to us today, but the content was clear, and presented in a lively fashion, winning him the admiration, and even adoration, of his congregations both in Antioch and later in Constantinople.

Chrysostom's skill as a church orator often led to him being viewed as a particularly good form of entertainment within the civic community, on a par with theatrical performances or sporting events. This is somewhat ironic, given his own intense disapproval of such spectacles. He saw them as prompting immorality and disorder in the lives of his charges. It was the display of actresses on the stage which he saw as leading to lustful thoughts in young men, while the gathering of citizens at sporting events such as horse races merely sponsored ostentation, gambling, and an excessive display of emotions. Throughout his career we see these sentiments being expressed by Chrysostom in his homilies, as he struggled to redirect the energies of his flock along more spiritual lines. On the surface it would seem to be the immorality of the dramas performed in the theatre that offended him, and he takes care to present the literary heritage of his flock, which displayed such dubious matters, as both ridiculous and contemptible:

> One man loved his stepmother, and a woman her step-son, and as a result hanged

herself ... And would you wish to see a son married to his mother? This too happened among them, and what is most horrible, although it was done in ignorance, the god whom they worshipped did not prevent it, but permitted this outrage against nature to be committed, even though she was a member of the nobility ... The wife of a certain man fell in love with another man, and with the help of her adulterer, killed her husband on his return home. Most of you probably know the story. The son of the murdered man killed the adulterer, and after that his mother, and then he himself went mad, and was haunted by the furies. After this the madman himself murdered another man, and took his wife for himself.[9]

This outburst occurs as part of an attempt by Chrysostom to demonstrate to his current audience the immorality of the Greek dramatic plots, and so he crudely summarises the plots of *Hippolytus*, *Oedipus Tyrannus*, and the *Oresteia* as shameful and ridiculous. Thus the cultural heritage held by almost everyone in his congregation, and indeed by John himself, is consistently and deliberately denigrated, paving the way for its replacement with Christian alternatives. As part of this project, the moral standing of the Greeks themselves is called into question, since they accepted the regular display of such nefarious deeds on their stages, and even allowed young virgin girls into night-time performances where they would both witness such shameful goings-on, and be thrown into the company of young, debauched, and unlicensed men. And indeed, in the above whistle-stop tour of Greek dramatic plots, Chrysostom has very cunningly blurred the distinction between fiction and reality, so that it seems as if he were speaking of the Greeks themselves, and regular occurrences within their community, instead of the creations of poets and playwrights. Elsewhere these same Greeks are dismissed as self-indulgent children, thus further underlining their unsuitability as cultural ancestors for Chrysostom's current audience:

For all the Greeks are children ... Now children cannot bear to take thought for anything useful; so also the Greeks would be forever at play; and they lie on the ground, grovelling in their posture and in their affections ... And as children expose their limbs unconsciously, and do not blush for shame; so the Greeks, wallowing in whoredoms and adulteries, and laying aside the laws of nature, and introducing unlawful intercourses are also unabashed.[10]

This carefully worked approach is in fact typical of Chrysostom's style, and was part of what made his preaching so popular among the citizens of the late antique cities in which he operated. He specialised in the presentation of vivid and evocative pen-pictures, which would capture and hold the attention of an audience all too prone to distraction, and which he would then proceed to undermine by demonstrating the dangers inherent in such behaviour. Thus, the congregation listening to the above extract would have been caught and held by his lively summary of stories and dramas well known to them through their education and entertainment systems, only to be shown at the end that this way of life was something to be shunned by them at all costs. The Greeks become the example of how not to act, and the more ridiculous and lowly such exempla are shown to be, the greater the encouragement to avoid similar actions. Thus these heathens are presented as mere children, spoilt and fractious, or as supporters of an anarchic society, where sons killed fathers and mothers turned against their children, all on account of their not having known Christ. For Chrysostom's congregation to show similar evidence of immorality and selfishness is for them to be no better than pagans, who are skilfully presented by the preacher as inhabiting the worst possible society.

There is a similar undermining of the philosophical theories which would have been familiar to the majority of a fourth-century Christian congregation. Revered and much-studied names are now dismissed as unlettered or misguided men, while well-known theories are presented in the abstract – divorced from their formulators as a mark of disrespect and denigration. Now St Paul is extolled as a teacher with a true philosophy, and one who was more effective in reaching his audience than any Plato or expensively educated classical philosopher. Christian oratory works in this way to remake classical culture in its own image.

Of course it was not just the immorality of theatrical spectacles or philosophical discourses that Chrysostom objected to in his tirades against these core aspects of civic life in the ancient world. It must be said that his vanity was frequently offended by the manner in which his congregation were lured away by such urban entertainments, instead of devoutly attending church and listening to his words of guidance. On many occasions he can be heard to reprimand a congregation for their absence on the previous day or week, decrying the fact that they preferred cheering for some horse on which they had a bet or drooling over a new actress, to the upkeep of their immortal souls. But it was also a matter of pride to Chrysostom that he should attract and hold the attention of this secular crowd on such a regular basis. It would seem that the worldly inhabitants of both Antioch and Constantinople considered their preacher to be merely another form of entertainment. Indeed, the demands placed on a man holding a public ministry within the church were well known to Chrysostom, as is evident from the following passage, delivered in some exasperation in the course of a sermon:

> He [the bishop] is distracted on every side and is expected to do many things that are beyond his power. If he does not know how to speak effectively, there is much complaining; and if he can speak, then he is accused of being vainglorious. If he cannot raise the dead, he is worthless, they say: such a person is pious, but this man must not be. If he eats a moderate meal, he is accused on this account, and they say that he ought to be strangled. If he is seen at the bath, he is greatly criticised. In short, he should not even look at the sun! [11]

In recognition of the demanding nature of his audience, Chrysostom throughout his career seems to have made the decision to pander to their expectations in order to hold their attention, and thereby effect some change in their lives. And so he embarks upon a competition with the secular attractions of the city, a kind of ratings war as it were. In this endeavour, rhetorical expertise became ever more important, and Chrysostom certainly pulled out all the stops. He knew best how to preach a dramatic and eloquent sermon which would both interest and enlighten his audience, but often he would reserve his greatest efforts for those days when attendance numbers were actually down, so that word would spread to the stay-at-homes that they had missed something remarkable. Points of contention with his flock would be dealt with through drama – hypothetical opponents would be created by Chrysostom for him to argue against strenuously and effectively. And evocative descriptions were employed to fasten any wandering thoughts to the subject in hand. His reputation as a golden-tongued speaker would indeed be much spoken of in the Christian communities within these cities, and it is even thought that non-Christians would attend church services at which Chrysostom was due to preach, such was the extent of his fame. Unfortunately, such successful campaigning for attendance figures could backfire on Chrysostom, as he was heard to complain on a number of occasions that his congregation had actually trooped back out of the church immediately after the close of his sermon, indicating that it was indeed the entertainment value of his rhetoric that they had come for, rather than for any higher moral purpose. [12] What we do see in all this, however, is the premium which was placed on effective speaking in the dissemination of the Christian message, and the extent to which

Chrysostom employed all the tricks of the trade in order to reach his own congregations.

His favourite strategy – the setting up of a fall-guy, or a negative exemplum, for his congregation to take note of and adjust their behaviour accordingly – is one employed by Chrysostom in two key areas of life in the ancient city, namely gender roles and the uses and abuses of wealth. His approach to these topics shows that it was more than simply the undivided attention of his audience that Chrysostom was aiming for, but actually a far more ambitious end. In targeting such core aspects in the lives of his flock with his most advanced rhetorical skills, Chrysostom in fact hoped to remodel the behaviour of each citizen of the ancient city-state (*polis*), and thereby transform the civic unit itself into one which clearly demonstrated the ethos of Christianity. To this end a series of vivid pictures was presented by the preacher to his congregation, in which contrasting modes of behaviour would be detailed, along with the ensuing circumstances. One of the best examples of this process at work can be seen in the preacher's discussion of behaviour appropriate to each of the sexes, so that men would demonstrate their intellectual and moral superiority through their adherence to God's law, and women would display suitable modesty and obedience to God and their husbands. In delineating these modes of behaviour through his preaching, we see Chrysostom display keen powers of observation with regard to ordinary human nature and its common flaws. He is aware that many in his congregation are more concerned with outward appearances than with inner spiritual health, and hopes to frighten them into more thoughtfulness:

> Observe the contestants and wrestlers in the games. Do they worry about their style of walk or their dress? No, but despising these things, and simply throwing about them a garment dripping with oil, they care only for one thing, to wound, and not be wounded. The devil stands grinding his teeth, waiting to destroy you in every way, and yet you remain unconcerned, or concerned only about this satanic ornament.[13]

Here pictures of worthy role models are juxtaposed with the literally hellish consequences for those who refuse to take heed. And if the devil does not terrify his congregation into more moral behaviour, Chrysostom can paint another picture which will work to achieve the same end through disgust if not fear:

> You would never choose to wear a piece of clothing which your slave wears,

being disgusted because of its filth, and you would rather go naked than use it. But will you abuse a body that is unclean and filthy, and which is used not only by your slave, but by numberless others, and not be disgusted? ... Tell me, what if you and your servant should go to the same woman? And I would hope it was only your servant, and not, let's say, the executioner! And yet you could not bear to take the executioner by the hand; but you kiss and embrace she who has become one body with him and you do not shudder, nor feel fear![14]

And so Chrysostom uses his skill with words to persuade his congregations that traditional attitudes to life, such as the privileging of rich appearances or the easy acceptance of adultery on the part of men, no longer have a place in the Christian scheme of things. He uses a constant, but no less carefully worked out, approach to convey this message. A picture of abhorrent behaviour or fearful consequences is graphically presented with all the rhetorical skill at his command. This is then set alongside a picture of the Christian alternatives or beside a recommendation as to how to avoid what has just been so dramatically conjured up in the mind's eye of every member of Chrysostom's congregation. And each instance of this approach forms a part of the preacher's overarching aim, which was to create a recognisably Christian city – one which would match the more devout examples he has spoken of.

A passage in which all of this can be seen to good effect is the one in which Chrysostom details the vanity of some women purporting to be ascetics, and yet who take more pains with their personal appearance than many an actress or a harlot.[15] The more John lingers on the finer points of their attire, the more he signals to his audience that this is not something to emulate. What is more admirable is his idealised portrait of the Christian housewife, who cares little for external appearances, seeking only to look modest and humble, and instead devotes her attention to the economical and righteous management of the household. Such a woman would not wear make-up or excessive jewellery, and her dresses would be simple and unremarkable with regard to colour or tailoring. This is one picture Chrysostom would like his audience to emulate.

But what is interesting to note throughout this process is the extent to which, in lingering on these vivid pictures, Chrysostom actually focuses the eyes of his audience on the very activities or people he wishes them to avoid – be it vanity with regard to dress or consorting with prostitutes. Paradoxically, therefore, we see John concentrate on providing his audience with the very type of entertainment which he so decried when it took place in the secular arena of the theatre. The intense focus on morally dubious acts or characters which was the crux of attending the theatre was what Chrysostom objected to, feeling that it presented his flock with more temptation than they could withstand. And yet here he creates a similar focus and does nothing to mitigate its intensity. All those attending his sermon – and it could be a large and socially diverse audience – are now encouraged to concentrate on pictures of wayward virgins, or even on their more admirable companions. This is in spite of the fact that Chrysostom firmly believes that it is through the eyes that lust enters the human soul, and so he would generally disapprove of men gazing on women with such intensity. When he discusses the evils of wealth, Chrysostom draws the eyes of his congregation to the personal peccadilloes of the rich and famous within their community, even as he denounces such a decadent way of life. One could almost describe it as 'tabloid' preaching. It is as if Chrysostom recognised the need of his audience to let off steam, and decided to make himself the safety valve, releasing their pent-up desires within the safer boundaries of the ecclesiastical service and building. He could then present his audience with an alternative behaviour system, to take the place of the desires they had just been encouraged to indulge on a temporary basis.

Unfortunately some of Chrysostom's wealthier audience members are proving hard to persuade, with their inappropriate behaviour becoming most manifest in their outward appearances. They insist on coming to church in all their finery, for example, and in his efforts to combat this fruitless display of worldly possessions Chrysostom presents his audience with many pictures of wealthy men and women whom he deliberately paints as ridiculous. He speaks of the woman who enters the church building in a particularly lavish outfit, turning this way and that to show herself off in a flattering light, and, rather than thinking of God and the respect due to him, she is merely concerned as to the feelings of admiration and envy she can arouse in other members of her sex.[16] On another occasion Chrysostom has cause to become particularly irate concerning the female love of gold and other precious metals. So bad has this current craze become that he sees even mules and carriage horses being adorned with gold,[17] and, if things do not improve, he does not doubt that the women themselves will start wanting their hair, lips, and eyebrows to be overlaid with the stuff.[18] And then of course there is the infamous occasion in which Chrysostom railed against his audience for possessing silver chamber pots:

Do you pay such honour to your excrements, as to receive them in silver? I know that you are shocked at hearing this; but those women who make these things ought to be shocked, and the husbands that minister to such distempers.[19]

In marked contrast to such vain and worldly women, we hear elsewhere of those young virgins who have transcended both the limitations of their sex and their gentle upbringing in order to embrace the exigencies of the ascetic lifestyle. Here Chrysostom provides both sides of the coin in his rhetorical display. First, he speaks of the tender nature of these women, the delicacy of their former style of living, and the many luxuries they were accustomed to. Then the contrasting state of their current existence is presented, and they are likened to athletes who have stripped off for the contest, thinking nothing of earthly belongings or comforts.[20] Thus the admiration due to such women is underlined by the focus on the very wealth that they had forsaken for love of God.

In this manner Chrysostom presents to his audience both the kind of behaviour that is judged ridiculous and immoral, and the attitude which is more becoming to women who claim to be Christian. Female members of the congregation can see both extremes, and can decide, on the basis of the rhetorical bias of the preacher, which path would be most beneficial for their moral well-being. But it is not just women who were targeted with such outbursts. Indeed these recommendations were not intended by Chrysostom for female ears alone. For the many men who would have been part of his congregation would also have been expected to take notice of the behaviour which met with their prelate's approval and disapproval. For Chrysostom had grave reason to be concerned as to the state of his male audience. Due to their excessive love of wealth and its ostentatious display, the men were in fact running the risk of becoming effeminate, or even worse. Men who cared too much for the latest fashions, and who wondered how their appearance would be greeted in public, were worse than the silly women who wore too much jewellery, since this kind of frivolity was unsurprising in the female sex, but deeply worrying when evidenced in the male sex. Where men have forsaken natural human compassion and restraint in return for rapaciousness and greed for wealth, Chrysostom likens them to wild dogs and other animals. His argument is that their desire to amass ever more wealth has negated their God-given intellectual and moral superiority, and so they become like dumb beasts. The use of the less pleasant members of the animal kingdom in such comparisons as these merely serves to underline Chrysostom's disgust for this kind of behaviour, since he can feel confident that none of his congregation would welcome being likened to slavering dogs, stubborn camels, or the monsters drawn from Greek mythology such as the chimaera.[21]

Thus, by caring for matters of personal appearance or for the vainglorious display of wealth, the men involved are in fact sinking to below the level of women. The frequent depictions of frivolous women as objects of contempt and derision which we have already seen make it clear that this is something to be avoided. Chrysostom is deeply concerned as to the blurring of gender boundaries inherent in such behaviour. Not only have men become more like women in their desires and shallow actions, but they have deliberately cast aside their divinely appointed superiority of virtue and intellect. Much of Chrysostom's rhetorical talent is devoted to showing the terrible consequences of such wilfulness.

Such is his concern for the moral salvation of his congregation, Chrysostom leaves few areas of civic life untouched in his preaching, and is certainly not slow to be gruesomely graphic if he feels it suits his purpose. The over-indulgences of the wealthy are often detailed, only to be highlighted for the vanities that they are or undermined by the equally detailed pictures of the sufferings that are the consequences of such indulgence. Speaking against the excesses of the dinner table, Chrysostom works hard to paint a lavish portrait of the rich person's dinner party, with all the ornaments and trappings that would be considered important by a host. And once this idealised picture is in place – like a photographic spread from a modern celebrity magazine – he immediately works to undermine it, detailing the nausea, hangovers, vomiting, and long-term physical illnesses that often result from such over-indulgence.[22] And so once again, Chrysostom's congregation are warned of the behaviour that will not be tolerated from them as professing to be Christians, through this comparison of two alternative ways of life.

Chrysostom's aim in this carefully worked presentation of the behaviour he hopes his audience will embrace is to make the society of the late antique city reminiscent of those ascetic communities he himself spent time in and admired so highly as a younger man. If Christian models of behaviour are appropriately adhered to, and if men and women each perform their allotted tasks with modesty, humility, and obedience, the resulting household will be harmonious and well-run. And if they can also be persuaded that money and its abuse leads to a host of other evils, and that a more moderate approach to economic matters is to be recommended, the household will also be a financial replica of the ascetic community, where there is no 'mine and thine', and no bother over storage chests or security guards for excess possessions.[23] This change in outlook will extend into the wider city landscape, since the Christian householder will no longer spend his days in the forum contracting business deals and working to accumulate vast sums of wealth to future generations. Instead he will dispense with his business as soon as possible and will hurry home to his family, to continue his task of bequeathing a spiritual rather than a financial inheritance to them.[24] Similarly, public gatherings and entertainments will be replaced by the regular convening of the faithful for church services, where we have already seen how a good preacher could be just as exciting as a chariot race, if he was on form. Civic building works would be replaced by the building of ecclesiastical structures, which would become the new public spaces of the urban landscape. And municipal euergetism, by which the rich citizens had been used to gather influence and notice, would be replaced by the more private and individual euergetism of almsgiving, so that all God's creatures would have the necessaries for survival in some kind of dignity.

This, then, is Chrysostom's planned city, a community of equally distributed wealth and devout, sober citizens. It is a transformed model of the traditional *polis*, and one in which Chrysostom passionately believed. In his efforts to realise his dream, he constantly strove to alter the behaviour of his flock through the medium of his preaching. Regular sermons were the most effective means available to Church authorities for disseminating the Christian message and influencing the lives of the faithful, since they were unparalleled in their accessibility to all inhabitants of the ancient world, regardless of age, sex, or social standing. What is most ironic, however, is that the best way to construct such a sermon, so as to capture and hold an audience, was to make use of the oratorical techniques available to the preachers, which were inherited from centuries of preceding Graeco-Roman culture. The skills employed by Chrysostom in his flamboyant preaching were those passed on to him by Libanius and were held by him in common with most of the inhabitants of the city. Such rhetorical bearing was in fact as natural to Chrysostom as breathing, and, while the culture of the Greeks and Romans is generally derided by him as pagan and uncouth, as we saw at the outset of this discussion, his best hope of success was actually to employ some of its techniques to suit his own ends. And so the style and structure of his homilies would have been familiar to almost every member of his audience. His rhetorical flourishes, his use of dramatic dialogue, his close similarities to the Cynic diatribe on occasion, and his vivid pen portraits of people and lifestyles were all part of the tool-kit of the ancient orator.[25] And indeed many of his argumentative strategies are reminiscent of the rhetorical tropes of the Cynic and Stoic schools of philosophy, and even of Plato and Aristotle themselves. What is different is the use to which Chrysostom put these skills. By employing techniques so familiar to his congregation, Chrysostom in fact lulled them into a sense of familiarity and security, which he then used to put forward his new ideas and his pleas for change. Thus a Christianised bias was placed over the traditional concepts of society. The well-known nature of the rhetoric involved and Chrysostom's own excellence as an orator meant that his audience were not as resistant as they might have been to these alien concepts. And so John hoped to transform the ancient city until it resembled one of the monastic communities he admired so much, using his skill as a public speaker as his primary weapon in this struggle. Unfortunately there is little evidence to show that he succeeded, and this is perhaps puzzling when we see how aware he was of the right way to go about manipulating his audience on so many occasions. I can only suggest that sometimes his frustrations as to their recalcitrance got the better of him, leading him to become shrill and offensive rather than simply persuasive and compelling. His outspokenness eventually lost him the goodwill of many wealthy and influential members of society, who were probably tired of him targeting their lifestyle and activities with such vigour. The loss of this support left him open to plotting from within the ecclesiastical hierarchy, and Chrysostom was eventually exiled from Constantinople, on a series of trumped-up charges, dying in 407 with his dream of a uniquely Christian city sadly unrealised.[26]

NOTES

1 My thanks go to Michael Edwards and Christopher Reid for their invitation to contribute to this volume. The extracts from John Chrysostom's homilies which I use throughout this article are adaptations of the translations contained in the *Nicene and Post-Nicene Fathers* (hereafter *NPNF*) collection of patristic writings.

2 I am very grateful to Allen and Mayer for allowing me to see some of this work in its initial stages. A discussion of their approach can be found in P. Allen, 'Homilies as a source for social history', *Studia Patristica*, 24 (1991), 1–5 (p. 1).

3 A. H. M. Jones, *The Later Roman Empire* (Oxford, 1969), pp. vi–viii.

4 See further A. Cameron, *Christianity and the Rhetoric of Empire* (Berkeley, 1991), and P. Brown, *Power and Persuasion in Late Antiquity: Aspects of the Christianisation of the Roman World* (Cambridge, 1992).

5 Sozomen, *Historia ecclesiastica* 8.2.

6 Augustine, *De doctrina Christiana* 4.2.

7 *De sacerdotio* 4.5, *NPNF* 9.66, *PG* 48.663.

8 Socrates, *Historia ecclesiastica* 6.4, *PG* 67.672.

9 *Homily V on Titus*, *NPNF* 13.538–9, *PG* 62.693. See also *Homily V on I Thessalonians*, *NPNF* 13.347, *PG* 62.428: 'When you see women displayed in the context of their physical bodies, and see spectacles and songs containing nothing but deviant loves, as when such a woman, it is said, loved such a man, and not being able to have him hanged herself; or unlawful loves which are felt for mothers; when you hear of these things as well as seeing them . . . tell me, how can you possibly remain chaste afterwards?'

10 *Homily IV on I Corinthians*, *NPNF* 12.22, *PG* 61.38–9. See also *Homily VII on I Corinthians*, *NPFNF* 12.39, *PG* 61.62.

11 *Homily I on Titus*, *NPNF* 13.523, *PG* 62.669.

12 See J. N. D. Kelly, *Golden Mouth* (London, 1995), pp. 57–8, and W. Liebeschuetz, *Barbarians and Bishops: Army, Church and State in the Age of Arcadius and Chrysostom* (Oxford, 1991), p. 158, for further discussion of Chrysostom's problems with the attention span of his audience.

13 *Homily VIII on I Timothy*, *NPNF* 13.434, *PG* 62.543.

14 *Homily V on I Thessalonians*, *NPNF* 13.347, *PG* 62.427.

15 *Homily VIII on I Timothy*, *NPNF* 13.434, *PG* 62.542: 'But what virgin, you ask, wears gold, or has decorated hair? But there can be such a careful refinement of a simple dress, that these are nothing to it. You may contrive the appearance of a common garment far more than those who wear gold. For when a very dark coloured robe is drawn closely round the breast with a girdle (as dancers on the stage are attired), with such daintiness that it neither spreads into breadth nor shrinks into scantiness, but is between the two; and when the bosom is shown off with many folds, is this not more alluring than any silken robes? and when the shoe, shining in its blackness, ends in a sharp point, and is as elegant as a painting, so that even the width of the sole is hardly visible – or when, though indeed you do not paint your face, you spend much time and effort washing it, and spread a veil across the forehead, whiter than the face itself – and above that put on a hood, of which the blackness may set off the white by contrast – is there not in all this the vanity of dress? What can one say about the constant rolling of the eyes? about the wearing of the stomacher, so skilfully as to sometimes conceal, and sometimes disclose, the fastening? For they sometimes expose this too, so as to show the exquisiteness of the belt, and they wind the hood entirely round the head. Then, like actors, they wear gloves so closely fitted, that they seem to grow upon their hands: and we could mention their walk, and other artifices more alluring than any ornament of gold.'

16 *Homily III on II Thessalonians*, *NPNF* 13.307, *PG* 62.371.

17 *Homily XI on Romans*, *NPNF* 11.415, *PG* 60.493.

18 *Homily VII on Colossians*, *NPNF* 13.293, *PG* 62.350.

19 *Homily VII on Colossians*, *NPNF* 13.292, *PG* 62.349.

20 *Homily XIII on Ephesians*, *NPNF* 13.115–6, *PG* 62.98: 'Girls who are not yet twenty years old, who have spent their whole lives in private quarters, and in a delicate and effeminate style of life, in inner rooms full of sweet ointments and perfumes, reclining on soft couches, themselves soft by nature, and made still more tender through their over indulgence, who all day long have had no other business other than to adorn themselves, to wear jewels, and to enjoy every luxury, who never waited on themselves, but had numerous handmaids standing beside them, who wore soft material softer than their own skin, fine and delicate linen, who revelled continually in roses and similarly sweet odours – yes these very women, all of a sudden, seized with Christ's flame, have put aside all that indolence and even their very nature, have forgotten their delicateness and youth, and like so many noble wrestlers, have stripped themselves of that soft clothing, and rushed into the midst of the contest. Perhaps I seem to be reporting incredible things, nevertheless they are true. These then, these very tender maidens, as I myself have heard, have brought themselves to such a level of severe training, that they will wrap the coarsest horsehair about their own naked bodies, and leave their tender feet unshod, and will lie upon a bed of leaves: and what is more, that they keep vigil for the greater part of the night, and that they take no heed of perfumes or of any of their old delights, but will even let their heads, once so carefully dressed, go without special care, with the hair just plainly and simply bound up, so it does not fall into impropriety.'

21 *Homily IX on I Corinthians*, *NPNF* 12.52, *PG* 61.80; *Homily III on II Thessalonians*, *NPNF* 13.386–7, *PG* 62.483; *Homily VII on Colossians*, *NPNF* 13.291, *PG* 62.349.

22 *Homily XII on II Corinthians*, *NPNF* 12.341, *PG* 61.489–90.

23 For a picture of Chrysostom's ideal ascetic community see his *Homily XIV on I Timothy*, *NPNF* 13.456–7, *PG* 62.575–7. The nostalgia and affection with which he speaks is evident, as he works to persuade his audience that such a trouble-free life can also be theirs if they follow his recommendations.

24 *Homily XX on Ephesians*, *NPNF* 13.151, *PG* 62.147.

25 See M. Cunningham, 'Preaching and the community', in R. Morris (ed.), *Church and People in Byzantium* (Birmingham, 1990), pp. 29–47, and P. Ryan, 'Chrysostom – a derived stylist?', *Vigiliae Christianae*, 36 (1982), 5–15.

26 For a detailed discussion of the end of Chrysostom's career see W. Liebescheutz, 'Friends and Enemies of John Chrysostom', in A. Moffat (ed.), *Maistor: Classical, Byzantine and Renaissance Studies for Robert Browning* (Canberra, 1984), and Kelly, *Golden Mouth*.

7

The Morning (Post) after: the vertiginous career of rhetoric in Coleridge's 'Fears in Solitude'[1]

MICHAEL SIMPSON

Etiam disjecti membra poetae
(Horace)

The later eighteenth century was one of the great periods of British political oratory. Events of world-historical importance, notably the revolutions in America and France, sharpened existing ideological divisions and domestic rivalries and made the House of Commons a place of dramatic rhetorical confrontations, where Burke, Fox, Sheridan, and Pitt were acclaimed for having equalled the achievements of their classical predecessors. Outside Parliament, the growth of the newspaper press made political information more generally available than ever before and helped to shape a political culture in which new forms of public speaking (in political clubs, county assemblies, and mass meetings of the unenfranchised) began to take root.

The poet Coleridge was an astute observer of – and indeed participant in – these events. A sympathiser with the principles of the French Revolution and a staunch opponent of British involvement in the war against the French Republic, in the 1790s he assumed the role of a spokesman for liberal opinion, delivering political lectures, addressing public meetings, and in his periodical miscellany *The Watchman* (1796) figuring himself as a guardian of the nation's freedoms and the cause of reform. The idea of the orator who addresses a large but in some sense knowable audience on issues of public importance clearly still had meaning for Coleridge in this period. To that extent, the orator was still available to him as a model for the poet. Yet the tendency of his best poetry was to withdraw from the scene of public action and to imagine new, smaller, and more local forms of political community, forged by acts of address which were more intimate than those prescribed by the conventions of public verse. As Michael Simpson shows in his chapter, the 'oscillation' between these oratorical and conversational models makes Coleridge's 'Fears in Solitude' a particularly eloquent (if unstable) exploration of the possibilities of writing a public poetry at a time of national crisis.

✳

Even if we cannot quite imagine what X-rated breakfast television might be like, the narrator of Coleridge's poem 'Fears in Solitude' seems to have found the late-eighteenth-century equivalent:

> Boys and girls
> And women, that would groan to see a child
> Pull off an insect's leg, all read of war,
> The best amusement for our morning meal!
>
> (104–7)[2]

The object of the poem's vigorous censure is the morning newspaper, in which women and children begin their day by reading about the end of someone else's. And yet four years after this poem was first published in a quarto pamphlet, extracts from it appeared in the *Morning Post* of 14 October 1802. What happens to project this text into a context that it previously deplored? How can the poem denigrate newspapers in 1798 and then fall into one in 1802? My answer to this question will be that the poem was at the outset so constitutively uncomfortable with itself that it could later accommodate itself to the Peace of Amiens and a historical defusing of the poem's topical anxiety. Caught between distinct versions of itself, 'Fears in Solitude' is able to shift its context from apocalypse to bathos, from virulent criticism of newspapers to an equable place in them.

To start the argument I've just summarised, I want to characterise this tension between the two versions that the text offers of itself with reference to a footnote that does not itself form part of the text and that features only on an autograph manuscript: 'NB The above is, perhaps not Poetry, – but rather a sort of middle thing between Poetry and Oratory – sermoni propriora – Some parts are, I am conscious, too tame even for animated prose.' That this stage direction is not included in the published version of the poem, while the same tag 'sermoni propriora' had already featured as the epigraph to 'Reflections on having left a Place of Retirement', suggests to me that the text is not in fact able to become a middle thing and that it oscillates instead between the alleged extremes of poetry and oratory. Such a suggestion is independently and much more emphatically prompted by a reading experience of the poem, as it is shunted between, on the one hand, a depiction of the dell and the speaker's response to it, and on the other his publicly phrased admonitions.

What is at stake in this oratory can be experienced empirically if we return to our first quotation:

> We send our mandates for the certain death
> Of thousands and ten thousands! Boys and girls,
> And women, that would groan to see a child
> Pull off an insect's leg, all read of war,
> The best amusement for our morning meal!

(103–7)

The allegation of this discourse's power of causation, asserted by the word 'mandate', is dramatised by the text itself, as we presume, on a cursive reading, that 'Boys and girls, / And women' are instances of, because in syntactic apposition to, the 'thousands and ten thousands', before we discover that they are, in fact, subjects of the verb 'read'. The potential force of language is proved affectively, since it can horrify us with the scenario of murdered innocents even when this event is unreal and only momentarily read. But this verb 'read' that resolves the syntax, and which lexically identifies us, does not identify us with the 'Boys and girls, / And women' who read, as we do, but who read the newspaper and not the poem. Whereas the real complicity of these 'innocents' in English aggression abroad rebounds on them merely as an 'amusement', as their 'mandates' are returned to them in accomplished but bathetic form, the poem deflects these amusing objects as they rebound and vectors them so that they can strike us with the possibility that they might literally rebound on these 'innocents'. Although these figures might be destroyed, as we first imagined that they might, they would this time be destroyed by 'all-avenging Providence' because of their unthinking complicity in the prosecution of the war. Tricked into seeing murdered innocents, we are just as quickly shown those victims as complicit bystanders who might now be murdered on quite other grounds.

Having thus demonstrated both the power and mendacious misuse of oratory, the text elaborates on how this oratory is capable of the most extreme imperial effects. The power and the problem of these mandates derives from the fact that there is nothing behind them to determine the limits of their application; they are not grounded in any empirical under-standing that might circumscribe their scope; driven by an absolute vacuum, they career forwards to an unstoppable completion. The speaker condemns this irresponsible discourse in terms that may recall the facile circulation, then as now, of technical terms in newspapers:

> All our dainty terms for fratricide,
> Terms which we trundle smoothly o'er our tongues
> Like mere abstractions. Empty sounds to which
> We join no feeling and attach no form.

> (113–16)

Tim Fulford and others have illuminated this kind of critique in Coleridge's earlier writing as a manifestation of his engagement with the philologist and parliamentary reformer Horne Tooke.[3] The ideal alternative to this empty but paradoxically powerful rhetoric is, of course, modelled in the Preface to *Lyrical Ballads*: 'a language arising out of repeated experience and regular feelings is a more permanent and a far more philosophical language than that which is frequently substituted for it by Poets'.[4] Such a language seems at first to be only an ideal because everyone is implicated in its prevailing antithesis:

> We gabble o'er the oaths we mean to break;
> For all must swear – all and in every place,
> All, all must swear, the briber and the bribed,
> Merchant and lawyer, senator and priest.

> (72–5)

By disrupting the customary codification that regulates the otherwise arbitrary relations between words and ideas, this hypocrisy also de-regulates the relations that the social contract entails. Once the institutional compact co-ordinating words and ideas is undone, the State, into which individuals are contracted, begins to lose coherence and so cannot enforce the ground rules of civil society. What remains, then, is an amorphous, debased national unity configured internally by a commonly corrupt semiosis and externally by an arrogant colonialism that bears 'to distant tribes slavery and pangs, / And deadlier far our vices, whose deep taint /Within slow perdition murders the whole man, /His body and his soul!' (50–3).

Since we are all said to be embroiled in this web of hypocritical corruption and decaying institutions, which seems to extend beyond the Test Acts[5] into the social contract itself, a desperate question is forced. Can we ever escape, and if so, how? There is a sense in which the text offers an escape clause in its very account of this ubiquitous perjury. By phrasing this account as a critique, the text begins to suggest that such auto-critique is at least an advance on, because a resistance to, a complacent indulgence in the debased and mendacious language of newspapers. What is more, the text actually offers such a position of auto-critique to us in its very representation of the omni-presence of a corrupt rhetoric. To the precise extent that the poem characterises itself and us as complicit in this rhetoric, by its sweeping public address in the first person, it provides us, vicariously, with a critical mission in relation to ourselves. Approximately half of the poem features a 'we', which on its first appearance is accompanied by the phrase 'Oh my countrymen', at 41. Variations of this phrase then appear at lines 124 and 154. The text thus speaks for, to and about the nation, as first, second, and third persons converge in a kind of integrated trinity characteristic of Unitarian doctrine.

Even as this travesty of the nation speaks its escape clause of auto-critique, it further empowers its audience, and ultimately itself, by offering a position from which mutual critique can be undertaken. Having excoriated the empty rhetoric of the newspaper as it complacently describes and prescribes 'megadeaths', the text then tries to distinguish its own desired war from the kind of hostility that it condemns. Of the French, who were in the process of invading Ireland in the spring of 1798, the poem declares:

> Stand we forth –
> Render them back upon the insulted ocean,
> And let them toss as idly on its waves
> As the vile sea-weed, which some mountain-blast
> Swept from our shores! And oh! May we return
> Not with a drunken triumph, but with fear,
> Repenting of the wrongs, with which we stung
> So fierce a foe to frenzy!

> (146–53)

Whether this martial passage is rationalised by the argument that it advo-cates a purely defensive war, as Kelvin Everest has suggested, or by the argument that the poem's critique of oratory has proleptically purified further uses of it, or indeed by the argument that this war is a punishment of our previous sins and a test of our present righteousness, there is still a sense in which this passage militates against the poem's earlier polemic against rhetoric.[6] The metaphorical phrasing of the exhortation seems to rehearse those same oratorical tropes that the text has critically identified both with newspapers and with the ceremonial moments of social contract-ing. Like those figures, the poem's image of 'sea-weed' and its portentous phrases 'Stand we forth', 'Render them back', seem to be both disposably bombastic and yet potentially lethal. To this extent the text becomes hypocritically susceptible to its own critique of hypocrisy.

Just as the poem criticised us, as part of its project of national address, so it furnishes grounds on which we can reciprocate that criticism. To reject the authority of this national address, however, is to accept it. By convicting the text of instantiating some of the very rhetoric that it con-demns, we accept and extend that gesture of condemnation. There is, then, no available vantage beyond the complementary exercises of using rhetoric as power and exposing rhetoric as trope: we are a nation of shopkeepers who take in and sell one another's dirty laundry without actually cleaning it. Such negative national bonding is not, however, a sufficient unity in the context of the alarm that seemed to confront Britain in 1798. The subtitle of 'Fears in Solitude' declares, after all, that the text was written 'during the alarm of an invasion'. As it disingenuously and self-consciously circu-lates its own dirt, the country is said to face the most apocalyptic prospect of all:

> And what if all-avenging Providence,
> Strong and retributive, should make us know
> The meaning of our words?

(125–7)

Just imagine the prospect of all the screaming in every word being suddenly unlocked. This question concerning 'our words', which are both intimate and public, serves to bring the apocalypse much closer to home than do comparable passages representing the war as apocalypse in either 'Religious Musings' or 'The Destiny of Nations'. To avoid answering the rhetorical question posed here in 'Fears in Solitude', we must do more than merely expose the vacuum that underlies the words of others and ourselves. Averting the apocalypse of actually experiencing the meaning of our unregenerate words requires us to use a new language that instantaneously conveys its meaning as it is used. But where might this language originate, and who might teach it to us?

'Fears in Solitude' answers the first part of this question by a discernible shift in tone and diction that resituates the poem in the landscape of the dell. Opening the poem, but then displaced by the lofty abstractions of the text's oratorical centre, the dell is the kind of rural scene favoured by the 'Preface' to *Lyrical Ballads*, a place of stable, reaffirmed relationship between word and experience. It is just this relationship that can configure a positive version of the nation capable both of replacing the regime of hypocrisy and of supplementing the polemic against it. The component in this relationship that renders it so capable is the fact that a language growing authentically out of nature into culture, as it must do, effectively constitutes the nation itself as the mediating category between nature and culture. Nation is the pivot between soil and society, and language is its visible, aural manifestation. Against the backdrop of a persistent humanising criticism of Romanticism, it is difficult to overemphasise this characteristically Romantic modulation from nature to nation. Love of nature leads to love of mankind, as Wordsworth maintained, but it does so only through the love of nation, which is the love, not always speaking its name, that links the other two loves.

'Fears in Solitude' discloses this largely organic process by remedially retracing its course from its most negative end product, which is irresponsible empire creating continental war, back to the emergence of nation from place. What the text actually retraces, however, are the very discursive vicissitudes in which it participates: the extreme product of reckless yet recriminating rhetoric is drawn back through a mode of patriotic address to a pastorally inflected locodescription. The mediating mode of patriotic address is marked by the apostrophes to 'Oh dear Britain! O my Mother Isle!' (176), 'O native Britain! O my Mother Isle' (182) and 'O divine / and beauteous island!' (193–4). The main function that these apostrophes seem to serve is to expose, by their evident artifice, both the conventional nature of the earlier address to 'my countrymen' and the fact that this address pretends otherwise by implicitly identifying the audience of the poem with the national public that it projects. As soon as the patriotic apostrophes to an abstraction appear, the previous address to 'we', etc., figures as similarly rhetorical. What, then, remains to the poem's audience, to us, as the text aspires to a poetry that measures its distance from the oratory previously embracing an audience?

In the event, we do seem to have an assigned function. As the text shifts gear from oratory to poetry, we are effectively offered a perspective from which we might distinguish between, on one hand, a rhetoric which claims that any gap between audience and national public is already closed, and, on the other, a poetry maintaining that their disjunction might eventually be closed. It may even be that 'Fears in Solitude' addressed one sector of its audience with the especially tantalising, and dangerous, prospect of that constituency joining the national public. In so far as the Unitarians were particularly averse to swearing the required oaths, the poetry of the text might well have offered an attractively conditional promise of incorporation. Whatever the case, locating the significant discursive distinctions is quite an awkward matter. Although the paragraphing of the verse seems to be correlated with significant shifts in tone, the latter occur just before or after the spatial breaks. Between lines 28 and 29 and lines 175 and 176 are obvious junctures, but even line 175 is divided between two verse paragraphs. Despite the typographical interval, the most plausible lexical division is postponed by half of a line. The converse of this minor disjunction between a lexical and a typographical mapping of the text occurs at line 201, where a modulation from the oratorical tone of public apostrophe to a description of landscape anticipates the change from one verse paragraph to another by one and a half lines. The effect of this disjunction is to multiply the possible separations indicated by the paragraphing. In addition to these shifting shifts, there is the more general difficulty that the Earl of Chesterfield had outlined: 'Though Poetry differs much from Oratory in many things; yet it makes use of the same figures of Rhetoric; nay it abounds in metaphors, similes, and allegories; and you may learn the purity of the language, and the ornaments of eloquence, as well by reading verse as prose'.[7]

In place of the hypocritical project of detecting hypocritical rhetoric, the text, as it becomes a poem, seems to promote us from this futile moral mission to the aesthetic practice of distinguishing between all forms of rhetoric, including our own, and its alleged antithesis, poetry. It is this change from moral to aesthetic criticism that permits the poem's audience to become a national public. Chopping up the text successfully, dividing it from itself, paradoxically connects audience to public. Such promotion into the aesthetic, however, involves a significant liability: our elevation above the merely moral comes at the expense of a demotion in relation to the disproportionately exalted poet who so transcends the moral and rhetorical that only he can perceive the positive moment of landscaped national unity around the Somersetshire village of Stowey, where he was living. Instead of being able to drag him down or pull ourselves up, as before, we are effectively obliged to accept the relationship that he offers and to apprehend the nation vicariously. The narrator speaks as a poet:

> This burst of prospect, here the shadowy main,
> Dim-tinted, there the mighty majesty
> Of that huge amphitheatre of rich
> And elmy fields, seems like society
> Conversing with the mind, and giving it
> A livelier impulse and a dance of thought.
>
> (215–20)

'Society' here is relegated, since the connection between itself and mind is forged exclusively by the mind, in an uneven triangulation. What is visible here is not society and the mind in equipoise, but the mind as subject actively pressing elements of experience into the service of an analogy involving society and mind as objects. So prominent is the poet's activity here that no precise correlation is established between the 'shadowy main' (215) and the 'huge amphitheatre' (217) on one side and mind and society on the other; more important than such details is the fact that the analogy is made. This analogy, moreover, is part and parcel of a larger process in which the 'I' of the poet detaches itself from the 'we' of rhetorical declamation in order to guarantee the necessary alternative of a national poetry. Emerging as late as line 153, the poet serves as an authenticating adjunct of this alleged poetry and is consequently instrumental in the modulation of nature into nation. He is cast, in fact, as the pivot between them, since his words remain anchored in a particular locale, ostensively described, and yet are addressed outwards to the same broad audience as the earlier rhetoric.

Despite this looming pre-eminence of the poet over nature and ourselves, our job remains that of differentiating this poetry from an ambient rhetoric. So long as we can divide up the poem, we know that we are looking over the poet's shoulder at our own nation; looking at the poem correctly entails that we can look at the national landscape.[8] It is because we are challenged, permissively but powerfully, to divide up the text that a particular biblical paradigm, otherwise registered by the text, is deflected and inverted. Since the text invites its readers to sift the graven images of rhetoric from the authentic inspiration of poetry, the poem's narrator can specifically eschew, at this juncture, the role of Moses on the mount. Even though the poet is a commanding figure, grounded in nature and speaking the nation to us, we are still equipped with our own mission. Not genuflecting to the false gods of rhetoric, and so able to assume the profile of the chosen people, we do not induce the narrator to break his tablets and then return to Sinai, or the Quantocks, for more. Able to make the crucial distinction, we approximate the figure of the autonomous national public and avoid the character of a mere audience that must be told which words to reject in order to accept ourselves.

Consequently unlike the outraged prophet, the narrator comes down from the mountain, neither bringing nor breaking any tablets, which are instead left behind as bombast in the dell, and he walks into the promised land while we remain behind, gazing after him because equipped with the promise of that land in the form of the talent to distinguish between talent and tablet, poetry and rhetoric. In this inversion of the Mosaic paradigm, the graven images are the tablets themselves, ultimately jettisoned as portentous 'bodings' (210). This inversion does not, however, entail that the poet can be plausibly identified with Christ, since the poet descends into a version of earthly paradise rather than ascending into heaven. Mighty as he is, and potentially constitutive, in his own estimate, of the nation, the poet ranks himself with neither of the great law-givers of the Old and New Testaments. Such delicacy permits at least the possibility of a terrestrial paradise for all within the nation. Although I agree with Morton Paley's argument that Coleridge's apocalypse becomes increasingly bereft of a millennium throughout the 1790s, I propose that our ability to carve the text from itself, on which depends both our ability to relate ourselves as audience to ourselves as public, and also the narrator's stalwart refusal of the Mosaic role, are all a composite of the millennium.[9] If, however, we cannot make this discrimination as readers, all bets are off, and we are lost in the empty but violently propulsive oratory of newspapers.

Although potentially displaced in 1798, the oratorical tablets do make their return in the *Morning Post and Gazeteer* of 14 October 1802. A good deal of the oratory is here recycled, little if any of the so-called poetry and none of the critique of newspapers. The passage recycled is, in effect, the section beginning at line 129 and ending at line 197 in the previously published poem. Just as the text encourages us to divide it up, so Coleridge himself accepts the invitation and cuts the text literally, not unlike the hypothetical child at the beginning of the poem who pulls off the insect's leg.[10] What is cut, or pulled, is, among other things, this very image of violence. And all this drastic slicing provokes a big question. Having engineered a symbolic escape from the mire of imperial rhetoric and the hypocritical polemic against it, why does Coleridge make a hypocritical return to it in the pages of the *Morning Post*? A predictable answer is baldly economic. Coleridge, as usual, needs the money.[11] Behind the transcendental claims that 'Fears in Solitude' makes on behalf of poetry and its legitimating adjunct of the poet lies the brutal commercial reality that Raymond Williams[12] first taught us to read Romantic poetry as cosmetically disguising. This reality is registered in the following letter to Thomas Wedgwood in which Coleridge describes his work for the *Morning Post*:

> And now I will tell you what I am doing. I dedicate three days in the week to the Morning Post ... The Poetry, which I have sent, has been merely the emptying out of my Desk. The Epigrams are wretched indeed; but they answered Stuart's purpose better than better things – /. I ought not to have given any signature to them whatsoever.[13] (CL, II, 876)

But a full signature he did give. Unlike the anonymous contributions, in verse and prose, that Coleridge often made to the *Morning Post*, the extracts from 'Fears in Solitude' were explicitly credited to 'S. T. Coleridge'. The fact that these extracts and the ode were reprints, or revisions, of earlier poems was also made clear. Introducing the poem 'France: An Ode', which accompanied the extract from 'Fears in Solitude', the editorial voice of the *Morning Post* declares:

> The following ODE was first published in this paper (in the beginning of the year 1798) in a less perfect state. The present state of France, and Switzerland, gives it so peculiar an interest at this present time, that we wished to re-publish it, and accordingly have procured from the Author, a corrected copy.

The extracts from 'Fears in Solitude' are then similarly described. One consequence of these disclosures is that the commercial circuitry of this writing was made at least partly visible: S. T. Coleridge had been and was again selling and being paid for these poems.

Even the earlier, larger version of 'Fears in Solitude' had registered the increasingly precarious working of patronage and, by implication, the corresponding force of the literary market:

> And now, beloved Stowey! I behold
> Thy church-tower, and, methinks, the four huge elms
> Clustering, which mark the mansion of my friend;
> And close behind them, hidden from my view,
> Is my own lowly cottage

(221–5)

Tom Poole's 'mansion' which might compositely incorporate the residences of Coleridge's other benefactors, the Wedgwood brothers, is prominent. The poet's own 'lowly cottage', however, is absent. Even in a national landscape of the poet's own figuring, in the portion of the text that most poetically renders the nation, the poet has no visible place. More than mere patronage is evidently necessary to pay the bills. Even Lord Byron would come to experience the limitations of his own considerable self-patronage and would resort instead to the literary market, in order to turbo-charge it. There is a sense, indeed, in which Coleridge's submissions to the *Morning Post* in 1802 and 1803 rehearse in microcosm the mutual infiltration of poetic writing and commercial society that Jerome Christensen has ascribed to Byronism after Waterloo and during the high tide of European commercial traffic.[14]

Selling off parts of 'Fears in Solitude' is more than a purely practical financial act, however. If it were not, it would be no more than a hypocritical regression to those very commercial values connected with buying and reading newspapers that the text has already condemned. As it is, there is much more at stake here. Intersecting with Coleridge's financial need is a partial transvaluation of commercial values wrought by the shifting sands of history. In the context of the Treaty of Amiens, which suspended hostilities between Britain and France from March 1802 to May 1803, the selling of this poem can be read as a moment of participation in a newly recharged matrix of commerce. After almost ten years of radically interrupted traffic between Britain and its largest trading partner, the channels of exchange and communication were again open, and a new old world of commercial possibility beckoned. In this world, the epic shifts between militarised colonialism and a new moral order, between war and peace, between oratory and poetry, between the eighteenth and the nineteenth centuries, between apocalypse and millennium, and between patronage and the market are all mediated, miniaturised, and dispersed by the market's governing paradigm of the circulation of the commodity. Even the selling and buying of images of war may sustain the peace. After his verse from 1798 completes one cycle of selling and buying, Coleridge then sells the expurgated version of 'Fears in Solitude' to Daniel Stuart, the proprietor of the *Morning Post*, and so ends a relationship with the text; Stuart simultaneously buys the text and so begins a relationship with it; he then sells the text and the newspaper to us and so ends his relationship; we buy the text at that same moment and begin our own relationship with it. Perhaps the culmination of this process is Stuart's selling of the *Morning Post* lock, stock, and barrel in 1803, just as the peace comes crashing down. The getting and spending of the market system may well lay waste our powers, as Wordsworth claimed, but these practices do so to others as well, in a process of taming and making banal the evils of history. While Wordsworth responded to the uneasy peace by visiting Annette Vallon, Coleridge instantly embarked on a journalistic jag that almost qualified him as a staff writer for the *Morning Post* throughout 1802.

Alan Liu has rightly characterised Coleridge's journalism for the *Morning Post* in this period, in both poetry and prose, as increasingly bellicose.[15] In doing so, however, Liu tells this phase as part of a process of tergiversation that seeks to make a virtue out of the *Post*'s known inconstancy of political alignment. Coleridge's similarly shifting commitments are thus presented as an enduring 'impartiality', loudly indifferent to the preferences and fixations of government and populace alike. The more cynical, and realistic, reading of Coleridge's changing investment in the counter-revolutionary war, as represented in the *Morning Post*, is that 'Recantation, quite simply, sold newspapers' (420). I have to concur with Liu's argument, as far as it goes, but I would want to push it further. Since Coleridge was evidently willing to cut up his earlier poem to make an 'extract', the content of the poem and what happens to the poem evidently bear a disjunctive relationship to one another. It is in this disjunction that we might read the extract as preaching war but practising peace through its vaunted functioning as a commodity in exchange. This disjunction might also be read in the recycled 'France: An Ode' and, by extension, in other examples of Coleridge's journalism in the *Post* during the Peace of Amiens. What might also signify the unlimited ironic status of the declaration of war in the extract are two further factors: firstly the perception of 'crying wolf' that it might otherwise provoke and secondly the sceptical question that all prophecies of impending doom, in the street or in print, ought to elicit: If it's all coming to an end, why aren't you doing something more rational than wasting your time telling me this?

Selling and buying images of war need not entail a selling out to and a buying into those images. The recycling of these images in the extract from 'Fears in Solitude' is, in one sense, a moving picture of peace coming out of war, and to that extent this extract contains within itself two of the numerous swerves that Liu identifies in Coleridge's shifting attitude to the hostilities. Peace here is the ongoing process of invoking the war as a finished product. It does so, however, not only as a logical contrary but also in the sense that wars, as the US President Andrew Jackson said, are assessed in relation to the peace that they do or do not achieve. How the counter-revolutionary war ending in 1802 will fare is, as Zhou Enlai would go on to say of the French Revolution, too soon to say. In the meantime, peace can be performed, cautiously, by merchandising images of war. Coleridge, in effect, had a good war, especially when it might have been over.

The set of assumptions on which this equation between peace and trade reposes is fully articulated in the debate about commerce and virtue that unfolded in the eighteenth century. In J. G. A. Pocock's compelling reconstruction of this debate, commerce and virtue are ultimately incompatible, but in 'the intermediate perspective', they can co-operate:

> In the intermediate perspective, commerce and the arts could be seen as contributing to sociability and even to liberty and virtue, just as it was possible to establish a positive relationship between passion and reason; but the ultimate incompatibility remained. Commerce had taken the place of fortune; the republic could not control its own history forever or resist its own corruption; the particular and the universal remained at war.
>
> It was possible at this point to restate the vision of history as an *anakuklosis*, in which republics were transformed into empires by their own *virtù* and then corrupted and destroyed by the subsequent luxury. But to the eighteenth century, highly confident in its own culture, the intermediate perspective could seem of a surpassing importance, more positively fortified than the *saeculum* or historical present of Christian thought, and the moment of corruption more remote than the tribulations of the Christian apocalypse.[16]

In contrast to Pocock's sequence here, Coleridge's Britain has already fallen into the corruption of empire and may now have emerged into another 'intermediate' phase in which buying, selling, and reinvestment might generate necessary social values. The alternative to such flowing traffic and the rhetoric that facilitates it is, of course, a civic virtue founded on the rural estate and its 'mansion', along with the vitally national poetry that the estate patronises. Although the terms 'commerce,' 'frugality', and 'luxury' that characterise eighteenth-century political debate do not translate precisely into those terms mobilised by 'Fears in Solitude', there is a considerable degree of overlap.[17] What there is can certainly ramify Mary Favret's fine reading of the text in which she argues that the public sphere, usually occupied by the upright 'citizen-soldier', is here rendered decadent and feminised, while the private domestic realm, normally the preserve of women, is here occupied by masculine virtue in the form of the 'Sons, brothers, husbands' (134) on whom the narrator calls to defend 'my Mother Isle' (176).[18] Since Favret does not pursue 'Fears in Solitude' into its later, compressed incarnation, however, she does not take account of the text's relaunching of rhetoric as a commodity that is both private property and yet available to all who can buy it. It is, in effect, this trick of the commodity that allows rhetoric to assume the same public value that a private poetry of the nation also possesses and yet hides, just as it hides itself in the cut poem.

Fuelled by virtuous wealth rooted in landed property, and thus impervious to speculative accumulation, the text's poetry is able to invoke the nation because this poetry is a form of words that is as close to nature as the disinterested possession of that nature. The commodity of rhetoric, in an internationally recharged commerce, is able to undertake a similar function from the opposite direction. Although propelled by a promiscuously mobile wealth, the rhetoric of this text, invested first in quarto pamphlet and then in the *Morning Post*, posits, by this repetition, an ideal public that links the two audiences receiving that rhetoric, and it is from this public that these words draw the legitimacy of their meaning. The commodity of rhetoric, in the event, begins to supersede rather than to oppose national poetry, symbolically securing the nation in a network of international trade and prompting an active, rehabilitated public to emerge from this matrix of exchange.

So the world has changed, from war to peace, and in doing so has changed the text; rhetoric, bought and sold, is now cool. But the text, in addition, has changed itself. Rhetoric may be back, without a vengeance, but the poetry of the nation has disappeared, and this event poses a question. How can such a mighty discourse vanish so? And what has happened to its ideal of the desirable proximity of its referents? One answer is that this poetry can disappear because it has already done its work of deactivating the oratory in 'Fears in Solitude'. After this poetry has immunised the nation against the contagion of French ideas, a freer circulation can begin. What we read in the *Morning Post* is the historical curiosity of a dumped discourse, quoted at a distance and so no longer replete with urgency. There may, indeed, be more than a mere coincidence in the fact that Scott's antiquarian *Minstrelsy of the Scottish Border* was published and sold successfully in this same year. Another, additional answer is that this poetry is simply elsewhere, awaiting the conclusion of the Peace of Amiens and ready either to remain silent in the case of success, or to reintroduce the tight relation between subjects and objects and between words and objects, should the renewed trading of objects and words between subjects collapse back into war. It is this historical uncertainty that reinstates us as readers into the kind of deciding position that we previously occupied in relation to the dichotomy between poetry and oratory in the earlier version of the text. Instead of trying to decide where the poetry and oratory lie, however, we are induced to read the portents, in the newspaper as elsewhere, about whether or not the peace will stand.[19] This difficulty is not unlike the British predicament in the recent Beef War, although the stakes are very different. The page of the *Morning Post* on which appears the abbreviated oratorical version of the text portends both rhetoric and poetry: on the one hand there is a report of British nobility attending a levée with the 'Chief consul', who diplomatically takes the occasion to enquire after English institutions, and on the other there are two contiguous accounts of the Chief Consul inspecting his troops in France while the Duke of York inspects the 'first battalion of the first Regiment of Guards' in England. Between these two opposed scenarios of peace and war is poised Coleridge's text, selling itself within a new dispensation of international commerce while haunted by its corona of exalted national poetry. How will it all end? The recantation in 'France: An Ode' might be endlessly republished, but will 'Fears in Solitude' reappear in its full apocalyptic extent or will it be excerpted and excerpted until it bathetically vanishes?[20] Whichever way we decide, and whichever contingency transpires between Britain and France and between the two versions of the text, there is now likely to be more oratory in action than poetry in motion.

NOTES

1 My own fears in solitude while drafting this piece were alleviated, even when also caused, by the helpful readings of Tim Fulford and Barbara Goff; and I thank Theresa M. Kelley for useful criticism of a very early draft. Audiences at the conference on 'Oratory in Action' at Queen Mary, University of London, and at the conference on 'Beginnings and Endings' at the University of Bristol were equally generous in their responses. Michael Edwards and Christopher Reid have been helpful and encouraging editors throughout.

2 All quotations of this poem are from *The Complete Poetical Works of Samuel Taylor Coleridge*, ed. Ernest Hartley Coleridge, 2 vols (Oxford, 1912), I.256–63.

3 Tim Fulford represents the critique of language in 'Fears in Solitude' as deriving from Horne Tooke's work and also suggests that the empirically divorced language castigated by the poem resembles Coleridge's later model of a specifically poetic language. See *Coleridge's Figurative Language* (London, 1991), pp. 22–3. Whether Coleridge's notion of language in the poem contradicts his subsequent model or not, the practical inefficacy of it is perhaps demonstrated by the fact that it is theoretically impossible according to the theories of a normative, working language enumerated for the period in Stephen K. Land's *From Signs to Propositions: The Concept of Form in Eighteenth-Century Semantic Theory* (London, 1974), pp. 21–74. For an amplification of Fulford's assumption that Coleridge's notions about language are thoroughly coherent see James C. McKusick's *Coleridge's Philosophy of Language* (New Haven, 1986), and especially pp. 38–52, where an accommodation with Tooke is alleged. Steven E. Cole in 'Coleridge, Language and the Production of Agency', *Modern Philology*, 88:2 (1990), 102–25 (pp. 109–12), provides a useful overview of how the criticism has discussed Coleridge's notion of figurative language.

4 *Lyrical Ballads*, ed. R. L Brett and A. R. Jones (London and New York, 1963, rev. 1965, repr. 1981), p. 245.

5 The Test Acts were designed to ascertain who was eligible for public office by virtue of their acceptance of the articles of faith and the liturgy of the Church of England. The test took the form of an oath.

6 Everest's account of the poem is especially alert to what it understands as the contradictions between the cultural position of the narrator, predicated partly on his politically eccentric argument for an exclusively defensive war, and the more aggressive popular opinion that the poem is addressing. He also regards the poem as 'Coleridge's best public poem', reading it as a 'sustained effort to move beyond the narrow audience of retirement'. See *Coleridge's Secret Ministry: The Context of the Conversation Poems 1795–1798* (Brighton and New York, 1979), pp. 270–80 (p. 271).

7 Lord Chesterfield (Philip Dormer Stanhope), *Letters Written by the Late Right Honourable Philip Dormer Stanhope, Earl of Chesterfield, to His Son, Philip Stanhope, Esq.* (1774). Published from the originals by Mrs Eugenia, 4 vols (London, 1806), I.146 (Letter XLIII).

8 Nicholas Roe reads this retreat into a domestic landscape as a more negative moment than I do. See *Wordsworth and Coleridge: The Radical Years* (Oxford, 1988), pp. 263–8. While I can acquiesce in a good deal of Roe's reading, I do see the poem as more resourceful, and more riven, in its ideological articulation.

9 See Paley's remarks on the attrition of a millenarian dimension in Coleridge's shorter poems in the 1790s in *Apocalypse and Millennium in English Romantic Poetry* (Oxford, 1999), p. 115. This argument is applied specifically to 'Fears in Solitude' at 138–9. What is left of this dimension, which was, in its turn, based on the pantisocratic endeavour, is the recurring figure of the dell in the revised 'Monody on the Death of Chatterton' and in 'Reflections on Having Left a Place of Retirement'. Tim Fulford shows how typical is the dell in 'Fears in Solitude' and how it, along with the nearby mount, is refracted through Cowper's modelling of retirement. See *Landscape, Liberty and Authority: Poetry, Criticism and Politics from Thomson to Wordsworth* (Cambridge, 1996), pp. 234–6. See also Peter Larkin's exploration of the dell in 'Fears in Solitude', *The Wordsworth Circle*, 22 (1991), 11–14.

10 The debate about Coleridge's revisions has recently become very interesting. For quite different approaches and arguments see Zachary Leader, *Revision and Romantic Authorship* (Oxford, 1996), and Jack Stillinger, *Coleridge and Textual Instability: The Multiple Versions of the Major Poems* (New York, 1994). My own 'Coleridge's swinging moods and the revision of "This Lime-Tree Bower My Prison"', *Style*, 33:1 (1999), 21–42, is partly an effort to negotiate between these notions of revision even as it tracks towards Stillinger's model.

11 Richard Holmes provides details of the annuities arranged by Poole and donated by the Wedgwood brothers in *Coleridge: Early Visions* (London, 1989), p. 176 and p. 119. See also p. 304 for Poole's refusal of a loan.

12 See *Culture and Society 1780–1950* (Harmondsworth, 1961, repr. 1976), pp. 48–64.

13 *Collected Letters of Samuel Taylor Coleridge*, ed. Earl Leslie Griggs, 6 vols (Oxford and New York, 1956–69), II.876.

14 See Jerome Christensen, *Lord Byron's Strength: Romantic Writing and Commercial Society* (Baltimore and London, 1993).

15 See *Wordsworth: The Sense of History* (Stanford, 1989), pp. 413–26.

16 J. G. A. Pocock, *The Machiavellian Moment* (Princeton, 1975), p. 493.

17 This overlap is very compelling in the case of 'The Destiny of Nations', which stands closely behind 'Fears in Solitude'.

18 Mary Favret, 'Coming home: the public spaces of Romantic war', *Studies in Romanticism*, 33 (1994), 539–48.

19 James Chandler's fixation on 1819 as a climax of historical self-consciousness is, on the evidence of 1802, no more than a climax. See James Chandler, *England in 1819: The Politics of Literary Culture and the Case of Romantic Historicism* (Chicago and London, 1998).

20 In the event, the cutting continued, but only in one instance, when Coleridge republished the poem in a version in *The Friend* of 8 June 1809. In 1803, however, anything could have been done to the poem.

8

Pronouncing sentence on medical murderers in the nineteeenth century

PAUL ROBERTSHAW [1]

❊

In the courts and trials of ancient Athens and Rome, which were considered in the opening chapters of this volume, there was no equivalent to the modern figure of the judge who presides over the legal drama, and lends it authority and legitimacy. The forensic speeches which have come down to us from classical times were delivered either by the litigants themselves (though they were often composed by professional speech writers) or by advocates. Even in the modern era judges are rarely thought of as orators, and in most records and representations of the courtroom the palm of forensic oratory is disputed by counsel speaking on either side of the case. In the three trials of Oscar Wilde (1895), for example, we think of Sir Edward Carson's electrifying cross-examination of Wilde in the first trial, when Wilde was the plaintiff. In the third trial, when Wilde was the accused, Sir Edward Clarke's principled, if doomed, defence and the Solicitor-General's relentless prosecution speeches stand out. Few recall anything that the judge said. Yet the modern trial is a complex and layered linguistic event made up of a number of different strands of more or less formal modes of speech. Its rhetoric extends beyond the adversarial exchanges of the advocates.

Paul Robertshaw's essay on trials of 'medical murderers' in the nineteenth century shifts attention to the oratorical action of the judge in pronouncing sentence. Since there was at this time only one sentence (death by hanging) for the judge to give for such crimes, this was on the face of it a rare occasion when rhetoric had no role . But as Robertshaw shows through his detailed examination of trial reports, these sentencing remarks often perform the traditional rhetorical functions of moving, teaching, and persuading. In making them, judges took care to justify the legal process which had led to the verdict and to articulate the shared moral values which that verdict was supposed to represent and protect. Perhaps for the first time in the course of the trial the accused, addressed directly by the judge, became the primary audience, and the judge's words began to take on a ceremonial, quasi-theological, and sermon-like character. Having done its work, forensic oratory made way for a solemn and epideictic moment.

❋

INTRODUCTION

This chapter was prompted by a recent event: the trial and conviction of Dr Harold Shipman in 2001 for the murder of fifteen of his female patients, the striking sentencing remarks of Mr Justice Forbes,[2] which, unusually, were reported in full in a number of newspapers, and the subsequent inquiry into a possible 466 further deaths of his patients held by Dame Janet Smith J.

The genre of sentencing remarks is ancient and continuous in the United Kingdom, especially in England, but the sub-genre of sentencing medical murderers is fortunately sparse and relatively recent. Before Shipman there was Dr Crippen, convicted for the murder of his wife in 1910, whose sentence was pronounced in intense, compressed remarks by Alverstone LCJ. Both pronouncements had nineteenth-century predecessors, and it is on these, four in number, that this chapter will focus. I shall concentrate on the judges' sentencing remarks, but add to this analysis a brief outline of their context in each case.

My source for all four of these cases is the Notable British Trials Series published by William Hodge until the ending of capital punishment. Each volume in the series consists of an introduction, followed by transcript material of the entire trial. It is from these introductions that my background sketches are drawn. The sentencing remarks are not simply reproduced here, as they have been transformed by me for presentation, in that they are broken down into their clauses and phrases (indicated by hyphenation: e.g. deprivation-and-invasion); additionally each generic segment is headlined in italics. This use of such segments has been developed from the complementary theories of genre produced independently by Rukaiya Hasan on compulsory and optional elements of resource in genre[3] and Susan Urmston Philips on compulsory and optional aspects of sequence of elements in genre.[4] My addition has been to consider the emergence historically of a genre, 'Sentencing Remarks', from within these perspectives. Briefly put, there were two phases: the first from 1300 to 1600 – when the first 'Exhortations to Repent' are recorded – was one of formal drafting, and the second phase of extemporised remarks continues. During the first phase eighteen elements emerged, such as: the Process/Verdict; Legitimation of Process; the Crime; the Offence; the Defendant; the Victim; Penal Policy. Of these eighteen elements two remain compulsory: that the defendant be addressed, almost invariably by name, and that the sanctions be fully cited. Although these two elements, Address and Sanctions, normally begin and end the pronouncement, I would not conclude that such a sequence and location is compulsory. In the period from 1600 to 1710 a further six elements emerged, such as degrees of Responsibility or Mitigation – all optional – and three fell into disuse in the twentieth century with the demise of capital punishment: the Exhortation to repent; discussion of the prerogative of Mercy; and the role of the jury regarding Mercy.

The deployment of these elements involves acts of interpretation and categorisation, so it is a constructive rather than 'scientific' activity. This format enables one to see the structure of any pronouncement. After giving a short résumé of the background of the offence and trial in each case to be analysed, I will then apply this method to the pronouncement with additional rhetorical analysis.

Firstly, however, to assist the reader I will present a selection of examples illustrating the eleven thematic elements that occur in the four cases.

EXAMPLES OF THEMATIC ELEMENTS IN THE GENRE OF SENTENCING REMARKS

Forms of Address (A)[5]
State Trials 4 Hugh le Despenser (1320):[6]
'Hugh le Despenser ... Hugh ... Hugh ... Hugh ... Hugh ... Hugh ...
Hugh ... you Hugh ... you Hugh ... you Hugh ... you Hugh ... you Hugh

... and you Hugh ... and you Hugh ... and you Hugh ... Go traitor, tyrant take thy punishment ...'

State Trials 60 Dr William Parry (1584):

'Parry, thou hast been before this time indicted ...'

Notable Trials Series; George Chapman (1909):[7]

'Severin Klosowski,

for I decline to call you by the English name you have assumed;

the only satisfactory feature in the case we have just completed is that I am able to address you as a foreigner and not as an Englishman ...'

Process/procedure/verdict (P)

State Trials 56 Thomas Howard Duke of Norfolk (1571):

'[Thomas Duke of Norfolk, (A)]

whereas thou hast been heretofore Indicted of High Treason

and hast been Arraigned upon the same

and hast pleaded Not guilty and hast put thyself upon thy peers

and the lords thy peers have found thee Guilty, wherefore ...'

State Trials 608 Maj. Sir Archibald Gordon Kinloch of Gilmerton (1759)
Scotland:

'and we have here conclusive evidence from the verdict which is our rule

that although the shocking deed of killing was committed,

yet the perpetrator was at the time by the will of God deprived

of that most invaluable gift of reason,

the distinguishing blessing-and-ornament of the human kind.

In this miserable situation could he be guilty of murder?'

Process legitimation (L)

State Trials 268 John Giles (1680):

'There is a jury has convicted you of this crime,

against whom had you any objection you might have made your challenge.'

State Trials 434 Daniel Lindsay (1704):

'and you must be convinced in your own conscience

that you have been convicted upon a full evidence proving the fact

which hath proceeded from your own mouth.'

State Trials New Series Kevin O'Doherty (1848) *Ireland*:[8]

'Now of that felony you have been found guilty by a jury of your country;

and I must add upon evidence sufficient not only to satisfy the requirements of the laws, but to satisfy the mind of every impartial person who heard the trial.'

The offence (O)

TREASON

State Trials 69 Sir John Perrot (1592):
'most wickedly conspiring Her Majesty's death,
and by deprivation-and-invasion of this realm by foreign enemies, and taking in the Spaniards
to the destruction of so many thousands of good-and-natural subjects.'
State Trials 277 Edward Fitzharris (1681):
'your design hath been to incite the people
to a rebellion and a popular insurrection
[that would have swept all away like a deluge
if it had taken effect.' (consequentialism [c])]

CORRUPTION

State Trials 683 Valentine Jones (1809):
'in short you stand convicted of having illegally-and-corruptly appropriated to your own use,
in violation of your duty and in fraud of His Majesty, the sum of £87,000;
a larger sum than has ever appeared in this or any other court,
to have been amassed by any pubic offender within our experience;
and this sum was but a moiety of that which was divided between you and others.'

Aggravation (a)
State Trials 323 Titus Oates (1685):
'but your perjury has all the aggravations that can be thought of to heighten it.
If a man kills another with his sword
and there be forethought malice in the case, he is to be hanged for it,
but when a man shall draw innocent blood upon himself
by a malicious, premeditated, false oath, there is not only blood in the case
but likewise perjury, corrupt-malicious perjury.'
State Trials 331 Lady Alice Lisle et al. (1685):
'and I cannot but deplore it withal as a sad-and-dismal thing,
that in this little case so many perjuries should be added to the crime of treason,
such as for my part I cannot but tremble to remember:

perjuries in defiance of all the instruction-and-justice that true Christian charity could express
and in defiance of the omniscience-and-justice of the all-seeing God of truth.'

State Trials 561 James Hill (1777):
'I shall not interrupt your feelings, which I trust you have,
by talking to you of the enormity of the offence you have committed,
because it is impossible for me or any man who hears me
to add a word of aggravation to it.'

State Trials 575 John Frost (1793):
'There is another circumstance which is an aggravation of your crime,
which is from the situation of life in which you are, as an attorney;
you must have taken oaths of allegiance to the King.
These words that you have uttered show in your conduct-and-your carriage
how very little regard you have paid to the oaths you have taken;
that therefore is a high aggravation of your offence.'

Intention/motivation (I)
State Trials 621 Thomas Williams (1797):
'You ... add that you were not aware you were committing an offence ...
or had any intention to detract from or vilify the established religion.
Can any man who calls himself a Christian pretend to say
the publication of such a work was without intention?
A child who had common attention shown to his education must know better.'

State Trials 632 John Tuite (1799) *Ireland*:
'You must have been activated by some strange delusion.
For what else but delusion could have led you to the commission of this act?'

The victim (V)
State Trials 570 George Gordon (1787):
'The other of these libels is calculated most daringly to asperse the character of her most Christian Majesty the Queen of France,
by imputing to her great tyranny-and-oppression
and to vilify the character of Monsieur de Barthelemy
(the chargé des affaires of the court of France),
as being the tool employed in carrying on

such supposed arbitrary-and-oppressive measures.'
State Trials 654 Edward Kearney (1803) *Ireland*:
'Upon that night, you and your associates hurried many an honourable man,
without warning, to an untimely grave.
You hurried on the savage pikeman to the charge
against the mild dispenser of benevolent justice.
He was the advocate of the oppressed,
and listened with patient kindness to the defence of the accused;
but the first effort of your provisional government was,
in the barbarous phrenzy of your republican tyranny,
to put that great-and-good man to cruel-and-instant death,
without one moment of preparation.'

Judicial response (Je)
State Trials 16 Sir John Hall (1399):
'John Hall deserved a grievous death ... '
State Trials 20 Sir John Oldcastle (1415):
'But forasmuch as we have experienced the said Sir John
to be incorrigible-and-irreclaimable,
we at last, with grief-and-heaviness of heart,
in obedience to what the law requires,
proceed to give sentence definitive against him ...'
State Trials 271 William Viscount Stafford (1680):
'My part therefore which remains is a very sad one:
for I never yet gave sentence of death upon any man,
and am extremely sorry that I must begin with your lordship.'
State Trials 505 Richard Earl of Anglesea et al. (1744) *Ireland*:
'My Lord, the concern I am under is very great,
to see your lordship here as an offender against the law.'
State Trials 596 William Skirving (1794) *Scotland*:
'My Lords, I could have wished, and it would have made me happy
if he could have given a proper vindication of his conduct,
so as to have got an acquittal from the crimes with which he is charged.'

The exhortation to repent (X)
State Trials 421 Col. Nicholas Bayard (1702) *New York*:
'I am sorry to find you so impenitent of your crime,

which is so heinous-and-abominable in the sight of God and man …
… but I hope God will open your eyes
that you may be convinced and repent of the crime …'
State Trials 426 Sarah Baynton et al. (1702):
'I hope you will reflect upon those evil courses that have brought you to
this end.
You have but a short time to live,
and therefore it would be well for you to consider your future state.
You may have better instructions for that than I can give you.'
State Trials 649 William Codling et al. (1802):
'The only office of kindness that I have to perform to you,
is to recommend to you to use the few days that may remain to you of life
to your best advantage;
for the circumstances of your case afford no reasonable prospect of mercy.
It is a late wisdom, but the only wisdom, which now remains for you to
practise:
to prepare yourself for the conclusion that awaits you.'
Notable Scottish Trials Series; Eugene Marie Chantrelle (1878):[9]
'I shall not say one word to aggravate your feelings
in the position in which you stand;
but shall only exhort you
to make the most of the few remaining days that you have to spend on
earth,
to repent your past life and make your peace with God.'
Famous Trials Series; Herbert John Bennett (1909):[10]
'I can hold out no hope for you,
and I implore you to make your peace with your Maker.'

Penal policy (p)
State Trials 389 Peter Cook (1696):
'Mr Cook, you are an Englishman
and must needs know that in this place we frequently condemn to death
clippers-coiners-thieves-and-robbers and other such criminals,
for the preservation of the innocent and for the common good.'
State Trials 554 Elizabeth Canning (1754):
'but it is your particular happiness that you are in a country,
where severe-and-sanguinary laws are not so familiar,
and though many may expect, and the court surely in this case could justify

the most severe exemplary punishment which the law can inflict;
yet you will soon be convinced that your sentence
is in no degree adequate to the greatness of your offence.'
State Trials 564 Francis Henry de la Motte (1781):
'In such a case therefore as yours,
you must expect to receive from an English court of justice
that punishment which every country would inflict for the same offence.
Such efforts as yours have hitherto proved ineffectual,
and I trust in God they ever will;
but the safety of the state requires that you should be made an example of,
to deter others from meriting the fate which awaits you.'

The judicial role (Jo)
State Trials 519 Simon Lord Lovat (1746):
'and there remains now no more with the court
but to perform their duty, which is to pronounce that sentence,
that dismal sentence of death,
which the law has provided for such offenders.'
State Trials 632 John MacCann (1748) *Ireland*:
'It remains only for me to pronounce that sentence,
which the law prescribed for the offence of which you have been guilty.
It is an awful ceremony, that the soul of man shrinks from,
but in this I am the instrument of the law only, and the sentence of the
law is ... '
Old Bailey Sessional Papers; Dr William Dodd (1777):
'and now the very painful duty,
that the necessity of the law imposes upon the court,
to pronounce the sentence of the law against you, remains to be performed.'
State Trials 599 Joseph Gerrald (1794) *Scotland*:
'but my Lords, the happiness of the innocent part of mankind requires us
to punish the guilty and to protect the innocent;
and we cannot give protection to the innocent part of society,
unless we inflict adequate punishments upon crimes committed against society.'

ANALYSIS OF SENTENCING PRONOUNCEMENTS

The thematic elements identified in these examples from *State Trials* are
deployed in various forms and combinations in trials of medical murderers.

The analysis of these elements helps us to understand the rhetorical function of the judges' remarks in each of the four cases discussed below.

DR THOMAS SMETHURST (1859)

THE CONTEXT

Dr Smethurst's medical qualifications were unorthodox. He was a member of the Society of Apothecaries, but that did not entitle him to call himself 'Doctor'; that came from gaining the Archbishop of Canterbury's medical degree (abolished in 1857) through two certificates of reference from members of the College of Physicians.[11]

Dr Smethurst's mistress was Isabella Bankes, whom he had bigamously married. His motive was apparently to obtain her property, valued at around £1800, which she left him in her will, prepared by Dr Smethurst, and executed by her shortly before her death. The allegation was that Isabella Bankes had been poisoned by an unspecified irritant substance, but no poison was traced to Dr Smethurst. There was strong conflict in the expert medical evidence: ten spoke for the prosecution in support of the poison theory; seven spoke for the defendant, supporting death by natural causes from either dysentery or the effects of pregnancy, or a combination of the two.

The jury took forty minutes to reach their verdict. Dr Smethurst was then allowed to make a statement,[12] which was much longer than Lord Pollock's sentencing pronouncement, and was somewhat rambling and incoherent. What was not clear to me, before I read the context of the sentencing remarks, was the extent to which they address and attempt to demolish the condemned man's statement. Because of the conflict of medical opinion the Home Secretary took an eminent 'second opinion', which happened to favour the defendant, and on that basis he exercised the prerogative of mercy in Dr Smethurst's favour. Dr Smethurst was nevertheless convicted of bigamy and imprisoned, but he succeeded in a civil action regarding Isabella's will in his favour.

It is interesting to note what would today be hidden by the Contempt of Court Act 1981, that one of the jury wrote a letter, published in *The Times* on 23 August 1859, stating that eleven of the jurors had decided against Dr Smethurst at the close of the defence, and the summing up of the judge confirmed their opinions. Furthermore, Lord Pollock intervened with the Home Secretary, supporting the jury and opposing clemency.[13]

Parry, in *Trial of Dr Smethurst* (p. 29), sides with the Home Secretary and takes the view that, if there had been a Court of Criminal Appeal in existence, it would have reversed the conviction because of one continuing lapse in the medical evidence. One might also consider this case a candidate for a Scottish 'Not Proven' verdict.

THE PRONOUNCEMENT PER POLLOCK LCB

Address
'Thomas Smethurst,'

Verdict
'you have been found guilty of the murder of Isabella Bankes,'

The victim
'with whom you underwent the ceremony of marriage on the 9th of December,
with whom you lived till the 2nd of May,'

The offence
'when you were apprehended on a charge of administering poison.
She died on the following morning and you were then charged
with having committed the act of murdering her by secret poisoning.'

Process legitimation I
'You have had a long, I hope a patient trial.
You have had the benefit of most able advocacy on your part.
The jury after due deliberation have found you guilty,
and I think it is difficult for anyone carefully to consider the evidence,
both for and against you,
without coming to the same conclusion which the jury have pronounced
by their verdict.'

Process
'You have addressed the court at considerable length.
You have dwelt upon some matters of little or no moment.

You have opposed the testimony of the witnesses
with some statements made by you now,
which you must be aware are made too late,
and some of which are directly opposed to evidence under your hand
and about which there can be no doubt.'

Sanctions I: introduction; Judicial role I
'The details which you have given with respect to Dr Julius and Dr Todd,
or your sacrifices for your wife are all now of little importance
with reference to the solemn duty that remains to me to discharge,'

Process legitimation II: forensic I
'but I cannot help alluding to some matters that have fallen from you,
which are contradicted by the strongest testimony.
You state you never kept the sister away.
You state that she was with her sister for half an hour at a time.
That hath been upon the oath of Louisa Bankes positively contradicted,
and there are two letters in your own handwriting,
which almost amount to a prohibition to her to come;
you stating that the doctors had forbidden the access of the sister,
which one doctor positively denies;
and the other states that he gave a conditional assent,
if it turned out to be pernicious to the dying patient.
It is manifest from the evidence.
It is confirmed by your own letters
that you kept the sister Louisa Bankes from seeing Isabella when she was dying,
at the very time when you yourself were introducing a strange attorney
to make a Will in your favour.'

Motive: forensic II
'You state that
the Will was of no importance, for you could have got the property at any time,
and that you had the means of obtaining it whenever you chose to ask for it.
It is incredible that you should, if that was the case,
have introduced, within two days of the death of Isabella Bankes,

a strange attorney, to whom you made a false representation;
and if you could have got the property at any time you liked,
how is it credible that you took at that fatal moment a strange attorney
to insult the ears of the woman who you had apparently made your wife,
by being called a spinster and signing her Will in her maiden name?
When the sister did see her afterwards she was unable to speak.
It is impossible therefore for you to say that
you did not prevent persons from coming to see her.
It is impossible for you to say, with any colour of truth,
that the Will was a matter of indifference,
or that you could have got the property at any time you liked,
when it appears you took such pains to make the Will.'

Process legitimation III: forensic III
'You say you thought she was in no danger,
and you even now ascribe her danger and her death,
to your being taken away from her, and yet you prevailed upon the attorney
reluctantly to go on a Sunday to make that Will,
at a time when you stated to the sister that
it was important that she should be kept perfectly quiet.
You now say that it was a matter of . . . indifference whether that Will was
made or not.
All this is exceedingly incredible,
and part of it under your handwriting is undoubtedly not true.
If anything could add to the evidence given against you,
I own it now appears to me that
the statement you are now making and the course of those observations,
has a strong tendency to confirm the result of the evidence that was given
during the trial.
You admit now that you said:
*Let Dr Julius provide those things at his own expense; I am told to interfere no
more.*
I think that observation is little in accordance with the acuteness
that you have displayed during some parts of this transaction.
When the magistrate told you to interfere no more as a medical man,
he did not mean that you should not give money.
You said, as you yourself now admit:
Let Dr Julius provide at his own expense, and that you would not.

You having at that moment in your banker's hands
seventy-one pounds and upwards of Isabella Bankes' money,
and her life then being in danger, you refused,
and now seem to think you were acting correctly
in refusing to advance any money that might have been of any service to
her.
This address of yours to me is very unintelligible.'

Sanctions II; Judicial role II
'I think you must be perfectly aware that if the whole of it were true,
it could not interfere with the painful-and-awful duty I have to discharge,
and it remains for me only to pass the sentence of the law which is:
that you be TAKEN to the place from whence you came
and from there to a place of execution and that there
you be HANGED by the neck until you be dead
and that your body afterwards be BURIED
in the prison in which you were confined previous to your execution
and may the Lord have mercy on your soul.
The execution of the judgment is committed to the Sheriff of the County
of Surrey
where the offence was committed.'
'I declare Dr Julius to be the murderer.
I am innocent before God.'

THE RHETORIC OF LORD POLLOCK'S REMARKS
STRUCTURE
As was stated in the introduction to this chapter, the only rigid requirements
of this legal genre are that the convicted person be named (usually, but
not necessarily, at the commencement – as here) and that the sanctions be
expressed (usually, but not necessarily, at the conclusion – as here). There
were twenty-four possible elements conventionally – but not consciously
– available to any sentencing judge at this time, of which nine were actually
used. What is significant here is the particular emphasis on Process Legitimation (itself the most commonly used of all the elements in the genre)
with three separate segments, and also the use of Narrative with much
forensic argument. As omissions one can single out the lack of Defendant
characterisation and the common – for capital offenders – Exhortation to
repent.

Particular elements *seriatim*

The victim: Although named, the victim is treated entirely by indirect reference and passively in relation to her murderer, 'with whom you ... with whom you'. The form employed stresses the use made of his victim, with its chronology of dates exposing the short term of the relationship, in which the judge signals the bigamy, 'underwent the ceremony of marriage'.

The offence: The sequential mode in the Victim segment continues with the first holding charge, then the victim's death, and the final charge.

Process legitimation I: The modes of legitimation employed in this segment are common, but are emphasised ('You have had ... You have had', and with judicial parentheses, 'I hope ... I think'): fair trial, good counsel, and that an objective observer would accept the verdict.

Process: Without the knowledge that the defendant had addressed the court at length immediately before sentence, one might think that this reference was to the general trial process, rather than to a post-verdict moment. The remainder of these judicial remarks are predicated on this segment, in which the defendant's peroration is first emphasised, 'You have ... You have ... You have', and then contradicted both in terms of process, 'you must be aware are made too late', and forensically, '... directly opposed to evidence under your hand ...'.

Judicial role I: The defendant's remarks against the other doctors and in favour of himself are also marginalised against the first reference to the judge's capital sentencing role. In this and the preceding segment begins the reiteration of the adverb 'now' which will permeate *Process legitimation III*.

Process legitimation II: This segment is specifically forensic, which may again be unique within the genre, and arises from the judge's reaction to the defendant's peroration, 'but I cannot help alluding to some matters that have fallen from you'. The primary rhetorical mode is by antitheses: 'You state ... You state that ... you stating that ...' as against, 'the oath of Louisa Bankes positively contradicted, and there are two letters in your own handwriting ... one doctor positively denies; and the other states that he gave a conditional assent ...'. The other rhetorical mode is climax, including a further temporal antithesis, '*It is* manifest ... *It is* confirmed ... that you kept the sister ... from seeing Isabella ... at the *very time* when *you yourself* were introducing ... to make a Will in *your favour*'. (The 'strange attorney' is introduced here.)

Motive: This segment commences with the defendant's denial of motive, which is repeated and then subjected to multiple contradiction, 'You state that ... you could have got the property at any time ... you could have got the property at any time you liked ... you could have got the property at any time you liked ...'. The contradictions are modulated, but negatively, 'It is incredible', then interrogatively, 'how is it credible', and finally by climaxed closure, 'It is impossible ... It is impossible for you to say, with any colour of truth ...'. There are also denigrations: the parenthesis, 'a strange attorney, to whom you made a false representation' and the metonymised personification, 'to insult the ears of the woman who you had apparently made your wife, by being called a spinster and signing her Will in her maiden name'.

Process legitimation III: The forensic mode continues in the third legitimation segment, in which the defendant's peroration statements are consistently stated to lack credibility or present other contradictions, and in which those immediately past moments, including quotations, are repeatedly contrasted with the present, 'You say you thought she was in no danger ... and you even now ascribe her danger-and-death ... when you stated ... the statement you are now making ... You admit now that you said: *Let Dr Julius provide those things at his own expense; I am told to interfere no more* ... You said, as you yourself now admit: *Let Dr Julius provide at his own expense* ... and now seem to think you were acting correctly.' The contradictions on credibility are, 'All this is exceedingly incredible, and part of it under your handwriting is undoubtedly not true ... has a strong tendency to confirm the result of the evidence that was given during the trial'. There are denigrations, 'I think that observation is little in accordance with the acuteness that you have displayed during some parts of this transaction', and the conclusion moves from asserting incredibility to asserting incomprehension, 'This address of yours to me is very unintelligible'.

Judicial role II: There is a further conclusion and brief reiteration of the judicial role in capital cases to introduce the promulgation of the sanctions: 'I think you must be perfectly aware that if the whole of it were true, it could not interfere with the painful-and-awful duty I have to discharge ...'.

CONCLUSIONS ON LORD POLLOCK'S REMARKS
Dr Smethurst's unusual attempt at a self-serving peroration appears to have prompted this equally unusual set of remarks. Lord Pollock bases his legitimation of the trial on the process itself, citing defence advocacy and

the jury. The degree of forensicism is unique, but consists largely of contradiction and the defendant's auto-contradictions. The focus on motive also counters the vexed issue of poisoning and employs the rhetorically forensic mode of *deixis*. Deixis is a technique of argument particularly relevant to forensic rhetoric; it involves focus on the specificity of space – here, the chamber of death – and of time – here 'at the very time … at that fatal moment', that is, the Sunday morning. This deixis also combines a classical conjunction of mutually contradicting binary oppositions: the insider – female kin – is *ex*cluded, whilst the male outsider – 'strange attorney' – is *in*cluded by the malefactor. I suggest that this overlap of complex tropes is evidence of a strong determination to persuade. In my concluding discussion I shall argue that Lord Pollock had special rhetorical purposes in using the themes and tropes that have been discussed here.

DR EDWARD WILLIAM PRITCHARD (1865) [14]

THE CONTEXT

Dr Pritchard was of English origin. His wife was a Scot and her family lived in Edinburgh. His medical qualifications were insecure; he served an apprenticeship with Portsmouth surgeons and then served as an assistant surgeon on various Royal Navy vessels around the globe. Later he purchased a Doctorate of Medicine *in absentia* from the University of Erlangen and joined the Society of Apothecaries. His wife's people were well off and facilitated his move to settled private practice in the East Riding of Yorkshire. Here his reputation was extremely negative, as a social climber, fantasist – known to speak the truth only by accident – and a would-be adulterer with his patients. After six years he sold his practice and went to the Middle East as a medical companion to a gentleman. His wife returned to her parents in Edinburgh.

When he returned a year later, her family again helped him set up in practice, in Glasgow. He then attempted to join the Faculty of Physicians and Surgeons, but could find no referee. He took to giving public lectures, which clearly gave full rein to his fantasies (e.g. hunting the Nubian lion in the American prairies). A fire of dubious origins then occurred in his house, at which he was present and in which a maidservant died – probably because she was already unconscious – and after which he made an equally dubious – and unsuccessful – insurance claim. The family then moved to another Glasgow house with a new, fifteen-year-old maid, whom he seduced. Soon they all moved again. It is clear that he was in financial difficulties, which necessitated taking in medical students as lodgers. The maid then became pregnant by him, so he procured her miscarriage. Shortly after this Mrs Pritchard became unwell with symptoms of sickness and vomiting. These disappeared when she went to stay with her parents in Edinburgh but reoccurred on her return to Glasgow. Later the first serious attack occurred with cramps and spasms of pain. These attacks followed liquid meals prepared by her husband. He was later proved to have made many purchases of antimony and aconite. Other doctors were called in, who were concerned and dissatisfied, but Dr Pritchard prevented her from travelling to stay with her brother, a doctor in Cumberland. On one occasion a tapioca meal was taken up to her by her mother, who as it turned out alone partook of it and then suffered the same symptoms; this tapioca was demonstrated to have been contaminated by antimony.

The mother-in-law regularly took opium as 'Battley's Sedative Solution', which was kept by her in her own bottle. She sent the maid out to get it refilled at the local chemist's. On its return she drank some and then collapsed and later died in her daughter's room. A new physician was present and was suspicious. Dr Pritchard removed the bottle, but it was later found and shown to contain antimony and aconite. Mrs Pritchard continued to suffer with daytime retching and vomiting in her sleep. The household servants all became ill when they tasted any food for her prepared by Dr Pritchard. Eventually Mrs Pritchard died. Dr Pritchard entered death certificates for both her and her mother, which were considered to be medically irrelevant and incompetent.

The Procurator-Fiscal, acting on an anonymous letter, instigated an investigation. Exhumations of both bodies were made for chemical analysis, and antimony was detected in them. Eventually it was decided not to proceed against the maid, but Dr Pritchard was tried for the murder of his mother-in-law and wife. The jury convicted on both counts. In prison, awaiting death, Dr Pritchard made various confessions [15] and made no attempt to have the sentence commuted.

Dr Pritchard's hanging at Glasgow Green was the last public execution in Scotland and reportedly was attended by one hundred thousand people without dissent.

THE PRONOUNCEMENT PER LORD JUSTICE-CLERK INGLIS

Address
'Edward William Pritchard,'

Process legitimation
'you have been found guilty by the unanimous verdict of the jury
of the two murders charged against you in this libel,
and the verdict proceeds upon evidence, which I believe
leaves in the minds of no reasonable being, the slightest doubt of your
guilt.'

Sanctions I: introduction; Judicial role
'You are aware that upon such a verdict one sentence only can be pro-
nounced.'
[The prisoner bowed.]
'You must be condemned to suffer the last penalty of the law.'
[The prisoner again bowed.]

Exhortation I: introduction
'It is neither my duty nor my inclination,
to say one word which shall have the effect
of aggravating the horror of your position,
and I leave it to ministers of religion to address you
exhortations of repentence,
which by God's blessing I hope may be attended with a good result.'

Exhortation II
'Let me remind you that you have but a short time left on this earth,
and I beseech you to devote that short space
to making your peace with Heaven.'

Sanctions II
'Listen now to the sentence of the Court:'
[assumes the black cap etc.]

THE RHETORIC OF LORD INGLIS'S REMARKS

Process legitimation: There is a specifically Scots feature here; the unanimity of the jury is noteworthy. The Scots jury comprises fifteen persons and may decide guilt by a simple majority of eight; to convict without dissent does indeed provide a strong element of legitimacy to the verdict. In addition the judge draws on one of the standard legitimation devices, that the evidence strongly supported the verdict.

Introduction to sanctions and the judicial role: Further legitimation is provided – for the sentence – by the defendant's two bows to the Court.

The exhortations: Exhortations to repent for those condemned to death were frequent from 1600 in England and Wales and from 1788 in Scotland; though this element in the genre disappeared after 1910, at least in the Notable British Trials series. This example is unusual in that the introductory segment contains both an example of what I call rhetorical silence, 'neither ... nor ... to say one word which shall have the effect of aggravating the horror of your position', and also an apparent disavowal of the role, 'and I leave it to ministers of religion to address to you exhortations of repentance ...', but paradoxically this enables the judge to repeat the exhortation, 'Let me remind you that you have but a short time left on this earth, and I beseech you to devote that short space to making your peace with Heaven ...'.

CONCLUSIONS ON LORD INGLIS'S REMARKS

By comparison with the remarks made to Dr Smethurst, these are brief, as are many of the rarer Scots pronouncements; there is a precise legitimation of process – the most common of all the genre's elements – and a rhetorically ingenious double exhortation. That is all, and there is no reason to suggest that more was required. The ensuing sanctions were:

'Decern and Adjudge the panel Edward William Pritchard,

to be Carried from the bar back to the prison of Edinburgh,

and from thence forthwith to be Transmitted under a sure guard

till Brought to and Incarcerated in the prison of Glasgow,

therein to be Detained, and Fed on bread and water only, till the 28th day of July current;

and upon that day between the hours of eight and ten o'clock forenoon, Ordain the said Edward William Pritchard to be Taken furth of said prison to the common place of execution of the burgh of Glasgow,

... and there, by the hands of the common executioner,

be Hanged by the neck upon a gibbet till he be dead,
and Ordain that his body thereafter be Buried within the precincts of the
prison of Glasgow; and further Ordain his whole moveable goods and gear
to be Escheat and Inbrought
to Her Majesty's use'
[removing the black cap]
'which is Pronounced for doom
and may God Almighty have mercy upon your soul.'
[The prisoner again bowed to the bench and also to the jury.]

It is the visible physical concurrence of Dr Pritchard in these remarks
that is special – even unique – and can explain their brevity. He submits
to the court and its audience three times in all. Thus by a shift in semiotic
form from verbal to deferential corporeal gesture he signals, without
interrupting the flow of judicial remarks, that he accepts both the unanimous
jury verdict and later the sentence and its form. Any legitimation problem
for the court was thus removed.

DR GEORGE HENRY LAMSON (1882) [16]

THE CONTEXT

Dr Lamson settled, as a married man, into general practice in Bournemouth,
but previously he had been a volunteer surgeon in Romania and Serbia.
The practice failed and he was in considerable financial difficulties. The
Married Women's Property Act had not been passed, so he stood to benefit
from control of any money that passed to his wife. It was suggested that
he had murdered one of his wife's brothers, so that he could benefit from
the money that passed to her under that brother's will. He was an atropine
and morphia addict.[17] His wife had another younger brother, Percy John,
a cripple with curvature of the spine and paralysed legs; he was in a boarding
school in Wimbledon. Dr Lamson visited him there. With witnesses present, he gave him a slice of cake and some sugar capsules. The cake was
already cut; it had been previously treated with aconite. This is an uncom-
mon poison derived from the plant Monkshood, which to my knowledge
grows where there are strong traces of the heavy metal manganese in the
soil. The pills were harmless: a diversion. Dr Lamson then left.

That night the boy suffered grievously, first with a burning throat,
which was relieved through morphia administered by the two doctors who

were called in; in addition he went through a series of tetanic convulsions and eventually died. The doctors were suspicious and kept samples of his vomit for analysis. Dr Lamson was arrested, tried at the Old Bailey, and convicted by the jury of murder.

THE PRONOUNCEMENT PER HAWKINS J
'Prisoner at the bar, have you anything to say why the Court should not give judgment according to law?'
'Merely to protest my innocence before God.'

Address
'George Henry Lamson,'

Process
'the jury having convicted you of the crime of wilful murder,'

Judicial role
'the law commands me to pass upon you the sentence of death.'

The offence
'It would serve no good end, were I to recapitulate
the harrowing details of your cruel-base-and-treacherous crime;'

Exhortation
'nor is it part of my office to admonish you
how to meet the dread doom which awaits you.
Suffice it to say that I entreat you to prepare to meet Almighty God,
and may He pardon you your great sin.'

Sanctions
'The sentence of the Court upon you is that you be ... hanged ...'

THE RHETORIC OF HAWKINS J'S REMARKS
Process: The judge's words are simply descriptive and too bare to amount to an underwriting of the legitimacy of the process, presumably because he did not think it necessary.
Judicial role: The law is personified and the judge is subjected to its imperative mood.

The offence: Here is another example of 'rhetorical silence', in which the offence is nevertheless categorised pejoratively with four adjectives, 'harrowing ... cruel ... base ... treacherous'.

Exhortation: As in the previous case the judge uses his introductory disclaimer, 'nor is it ... how to meet the dread doom', to make two brief exhortations to repent, 'I entreat you to prepare ...'.

CONCLUSIONS ON HAWKINS J'S REMARKS

This pronouncement exemplifies those from the late nineteenth century, in that it is much shorter than those of a century earlier, without abbreviating to the Address-and-Sanctions only form, which had always been available. Within that restricted scope it characterises the crime and exhorts repentence. It can, however, be criticised in that Lamson responded to the invitation preceding the pronouncement (with its expectation of confession and even contrition) by asserting his innocence. The pronouncement does contain an exhortation to repent, but it is not couched in persuasive language. My interpretation of this is that Hawkins J was content to let these remarks guide the Prison Chaplain's later services.

DR THOMAS NEILL CREAM (1892)[18]

THE CONTEXT

The defendant was born in Glasgow, but his family emigrated to Canada, where he graduated in medicine at McGill University. After a shotgun marriage with a woman whom he had aborted, he left for England. He attended lectures at St Thomas's Hospital but failed his examinations, though he did later pass for the Royal College of Physicians and Surgeons of Edinburgh. He then returned to Canada, where there were strong suspicions that he murdered an abortion patient. He moved again, this time to the USA, where he practised in Chicago as an abortionist. He was convicted of murder by poisoning with strychnine and sentenced to life imprisonment. Eventually this was commuted, whereupon he moved back, first to Canada then to England.

He settled in a red-light district of the South Bank in London and frequented low-life women. He purchased quantities of *nux vomica*, which is the base for strychnine, the back-breaking poison. He was already a morphia addict, which he cocktailed with cocaine and gin. He always carried pornographic photographs with him. There were doubts about his sanity in the USA, and in due course in England. (He is, incidentally, a candidate for Jack the Ripper.)

The victims of whose murders he was charged were: Matilda Clover, who died of strychnine poisoning; Ellen Donworth, Alice Marsh, and Emma Shrivell, all of whom died of tetanic convulsions, and the analyses of whose stomach contents revealed strychnine; he was also charged with the attempted murder of Louisa Harvey, who had survived and is referred to in the pronouncement.

The prosecution had a problem in that the Crown wished to adduce evidence as to a systematic course of action by the defendant regarding all the murders, rather than direct evidence regarding each one specifically. This was admitted by the trial judge Hawkins J, who had also been the judge in the trial of Dr George Lamson discussed above.

THE PRONOUNCEMENT PER HAWKINS J
[The prisoner did not make any reply.]

Address
'Thomas Neill,'

Process legitimation
'the jury having listened with the most patient attention to the evidence, which has been offered against you in respect of this most terrible crime; and having paid all attention to the most able arguments and the very eloquent speech,
which your learned counsel addressed to them on your behalf,'

Process: verdict
'have felt it their bounden duty to find you guilty of the crime of wilful murder;'

The offence
'of a murder so diabolical in its character,
fraught with so much cold-blooded cruelty,
that one dare hardly trust oneself to speak of the details of your wickedness.'

Motive: aggravation
'What motive could have actuated you to take the life of that girl away,

and with so much torture to that poor creature, who could not have offended you,
I know not;'

Judicial response
'But I do know that your cruelty towards her and the crime that you have committed,
are to my mind of unparalleled atrocity.'

Penal policy I
'For the crime of which you have been convicted, our law knows but one penalty,
the penalty of death.'

Judicial role I
'That sentence I must now pronounce upon you in accordance with my duty;'

Exhortation
'I would add one word:
to beseech you during the short time that life remains to you – for remember that when you descend the steps from the spot where you now stand,
this world will be no more to you –
to endeavour to seek your peace with Almighty God.
Pray Him to pardon you for your great sin;
He alone can grant you pardon.'

Penal policy II
'The crime which you have committed,
I have already said, can only be expiated by your death.'

Judicial role II
'I proceed therefore to pass upon you the dread sentence of the law,'

Sanctions
'which is that you be ... hanged ...'.

THE RHETORIC OF HAWKINS J'S REMARKS

Although this is not a long pronouncement, it is much more complex than the same judge's remarks to Dr Lamson. Penal policy for wilful murder, although simple – indeed obvious – at the time, was stated and repeated; penal policy has not appeared before in these cases.

There is no separate segment for the victims, but they are referred to by type, '... that girl', but in sympathetic terms, 'that poor creature'.

THE ELEMENTS

Process legitimation: The means employed are standard, first the jury's role, in superlative terms: 'the most patient attention ... in respect of this most terrible crime; and having paid all attention ...'; and second the role of the defence advocate, again in superlatives, 'the most able arguments and the very eloquent speech ...'.

Process: verdict: The use of language from the Book of Common Prayer, 'their bounden duty', is an implicit *antitheton* to the characterisation of the murder that follows and heralds the theological language in the Exhortation.

The offence: The *antitheton* is completed with 'so diabolical' and motivated, 'so much cold-blooded cruelty'; this was already a 'dead metaphor', but one should remember its additional non-human, reptilian connotations. The characterisation is completed, typically, with another rhetorical silence, 'that one dare hardly trust oneself to speak ... '.

Motive; Aggravation; Judicial response are elided. They comprise Question and negative Answer (*Erotesis–Apocrisis*), 'What motive could have ... I know not', in which the Aggravation is embedded, 'so much torture ... could not have offended you'. There is another *antitheton*, 'But I do know ...' introduces the judicial response of anarhymed climax, 'cruelty ... crime ... unparalleled atrocity'.

Penal policy I; Judicial role I: These will be repeated for emphasis after the Exhortation; they include a personified redundancy, 'our law knows but one penalty, the penalty of death'.

Exhortation: The precatory 'beseech' is followed by imperative parentheses, 'for remember' (and 'Pray Him ...'), a contradiction (since this 'remember' anticipates) to introduce a further contradiction in the graphic actualisation of 'descend the steps from the spot where you now stand' and 'this world will be no more ... '.

CONCLUSIONS ON HAWKINS J'S REMARKS

It is valuable to have had two pronouncements by Hawkins J available to us. They demonstrate well the voluntaristic nature of the genre. Not only was there never an obligation to add remarks to the Address and Sanctions, but there was no formulaic settling down over the centuries. Consider these shorthand abbrevations of their structures:

Lamson: Address, Process, Judicial role, Offence, Exhortation, Sanctions: six elements, all present in *Neill Cream*. These may be presented 'algebraically' as: A P Jo O X S.

Neill Cream: Address, Process legitimation, Process, Offence, Intention/Motive, Aggravation, Judicial response, Penal policy I, Judicial role I, Exhortation, Penal policy II, Judicial role II, Sanctions: eleven elements, two of which are repeated, five not present in Lamson: A L P O I a Je p1 Jo1 X p2 Jo2 S.

However there is more to it than simple selection and deployment of the thematic elements which comprise each pronouncement's structure. In *Neill Cream* there is also a much greater complexity of tropic usage. In this we can witness the 'individuation' of the otherwise totally constrained and stereotypical sentencing of capital offences at that time. It may also be the case that judges respond differentially to the public interest in a particular case, through such matters as public gallery attendance and press coverage. In *Lamson* the crime was after all of greed, an all too mundane failing. *Neill Cream*, however, moves us into psychopathology, in that his motive plainly defeats the judge and this always raises a spectre for the penal system, for, if we cannot understand a crime, how can we control it? This is managed by Hawkins J by his resort to the theological language of the diabolic and sin.

CONCLUDING DISCUSSION

I have considered four sentencing pronouncements concerning doctors convicted of murder in the second half of the nineteenth century. What they had in common apart from their apparent medical qualifications (these were frequently doubtful) was their access to drugs. These they used in some instances to addict themselves. They also used them to cause first, extreme distress, then death, sometimes to more than one victim. They often had problems with their medical practices and associated financial difficulties. Only in the case of Dr Neill Cream were the victims not well known to the murderer. His motivation does not appear to have been rational, possibly a morbid misogyny or a paranoid loathing of women lacking conventional virtues (it has been suggested that he had contracted syphilis from his encounters). The other doctors saw the possibility of financial gain, though in Dr Pritchard's case the urge to liberate himself from marriage to indulge his passion for his underage maid-mistress was paramount.

In this conclusion I shall raise what I believe to be a problem for rhetoric, which although acknowledged, needs to be systematically addressed: the issue of audience. I shall enter this by way of a critique of these pronouncements.

Given the axiomatic relationship between doctors and drugs by the mid nineteenth century, what is remarkable about these often rhetorically powerful pronouncements is their lack of content concerning such obvious matters. One would not know from reading these remarks, taken without context, that the murders were committed by doctors, or that they were poisoners. These blatant omissions foreclose any judicial remarks on the problem of power in the doctor–patient relationship and the collective responsibility of the medical profession for this, and for the health or sanity of its practitioners. Of the four cases it is only in *Smethurst* that there is just enough to make such connections. Both the original and final charges cite 'poison'. It is also possible to make out that he is a doctor (of sorts), despite the various references to 'Dr Julius' and 'Dr Todd', from one sentence in Process legitimation III, 'When the magistrate told you to interfere no more as a medical man ... '. *Smethurst* also differs from the other cases in that whether poisoning caused death was the key issue, and no acquisitive connection between poison and Dr Smethurst was established. In all the other cases such connection was blatant. So, in the case where the links were weakest, the remarks do refer, at least briefly, to poison as the alleged cause of death and to the defendant's professional status.

By contrast, with Drs Pritchard, Lamson, and Neill Cream, there is absolutely no mention of the defendants' medical status, nor any direct reference to poison or poisoning. In fact, 'The Defendant' thematic element of the genre does not figure in any of them, including *Smethurst*, nor is the potential for use of the 'Consequence/Consequentialism' thematic element taken up. The single 'Aggravation' element that occurs is in *Neill Cream* and makes no point of the torture caused by a purported healer.

These criticisms, perhaps because so easy to make, may miss the point, since they assume an external audience or audiences of certain types, or at least some degree of differentiation in potential audiences. The counter-argument that I entertain – for the time being – is that the audience the judges address is, at least as a priority, the narrowest possible; so despite their rhetorical power, not even the public gallery or the (print) media are in the foreground. The judge's audience is the condemned man, and one may as well add, just that, a man – not a doctor or a poisoner – soon to die ignominiously.

We can see this from all three of the post-*Smethurst* pronouncements. In *Pritchard* the short pronouncement is dominated by the double Exhortation to repent; similarly in the even briefer pronouncement in *Lamson* the Exhortation is delivered; the pronouncement in *Neill Cream* is more complex, but its longest element is its Exhortation. In attending to the defendant the judges are 'individuating' and so fulfilling a major role-expectation of the Common Law.

However, to weaken this line of argument somewhat, I shall now suggest that even in these three pronouncements one can perceive an actual or potential external audience, whether or not mediated by external sources such as newspapers. In *Pritchard* the capital sentence is taken as being unproblematic in that the introductory Processs legitimation commences with the reminder that this Scots jury of fifteen was unanimous; this implies that appeals for the Prerogative of Mercy are wasted, thus *excluding* an external political audience. Hawkins J's brief pronouncement in *Lamson* does not help or hinder my argument, but his pronouncement in *Neill Cream* does. Here Hawkins J ends the Exhortation, 'He alone can grant you pardon'. As with *Pritchard* the external political audience is excluded, but this time it is done explicitly.

This brings us back to *Smethurst*. Its context enables us to intepret it in a different way from my first reading. There was a major conflict within the seventeen expert witnesses on the poison and poisoning, so an appeal for clemency to the Home Secretary was highly probable, and, as we know with hindsight, Lord Pollock was at one with the jury and opposed to clemency as an evasion of guilt. There are therefore *tactical* aspects to the pronouncement and these are not aimed primarily at Smethurst; if Smethurst had been his primary audience and if guilt was not problematic, an Exhortation to repent would have been present. The tactical aspects are firstly the particularly strong emphasis on Process legitimation, and within it on forensic argumentation; and secondly the forensic approach to motivation. Lord Pollock does not enter the vexed question of the poisoning at all, and pragmatically bypasses it by providing, in the strongest terms, reasons for such poisoning: these remarks are *advocacy* aimed not at Smethurst but primarily at the Home Secretary.

So I conclude that judges pronouncing capital sentences had two audiences in mind, the defendant first and foremost, and then the Home Secretary, who would always receive the judges' remarks. There may have been others in mind, such as the relatives of victims. They would lie at the periphery of the pragmatics of presentation, because multiple audiences are difficult to address, and may be best managed by address to them in particular segments of a pronouncement. Finally, this omits a paradox, that in cases such as these a contingency continually hovers above the pronouncement, over which the judge has no control at all – as in the terse, staccato concision of Alverstone LCJ in sentencing Dr Crippen in 1910, or Forbes J in sentencing Dr Shipman in 2001 – that the remarks may survive for posterity as pure rhetoric for audiences not then in being.

NOTES

1 I would like to record my thanks to my colleague Jackie Davies for her thoughtful and constructive criticisms of my first draft, and the editors for providing more of the same; all remaining errors and faults lie entirely at my door.

2 Hereafter I use the standard legal formulation, thus: 'Forbes J' = Mr Justice Forbes; 'Alverstone LCJ' = Lord Chief Justice Alverstone; 'Pollock LCB' = Lord Chief Baron Pollock.

3 'The nursery tale as a genre', *Nottingham Linguistics Circular*, 13 (1984), 71–101.

4 *Ideology in the Language of Judges: How Judges Practise Law, Politics and Courtroom Control* (Oxford, 1998).

5 Each thematic element is given a letter in either upper or lower case, e.g. A = Address, L = Legitimation, a = aggravation, p = penal policy.

6 State Trials = *A Complete Collection of State Trials and Proceedings for High Treason and Other Crimes and Misdemeanors from the Earliest Period*, ed. W. Cobbett, T. B. Howell and T. J. Howell, 33 vols (London, 1809–26).

7 H. L. Adam (ed.), *Trial of George Chapman* (Edinburgh and London, 1930).

8 *Reports of State Trials. New Series 1820–1858*, 8 vols, ed. J. Macdonnell and J. E. P. Wallis (London, 1888, 1898).

9 A. D. Smith (ed.), *Trial of Eugene Marie Chantrelle* (Glasgow and Edinburgh, 1906).

10 *The Trial of Herbert John Bennett: The Yarmouth Beach Murder* (London, 1929).

11 L. A. Parry (ed.), *Trial of Dr Smethurst* (Edinburgh and London, 1931).

12 Parry, *Trial of Dr Smethurst*, pp. 135–44.

13 Parry, *Trial of Dr Smethurst*, Appendix J.
14 W. Roughead (ed.), *Trial of Doctor Pritchard* (Glasgow and Edinburgh, 1906).
15 Roughead, *Trial of Doctor Pritchard*, Appendix VIII.
16 H. L. Adam (ed.), *Trial of George Henry Lamson* (Edinburgh, 1913).
17 Adam, *Trial of George Henry Lamson*, Appendix VII.
18 W. T. Shore (ed.), *Trial of Thomas Neill Cream* (London and Edinburgh, 1923).

9

F. E. Smith's maiden speech

CHRISTOPHER SMITH

❊

'I know not what struck me, but I took a sudden resolution to say something ... I did say something; what it was, I know not upon my honour; I felt like a man drunk ... All I hoped was to plunge in, and get off the first horrors; I had no hopes of making a figure' (*The Correspondence of Edmund Burke*, ed. Thomas W. Copeland and others, 10 vols (Cambridge and Chicago, 1958–78), I. 232–3). This was Edmund Burke, soon to establish a reputation as one of the leading political orators of his time, describing his Parliamentary debut (or 'first trial', as he puts it) in January 1766. The anxiety, even panic, induced in the Parliamentary novice by this moment of initiation should not be underestimated. Burke's distinguished contemporary, the historian Edward Gibbon, sat through eight sessions in the Commons without once being able to summon up the courage to speak. In an era when few MPs thought of themselves primarily as politicians this silence was not in itself unusual, and yet for those with 'hopes of making a figure' on the public stage, especially when, like Burke, they lacked money and status, success as a speaker in the Commons was essential. For the future Prime Minister George Canning, writing in 1793, this was 'perhaps the most important day of my life': a day when 'perhaps the whole character of my future fortune, condition and reputation' was at stake (*The Letter-Journal of George Canning, 1793–5*, ed. Peter Jupp (London, 1991), p. 54).

The maiden speech thus presented (and arguably continues to present) a special kind of ordeal but also an opportunity for the orator to win a reputation through a display of eloquence. Its pronounced performative character, as a kind of rhetorical demonstration presented to a political assembly, places it somewhere between the epideictic and deliberative genres of oratory described by Aristotle. As this chapter by Christopher Smith shows, it was by means of carefully managed display that F. E. Smith (the future Earl of Birkenhead) achieved his celebrated success in the maiden speech he delivered in 1906. Already a distinguished forensic orator, Smith coped with the added pressure of high expectations by astutely selecting the most opportune moment to speak and by developing a mode of cool irony which not only conformed to the rhetorical conventions of the Edwardian Commons but reportedly gained admirers on both sides of the House. The maiden speech thus has a special role as a test of eloquence – a test of the orator's ability to construct a favourable *ethos* – but it does not bring that process to an end. In an adversarial assembly the Parliamentary speaker's character is always on trial, and even today, in the truncated oratory of Prime Minister's Questions, political reputations may be fatally damaged by rhetorical failure.

✽

Verba virumque cano. To alter 'arms and the man I sing', the celebrated opening line of Virgil's *Aeneid*, so that it becomes an invocation rather of 'words and the man' is not inappropriate in this case. For the maiden speech delivered by F. E. Smith – always F. E. to his friends and later Lord or else the First Earl of Birkenhead to the world at large – was both a consummate act of rhetoric and the very portrait of an orator who was always proud of his Latin learning.[1] If in this instance 'the style is the man himself', as Buffon's dictum would have it,[2] that would, however, not be grounds for assuming that in it we see the man here in his absolutely true nature. Many are the commentators who attest the fame he 'won overnight with a single dazzling display of rhetoric';[3] 'no more successful maiden speech has ever been made, before or since'.[4] That was just as Smith intended; never was a speech more cannily calculated to create a certain impression. The idea he put around that when he rose in the Commons after dinnertime on Monday 12 March 1906 he was known to fewer than one in twenty of his fellow MPs must, as we shall see, be dismissed as one of the many embellishments of mere work-a-day fact with which Smith characteristically enhanced his autobiography in the seventy pages of 'Milestones of My Life'. It is an account of progress in seven-league boots towards the 'Glittering Prizes', to borrow the title and somewhat pervert the purport of Smith's rectorial address to the students of Glasgow University in 1922, for, as Campbell puts it, 'F. E. was a great pretender [who] loved to enliven dull reality with fantasy'.[5]

The son of a thrusting businessman whose oratory had won him the mayorality of Birkenhead, Frederick Erwin Smith went up to Oxford in 1891, on a scholarship to Wadham College, only months after his father's death. Even in the company of such as the famous cricketer C.B. Fry and another future Lord Chancellor John Simon,[6] his triumphs were many, on the rugby field, in Schools, as Oxford men like to call their examinations, and in the Union. To dwell on the detail, as was Smith's surprisingly immature wont even after promotion so high as the Woolsack, would be otiose and also invidious, for not everything is quite what it was made to seem. Still, achievement was undeniable, for success in finals was confirmed by the Vinerian scholarship and a fellowship at Merton College. A legal career beckoned this young man whose ambitions for wealth and fame were without limit, and the bar was intended to serve as but a stepping-stone to a position of eminence in public life. Yet remedy needed to be found for the scantiness of his financial resources and his lack of connections in the powerful political circles of the day. After eating his dinners at Gray's Inn, another institution for which he maintained a lifelong all but excessive filial affection, Smith emerged as a barrister. In no time, both on the Northern Circuit and in London, he was showing his mastery of the art of combining honed intelligence in advocacy with a talent for oratory practised in the Union and readily converted to the conduct of cases.

Anecdotes abound, though confirmation of their veracity, if not of their value as pointers to Smith's style, is sadly lacking.[7] Often Smith seems to have told his friends not what he really said to the judge but what he might have retorted.[8] However that may be, Smith quickly made his reputation as a fluent, incisive, witty, and, when occasion demanded, compelling courtroom orator in the age of Marshall Hall, when justice was still tempered by – or tampered with by – rhetoric.[9] When Smith ventured into politics, he appreciated that it would be best to capitalise on his father's reputation. So he began by making speeches supporting the Conservative cause in the North-West. He soon won attention, and Joseph Chamberlain was quick to press for him to be found what in all normal circumstances could be regarded as a winnable seat.[10] Smith's opportunity soon came, and in January 1906 he was elected for the Walton division of Liverpool by a majority of 709, with 53 per cent of the 11,015 votes cast.[11] To win was no mean triumph, not in the general election that saw the Liberal landslide and the dismissal from office of the Conservatives.

On entering the Commons, Smith did not at once make his maiden speech. Though it is unlikely that he was oppressed by any sense of 'morbid self-doubt', there is evidence to suggest a certain 'anxious solicitude'.[12] He had already made one reputation in the Oxford Union,[13] another in the courts, but the House of Commons, as he well knew, was different.[14] Besides, the stakes were higher: Smith reckoned that a blunder at this point might set back his Parliamentary career by three or four years, and he could ill afford to wait so long. That was probably true, yet it would be incorrect to take him at his word when he remarked that he rose virtually unknown and then brought off a totally unexpected triumph. Rather, the reverse was the case: many knew of him by reputation, and much was expected, even if, as he suspected, some were hoping he would make as great a fool of himself as Disraeli had in his maiden speech.[15] The true situation emerges from Philip Snowden's *Autobiography*.[16]

The debate was winding towards its inevitable conclusion in a totally predictable division when an opportunity of winning their spurs was granted to not one but two new members, one on each side of the House and who were both reckoned to be very promising newcomers. The first was Snowden, 'boomed', as he put it himself in the idiom of the day,[17] as the coming orator of the Labour Party, and a House crowded to enjoy the fun gave him a generous response. After that (and after a minor contre-temps when another member by the name of Smith mistakenly supposed that he was being called)[18] the new Tory had his chance to trump Snowden's ace.[19]

Stressing Smith's good fortune in the timing of his Parliamentary debut is no less mistaken in general terms as in the detail of the particular debate in which he spoke. Opportunity makes the orator, as well as the thief. There is evidence that Smith, though typically tempted to speak earlier, was waiting for the right moment;[20] even that fact suggests the calculation of a new member not content to make a modest first appearance on a quiet day and, indeed, grateful to be able to do so without attracting too much attention. A further argument, though, is that Smith was probably waiting for the reappearance on the scene of his Party leader. After leading the Conservatives to disaster and compounding the ignominy of defeat by himself losing his seat at East Manchester, Arthur Balfour returned to the House as member for the City of London, by courtesy of the retiring Hon. Alban Gibbs.[21] An Irish member, Jeremy MacVeigh, cried 'Welcome, little stranger!' as Balfour entered the Chamber,[22] but for Smith the belated return of the Tory leader was an event of potential significance. Though picked out and supported by Chamberlain, Smith evidently did not plan to be patronised or monopolised by the former mayor of Birmingham while Balfour was still the leader of the Conservatives, even if he was in all conscience in no position to offer much at the time either.

When landslides occur, the Government benches are crammed with new members. They soon discover, sometimes to their chagrin, that their opportunities to shine in debate are, however, scant. The new Prime Minister and ministerial team claim the limelight; all they really ask of their backbenchers is obedience to the Whips. As for the Opposition, it tends to be both elderly and jaded. For not only will the strains of a dying administration and of subsequent defeat have been dispiriting, but it is only the safer seats that will have been retained, and for the most part they are, of course, the apanage of the older campaigners. In the drastically thinned ranks to Mr Speaker's left, Smith was in 1906 what he always liked to be, an exception, a young newcomer on the Opposition benches, and a promising one at that. Chamberlain most likely had no difficulty arranging for Smith to be called 'at the best hour in the debate, at 10 o'clock'.[23] Was Smith again improving the record when stressing how fortunate he was to be given the chance to speak at this particular hour? In an age of leisurely dinners, he would, of course, have a good chance of a full house, but speaking so late meant, as we shall see, that he was spoiling his chances of full press coverage. And did Chamberlain really say: 'This is the chance of your life, my friend; see that you use it'?[24] He may have, but the Newboltian sentiment seems implausible from such an experienced parliamentarian. He had taken his own in his stride,[25] listened to his son's, which had attracted a magnanimous compliment from Gladstone,[26] and was, besides, unlikely to have so misjudged Smith as to think that gingering up was what he needed at this juncture.

'Body-language' may perhaps be admitted as not too free a translation of *gestus*, one of the branches of oratory mentioned by Quintilian[27] and certainly not neglected by Smith. He adopted 'a pose of elaborate insolence.'[28] On occasion a strikingly dandified figure in his Union days,[29] he knew better than to try to impress the House as a latter-day Disraeli any more in dress, coiffure, and deportment than in style. He was content to be no more than well-groomed.[30] Far from holding notes in trembling hands or essaying gesture, he kept his hands shoved in his pockets. Headmasters in that period had impressed on every schoolboy what that meant: insouciant disrespect.[31] Smith made no endeavour to ingratiate with facial expression either; no smile, no more indication that what he was saying might provoke laughter than that he was under any pressure.

As for *pronuntiatio*, Smith kept his voice relatively low, quite unvaried and by no means melodious. At the opening of his Parliamentary career, he had already made a decision: the conversational style that had been making steady progress since the 1870s was what was needed in Parliament.[32] He did not choose to sound as if he were delivering an oration in ringing tones; instead he spoke to the House, in a style to which he had taken great pains to avoid giving an appearance of being overworked.[33] His decision was wise, and may have had the advantage of surprise, when something more obviously fiery might have been expected of a new member who had already gained quite a reputation as an advocate and public speaker.[34]

Maiden speeches normally provide new members with the opportunity of overcoming any diffidence they may feel about addressing the House. Modesty is expected, and a modest performance, in two senses of the adjective, will generally be well received. Smith, typically, did not see things in quite that light. His purpose was to show MPs on both sides of the Chamber what an exceedingly fine fellow he was. He was, however, clever enough to do so without any high-falutin rhetoric.

The debate had been devised as a showpiece, not to say as a display of Liberal self-congratulation. In the courts Smith had demonstrated how he relished the challenge of a lost cause; now he took up the cudgels for a Tory Party that had lost its credibility as well its majority in an election. The motion before the House commended the electorate on its rejection of tariff reform; it had been devised in a spirit of purest triumphalism by a Liberal backbencher, the Yorkshire baronet Sir James Kitson. With accuracy as well as irony Balfour roused himself to condemn it as a 'novel Parliamentary operation ... a vote of censure on the Opposition'. But the Tory leader was out of sorts and failed to make the impression that might have helped repair his reputation after his enforced absence from the House.

In the event, it was not within his powers to rouse his dispirited followers who had, in the manner of defeated Oppositions, been toying with the idea of finding someone else to guide them through the Wilderness.

Such was the situation when Smith rose and began. There is, unfortunately, some difficulty is knowing exactly what he said. Evidence is not lacking, only it remains incomplete. The problem hangs on Smith's method of preparing his speech, which links with Quintilian's insistence on *memoria*, that is to say on the need for an orator to cultivate a good memory so that he could speak fluently and apparently from the heart.[35] Smith had rehearsed his maiden speech a few days earlier while walking with a friend in Port Meadow at Oxford. Whether this means that Smith learned his speech parrot-fashion, as was Churchill's invariable practice after the debacle of 22 April 1904,[36] is questionable. What is known about its later history makes it appear more likely that what Smith was going through was the *dispositio*, that is, the layout and argument of his speech.[37] As he did so, he not unnaturally put the successive thoughts into words, in order to give his arguments some substance and in order to prepare appropriate phraseology and vocabulary so that it would be ready when needed.[38] A speaker whose fluency had already been developed by self-conscious training in other arenas, Smith no more intended to shackle himself to a text committed to memory than to encumber himself with notes. As a barrister he knew the importance of presenting himself as the master of his brief and of retaining a degree of flexibility in the face of any unexpected intervention. And his legal training had taught him too that it was equally folly to appear underprepared. To use Quintilian's terminology, on that walk in Oxford Smith gathered his thoughts on the *inventio* and the *dispositio* of his speech, which he then clothed in the *elocutio* apt for his purpose. Yet, though the general form of the speech was retained, it appears that the precise choice of words and phrases came largely on the spur of the moment, certainly not unprepared, but equally certainly not learned parrot-fashion either.[39]

The evidence for this also accounts for some difficulty in assessing the speech. An account of Parliamentary debates called *Hansard* does exist for 1906, but it is somewhat sketchy and not entirely trustworthy, for it is in effect only a summary. It was to be another couple of years before the House, in reformist mood, introduced the modern style of recording Parliamentary debates.[40] In the preface to his *Speeches Delivered in the House of Commons and Elsewhere*,[41] Smith himself draws attention to this fact, going on to state that in this collection

In nearly all the cases the speeches appear substantially as they were delivered, although I have allowed myself entire freedom of verbal correction. Many of the earlier speeches were delivered before the present verbatim reports were established, and the reports are necessarily imperfect. The first speech, for instance, took an hour in delivery, and, as I have no record, the report is incomplete. In this and similar cases I have supplemented the official report from others that appeared in the Press. In this connection the admirable Parliamentary report of the *Liverpool Courier* and the *Liverpool Daily Press* have been most helpful.

Though this appears, to take up Smith's words, 'most helpful', difficulties remain. A pilgrimage to the Newspaper Library at Colindale reveals that Smith was, again, improving facts somewhat when suggesting that both Liverpool papers gave full accounts of his speech, when only the *Liverpool Courier* devoted much space to it; the account in *The Times* is not especially long either. As has already been suggested, that speech was delivered too late in the evening for the next morning's papers, and it had become stale news by the day after. Besides, editors may well have deemed it more important to report the statements of the new Government than attacks by a new Opposition member.

If that casts some doubt on the significance of the speech, it must be noted too that we should be aware that the *elocutio* of Smith's maiden speech has, at least to some degree, evaporated, just as has the echo of his voice.[42] This means that criticism must be circumspect. The situation is, however, by no means without precedent with respect both to antiquity and to more recent times, as Smith points out in his essay on 'Eloquence',[43] and Bossuet is a French example[44] to be added to the instances he adduces of discrepancies between rhetoric in action and speeches on the page that have not been thought a bar to appreciation. All the same, it is a pity we have not the exact words Smith used, for his manner was, by all accounts, as important in creating an impression as his matter. The best we can do is follow Campbell and piece together what is found in Smith's own *Speeches, 1906–1909*, in *Hansard*, and in the three newspapers he mentions.

Starting by praising Snowden, Smith almost immediately showed that when bowing to convention, he stooped only to conquer. He picked on Snowden's comment that sixty years of free trade had failed to alleviate the conditions of the poor, immediately agreed, as a 'perfectly unrepentant member of the Tariff Reform League', and swept on to disparage all schemes of burdening the rich to help the poor, for, as he put it, with nice ambiguity, 'Labour, after all, is immobile, whereas capital is always fugitive'. Smith moved on quite swiftly, dropping some hints that even in a speech ostensibly on free trade he would be turning to Chinese slavery, and then spat some venom on Mr Austin Taylor. Though the member for East Toxteth deserves, as Campbell points out,[45] sympathy for certain personal problems, the attack was not without party-political justification. Returned unopposed as a Unionist Free Trader, he had, as soon as the Commons assembled, crossed the House to swell the crowd on the Government benches. The outrage of a fellow Liverpool MP is pardonable. In cold print, he 'entered the House, not like his new colleagues, on the crest of a wave, but rather by means of an opportune dive' is not a high-grade epigram, but, pronounced with some scorn, it added point to the gibe that Mr Taylor's constituents would doubtless welcome the chance of meeting him again.[46]

After this sniping, Smith turned on bigger game. Already he had dropped a hint about Chinese slavery. Now references to Tammanyism and Nonconformity were nothing other than aiming shots at his next target, the President of the Board of Trade. He, said Smith, had gone so far as to tell an audience of 'simple rustics' that 'if the Tories came to power they would introduce slavery on the hills of Wales'. That was too much for the pawky member representing Caernarvon. 'I did not say that,' shouted Lloyd George. The bellow of a man tumbling into a carefully prepared elephant trap rang out all the louder because it came from the throat of an experienced politician who had been enjoying walking unaccustomarily high in recent weeks. The barrister, like his audience, enjoyed their laugh: 'anticipating a temporary loss of memory,' Smith had taken the precaution of bringing along him a cutting from the *Manchester Guardian* for 16 January that contained a quotation that appeared to bear out the allegation. Jeer mingled with shout, and the truth of the matter was ignored in the rumpus. Contrary to the unwritten convention requiring maiden speeches to be uncontentious, Smith had locked horns with the most pugnacious of Government ministers, who had infringed the normal courtesy of listening to them without making interruptions. When Balfour had tangled with Campbell-Bannerman, the Tory leader had been worsted; now Lloyd George had conspicuously failed to repeat the trick with a mere newcomer, and the solicitor must have realised that he had been worsted by the barrister on a matter of evidence.

Smith still had not had his fill of provocation. In his essay 'Eloquence', he devoted some space to the use of quotation in parliamentary oratory.[47] As a species of imitation it has long had its place in rhetoric,[48] but, as Smith noted after praising Pitt's taste in the apt selection of a particularly sonorous Virgilian passage, such references that once were frequent had 'now ... almost wholly disappeared'. That was, of course, partly a reflection of the way the social composition of the House of Common evolved, especially with the election of members from the working classes. A speaker desiring to ingratiate himself would, then, have avoided Latin in the House of Commons of 1906. But that was not Smith's aim, and his Virgilian quotation, which was neither sonorous nor particularly apt, was intended solely to annoy. 'Proximus ardet Ucalegon', from the fourth book, lines 311–12, of the *Aeneid*,[49] could not by any stretch of the imagination have been reckoned part of the store of tags familiar to every educated person. From Virgil's account of the destruction of Troy, it means simply '[the house of] his neighbour Ucalegon is on fire'. Construing the text in the parody of a schoolmaster making its meaning clear to a dim-witted scholar afforded Smith a delicious double opportunity for poking fun, at those who admitted to needing a translation and at those who might wince at the free version Smith now offered: '*Proximus* – very close to him; *Ucalegon* – the hon. and learned member for East Manchester; *ardebat* – was letting off Chinese crackers.' Referring to Mr Horridge in the normal terms of Parliamentary courtesy added another twist of satire; the member was, of course, 'learned in law', but suggesting he needed help with his Latin could be counted on to touch a raw spot. It was too a novel way of raising the issue of Chinese indentured labour that had become rather stale.

Another trap Smith then laid, and to the delight of those around him those opposite fell into it. As after every election, psephologists had been poring over the figures, and Smith pointed out that though the results at the polls had been an overwhelming victory for the Liberals, the aggregate vote had been far closer: 3.3 million for the uneasy alliance of Liberals, Nationalists, and Labour members against 2.5 million for tariff reformers. Of course, the figures were doubted; Smith knew they would be; he fully intended that they should be. In fact, they 'probably were' wrong, he coolly admitted; after all, where had he found them? Why, in the *Liberal Magazine*.

Statistics had served their limited purpose, and rather more personal gibes showed how Smith had both taken the measure of the MPs opposite and also had the nimbleness to adjust his speech as they had expressed their views. This was the skill of the trained advocate who knew that the swift riposte was generally more damaging than an attack that had been more ponderously prepared.[50] The conclusion, however, was something of a set piece. Campbell rather spoils it by pointing out that it owes a good deal to Henry Labouchere's attack on Gladstone. Perhaps it does, but *imitatio* has its place in rhetoric,[51] and the apt borrowing also has, though hardly trite, a certain familiarity so that, like the reprise of a theme at the end of a symphony, it serves well to mark a conclusion.

What raised Smith's dander was not only the fact of defeat but a note of triumph that echoed the accents of revivalism. Noting, with a sniff no doubt, that Nonconformity claimed the loyalty of some two hundred of the Members sitting opposite, he referred to reports that the Free Church had publicly offered thanks to Providence for inspiring the voters in their choice at the election. This was too much: 'I do not in the least mind being cheated at cards; but I find it a trifle nauseating if my opponent then proceeds to ascribe his success to the Most High.' Note the detail: a reference to cards, as well as to cheating; the studied, evisceratingly ironic diminutions of 'in the least' and 'a trifle'; and finally 'nauseating' stands in unexpected balance with 'the Most High'. After that, with a warning to the Government not to abuse its huge majority standing proxy for the cus-tomary expression of gratitude for the House's patience with a novice, Smith, after talking for so long as an hour or so, sat down.

His speech had been received with roars of laughter from both sides. The Government front bench abandoned all trace of dignity to guffaw; the whole House followed suit, perhaps all the more since it was packed, for laughter is notoriously infectious.[52] Yet can this be accounted reward enough for Smith's artfully concealed efforts? We are told, it is true, that e'en the ranks of Tuscany could scarce forbear to cheer.[53] But they, it should be remembered, did not desert their commanders or help a doughty adversary up to his neck in the Tiber. The debate continued with tedious procedural wrangles. And when at last it came to the division, did the tellers report to unexpected totals? They did not. Though the painful experience of his own disastrous maiden speech did not by any means cure Disraeli of a foible for oratory, he was wise enough to give Coningsby an epigram that has the ring of truth: 'A majority is always the best repartee.'[54]

A distinguished constitutional commentator remarks that 'the tactics of the Opposition are ... directed to the conversion not of the Government's party but of the electorate outside'.[55] Doubtless that is true, yet nothing in the crowded electoral epoch before the First World War indicates that

Smith's maiden speech changed the voters' views. There was laughter, but treating satire as a joke blunts its teeth, and, if the Tories found satisfaction in Smith's jibes, that gave only momentary relief. Dissatisfaction might have been a spur to the more profitable occupation of organising effective opposition. Smith's maiden speech was indeed a Parliamentary performance, and a remarkable one at that. But saying so is, in a sense, disparagement, for on government it had no impact. It was, moreover, to Sir Henry Campbell-Bannerman's crushing response to the leader of the Conservative Party in the debate of 12 March 1906 that Lady Frances Balfour was referring when she wrote of 'the greatest Parliamentary triumph I have ever witnessed'.[56] Such judgement must always be to some degree subjective. Yet the fact of the matter is that by his performance in this debate Campbell-Bannerman confirmed his authority no less over his Liberal colleagues than over the country as a whole[57] and thus set a firm foundation for a great reforming government. Smith had gained only a certain instant fame for himself. For nine years he was to serve as a gladiator for the Opposition with scant practical success. He owed his appointment to the Privy Council in the 1911 coronation honours to Winston Churchill's personal friendship rather than general recognition of his particular services to public life.[58] It was only in 1915, when the exceptional strains of the First World War, rather than a resurgence of the Conservative Party, led to the decline of Asquithian Liberalism and the formation of a coalition, that Smith at last joined the Government, at first as Solicitor-General. Steadiness is, in fact, often rated higher than brilliancy by the Commons, by the Whips, and, when it comes to picking ministers, by Prime Ministers, and it's not half a mistake to appear too clever by half, especially in early days.[59]

NOTES

1 John Campbell's *F. E. Smith, First Earl of Birkenhead* (London, 1983) is, with its survey of earlier material, the indispensable modern source of information.

2 First observing that Buffon's dictum – 'le style est l'homme même' – from his *Discours sur le style* (1753) is commonly misquoted, F. L. Lucas also notes an apt parallel in Gibbon's view that 'style is the image of character' (*Style* (London, 1964), p. 40, n. 1).

3 The phrase comes from *Rufus Isaacs*, 2 vols (London, 1942), I.160, by the Second Marquess of Reading; he goes on to argue that his father succeeded in making his particular oratorical impact by knowing better than to emulate Smith's 'historic *tour de force*'.

4 J. L. Garvin and J. Amery, *Joseph Chamberlain*, 6 vols (London, 1932–69), IV.866.

5 Campbell, *Smith*, p. 80; on the 'Glittering Prizes', cf. Campbell, *Smith*, pp. 632–40.

6 David Dutton, *Simon* (London, 1992). There are many parallels between the life and career of Smith and those of his Wadham contemporary who, surviving longer, enjoyed longer periods in high office. It is both striking and characteristic that Simon was far more cautious when making his maiden speech (p. 13).

7 Campbell, *Smith*, pp. 112–14. See too Paul Johnson's entertaining *Oxford Book of Political Anecdotes* (Oxford, 1986), *s.v.* Birkenhead.

8 In a similar spirit, but with more discretion, John Mortimer appears to give in to the temptations of enhancing experience when he allows Horace Rumpole, his fictional *alter ego*, to express sentiments that he might himself have liked to address to Old Bailey judges. Mortimer reveals that, when writing *Dock Brief*, his early one-act legal comedy, he found himself 'working with ease at a new level of reality ... one that was approximately two feet above ground' (*Clinging to the Wreckage* (London, 1982), p. 128).

9 Edward Majoribanks, *Edward Marshall Hall*, with an introduction by the Earl of Birkenhead (London, 1930).

10 Garvin and Amery, *Chamberlain*, IV.493.

11 Campbell, *Smith*, p. 135.

12 The Earl of Birkenhead, 'Milestones of My Life', in *Law, Life and Letters*, 2 vols (London, 1927), II.182–249.

13 Did Smith make too much both of his Oxford Union triumphs and also of the importance of this debating club as a nursery of oratory and statesmanship? Not even he could resist remarking that he and Raymond Asquith, on whom his cloak fell some six years later, were quite possibly 'both nothing but the instruments of a common tradition based on the desire of pleasing the ladies in Eights week' ('The Oxford Union Society', in Birkenhead, *Points of View*, 2 vols (London, 1922), I.76–91 (p. 83); see too, on the general point, 'Milestones', pp. 196–8). No less an orator, however, than Winston Churchill regretted that he 'had never the practice which comes to young men at the university of speaking in small debating societies impromptu on all sorts of subjects' (Robert Rhodes James, 'The parliamentarian, orator, statesman', Robert Blake and Wm Roger Louis (eds), *Churchill* (Oxford, 1996), pp. 503–17 (p. 507).

14 See Smith's 'Eloquence' in *Law, Life and Letters*, II.98–160. It should, however, be noted that Smith wrote this essay more than two decades after making his maiden speech and thus, to quite a marked degree, reveals his mature conclusions on Parliamentary oratory, not his thoughts when preparing to speak in the Commons for the first time.

15 Robert Blake, *Disraeli* (London, 1966), pp. 148–50.

16 Philip, Viscount Snowden, *An Autobiography*, 2 vols (Liverpool, 1934), I.137–45.

17 The *Oxford English Dictionary*, 2nd edn (henceforth *OED2*) identifies the usage, in the sense of 'build up a (possibly unmerited) reputation' as an Americanism dating from the last quarter of the nineteenth century; Snowden's comment indicates that in the reign of Edward VII it was still regarded as slang.

18 Campbell, *Smith*, p. 145.

19 According to Arthur Hamilton, he had been 'elaborately groomed for his meteoric maiden speech' (Alan Clark, *'A Good Innings': The Private papers of Viscount Lee*

(London, 1974), p. 90). Whether this is true is doubtful. There is no evidence to show what form this grooming may have taken, and little in Smith's character suggests he would have welcomed or taken advice. In 1901 *The Pall Mall Gazette* had congratulated Hamilton on 'one of the best maiden speeches ever made in the House' (p. 79); perhaps he was not entirely happy when the palm was wrested from his grasp by a man who was never his 'friend, in an intimate sense' and whose speech, he avers, struck him 'as "smarty" and over-redolent of midnight oil' (pp. 90–1). The redundant intensifier – '*over*-redolent' – suggests animus.

20 'Milestones', p. 235.

21 Gibbs did not make a great sacrifice: in 1907 he entered the House of Lords, in succession to his eighty-eight-year-old father, as the second Baron Aldenham.

22 Snowden, *Autobiography*, I.137.

23 'Milestones', p. 236.

24 'Milestones', p. 236.

25 Garvin and Amery, *Chamberlain*, I.232–3.

26 J. Enoch Powell, *Joseph Chamberlain* (London, 1977), p. 90.

27 In *Quintilian*, Twayne World Author Series, no. 59 (New York, 1969), George Kennedy gives a succinct account of the Roman authority on rhetoric; he has a section (pp. 98–100) on Quintilian's views on the delivery of speeches.

28 Clark, *Lee*, p. 90.

29 Campbell, *Smith*, p. 72.

30 Campbell, *Smith*, pp. 44–5.

31 The first headmaster of Gresham's School, Norfolk, after its great reform, went so far as to demand that his pupils' trousers should be made without pockets, apparently so that they should not 'slouch' (J. H. Simpson, *Howson of Holt* (London, 1925), p. 24).

32 Garvin and Amery, *Chamberlain*, I.232: Chamberlain 'struck the conversational key and tone of argument which characterises the present House of Commons' (*Birmingham Daily Post*, 5 August 1876). Winston Churchill reverted to the older style of rhetoric, not, suggests Violet Bonham Carter, out of affectation but because it was his nature (James, 'The parliamentarian, orator, statesman', pp. 507–9).

33 Smith tempers praise of his great friend Winston Churchill's oratory: 'he elaborates and sometimes overelaborates', and the judgement that 'he is more instinct with the House of Commons spirit than any of the new generation' could be read as an half-concealed suggestion that his style was somewhat outmoded ('Eloquence', in *Law, Life and Letters*, II.147–50).

34 Lawyers generally appear to prefer, however, to make their mark with presenting themselves as cool, thoughtful orators; see Eric Estorickj, *Stafford Cripps* (London, 1949), p. 83.

35 Kennedy, *Quintilian*, pp. 96–8.

36 James, 'The parliamentarian, orator, statesman', p. 509.

37 Kennedy, *Quintilian*, pp. 77–9.

38 Quintilian's specific points on style (Kennedy, *Quintilian*, pp. 79–96) have scant application to Smith's speech, but the need to find the right wording was none the less pressing.

39 'Birkenhead spoke brilliantly and without a note', according to Lord Mersey in 1921.

A few months later, he also recorded Lord Lansdowne's appraisal: Birkenhead's 'powers of collecting together all the threads of an argument or a debate and answering them, apparently without attention or preparation, was he imagined, the highest form of forensic art' (*A Picture of Life* (London, 1941), pp. 317–18).

40 In 1907 a Select Committee enquired into the recording of debates and, concluding that existing arrangements were unsatisfactory, proposed a new-style *Official Report*, with speeches recorded in full and verbatim. It first appeared in 1909, the name 'Hansard' being restored to its title-page in 1943. See Norma Wilding and Peter Laundy, *An Encyclopedia of Parliament*, 4th edn (London, 1972), pp. 340–5.

41 Smith, *Speeches Delivered in the House of Commons and Elsewhere, 1906–1909* (Liverpool, 1910), p. viii.

42 The National Sound Archive has kindly reported that it has no reason to think that any recording of Smith's voice is in existence.

43 'Eloquence', in *Law, Life and Letters*, II.98–160.

44 Christopher Smith, 'Bossuet's self-improvement: reading the variants in the *Oraison funèbre d'Yolande de Konterby*', in C. Smith (ed.), *Essays in Memory of Michael Parkinson and Janine Dakyns*, Norwich Papers 4 (Norwich, 1996), pp. 51–6.

45 Campbell, *Smith*, p. 146.

46 Taylor relinquished his seat in 1910, not risking the verdict of his constituents on his defection (M. Stenton and S. Lees, *Who's Who of British Members of Parliament*, 5 vols (Hassocks, 1978), II.347).

47 'Eloquence', in *Law, Life and Letters*, II.120–1.

48 Kennedy, *Quintilian*, p. 115.

49 *Virgil*, with a translation by H. Rushton Fairclough, 2 vols, Loeb Classical Library (London, 1914), II.314.

50 A weakness of Churchill's was his inability to change tack once embarked on his over-prepared oratory (James, 'The parliamentarian, statesman, orator', p. 510).

51 Kennedy, *Quintilian*, pp. 113–15. For an excellent concise account of the role of imitation in classical poetics generally see John Sparrow's 'Latin verse of the High Renaissance' in E. F. Jacob (ed.), *Italian Renaissance Studies* (London, 1960), pp. 354–409.

52 As Bergson put it, 'on ne goûterait pas le comique si l'on se sentait isolé. Il semble que le rire ait besoin d'un écho' (*Le Rire*, Bibliothèque de philosophie contemporaine (1924; Paris, 1969), p. 4).

53 It was Simon who made the allusion to Macaulay's 'How Horatio Kept the Bridge' (Campbell, *Smith*, p. 153).

54 Benjamin Disraeli, *Tancred* (1847; London, 1905), p. 191.

55 W. Ivor Jennings, *Parliament* (Cambridge, 1939), p. 153.

56 Quoted by John Wilson, *CB: A Life of Sir Henry Campbell-Bannerman* (London, 1973), p. 49.

57 Earl of Asquith and Oxford, *Memories and Reflections*, 2 vols (London, 1928), II.193–6. Asquith puts as good a gloss as possible on Liberals' attempts to replace Campbell-Bannerman in their party's hour of triumph or at least send him to the House of Lords.

58 Randolph S. Churchill, *Winston S. Churchill: The Young Statesman* (Boston, 1967), pp. 342–3. Winston Churchill remarks that the grant of the honour, to which Balfour,

Smith's own party leader was opposed, was the subject of a 'lot of soft sawder'; that means 'much silly talk', rather than 'a great deal of flattery' (cf. *OED2 s.v.* sawder).

59 As late as 1919, on his appointment as Lord Chancellor, the Legal Correspondent of *The Times* was to make a comment revealing that, though Smith had made a reputation, it was not altogether a good one: 'a fatal fluency of thought and speech has tended to defeat great natural ability by the production of temporising superficiality' (Campbell, *Smith*, p. 462).

10

Margaret Thatcher and the gendering of political oratory[1]

CHRISTOPHER REID

❋

In 1919 the participation of women as orators on the public stage was given a new impetus when Nancy Astor became the first woman to take her seat in the British House of Commons. Her achievement, however, was not universally applauded. For Winston Churchill, the entrance of a woman into what had for long been an exclusively male space was a troubling and even transgressive event. Although he knew Astor socially, he reportedly declined to converse with her during her early years in the House. Astor might have been forgiven for feeling vulnerable in her gendered isolation but a remark Churchill made to her two years after she took her seat suggests, albeit humorously, that the presence of a woman in the House undermined the confidence of the male majority. 'When you entered the House of Commons,' he told her, 'I felt like a woman had entered my bathroom and I had nothing to protect myself with except a sponge' (cited in Christopher Silvester (ed.), *The Pimlico Companion to Parliament: A Literary Anthology* (London, 1997), p. 584). A generation later the inflexible *ethos*, withering gaze, and uncompromising rhetoric of Margaret Thatcher often had a similarly emasculating effect on the men who surrounded her in the Commons Chamber, conference hall, or, indeed, around the Cabinet table.

Thatcher yielded to no one in her admiration for Churchill, whose powerful wartime oratory had a profound impact on her in her teenage years as she listened to radio broadcasts in her Grantham home. One of her first acts as Prime Minister was to remove 'a powerful portrait' of Churchill from her room in the Commons and to hang it in 10 Downing Street where with patriarchal authority it 'looked down on those who assembled in the antechamber to the Cabinet Room' (Margaret Thatcher, *The Downing Street Years* (London, 1993), p. 23). When Thatcher had first entered Parliament, speakers (especially those who belonged to her own party) still lived in the shadow of the grand and heroic eloquence which Churchill had established as a supreme idiom of political leadership. Christopher Reid's chapter shows how Thatcher was

able to build on the rhetorical legacies both of Churchill and of Astor who, when asked how as the mother of six children she could justify entering Parliament, replied, 'I feel someone ought to be looking after the more unfortunate children' (see Karen J. Musolf, *From Plymouth to Parliament: A Rhetorical History of Nancy Astor's 1919 Campaign* (London, 1999), p. 29). In this way the Iron Lady made herself the most plausible postwar inheritor of the Churchillian idiom while at the same time appealing to private interests and ambitions with an authenticity that Churchill was never able to claim.

✳

INTRODUCTION

On 26 November 1984, as the long-running miners' strike entered a critical phase, Margaret Thatcher delivered a lecture entitled 'Why democracy will last' at the Carlton Club.[2] With its thinly veiled attack on the miners' leaders as among the most dangerous domestic enemies of democracy, the Prime Minister's performance was typically unequivocal and insistent. The occasion itself, however, was shot through with paradox. Two years earlier Harold Macmillan had given the first Carlton Lecture with the title 'Civilization under threat'. Two weeks earlier, as the recently ennobled Earl of Stockton, he had made a widely acclaimed maiden speech in the House of Lords. Speaking without the benefit of notes (for his eyesight had failed him), the ninety-year-old Earl led his audience through a wide-ranging survey of the state of the nation, pausing along the way to make some teasing remarks about the theorists of monetarism who were said to have shaped Thatcherite economic policy ('nobody knows where they come from; they say that some come from America, and some from Tibet').[3] As he moved towards his peroration, and turned to the social divisions which currently racked the nation, the Earl struck an altogether more sombre note. 'It breaks my heart to see what is happening in our country today', he confessed to the assembled Lords. 'A terrible strike is being carried on by the best men in the world. They beat the Kaiser's army and they beat Hitler's army. They never gave in.'[4]

Although she does not mention it in her lecture, the Earl's maiden speech can hardly have been far from Thatcher's thoughts as she addressed the Club. While she took care to pay tribute to her distinguished predecessor, and to praise the 'inimitable style' of his earlier Carlton Lecture, in the broader context of debate it is difficult not to read her argument as a critical reply to – even a repudiation of – his political creed. Implicit in her tribute is a rhetorical contrast between the style of the ageing Earl and her own political personality. The magisterial sweep of his eloquence ('Civilization under threat') is, read negatively, the sign of a speaker who is politically *hors de combat*.[5] Thatcher herself, 'still in the business of building defences' for freedom and democracy 'in the immediate hurly-burly of political life', has no time for such expansive gestures. More pointedly, she took issue with the values of the postwar political settlement with which Macmillan's premiership had long been associated. If democracy was to last, she insisted, what was required was not consensus but conviction, not a readiness to negotiate but a determination 'to stand up and be counted'.[6]

Wrapping a rebuke inside a compliment, Thatcher characteristically distances herself from the mindset of a Tory patrician, and does so as an interloper in what might be thought of as his natural habitat. For Thatcher to speak thus at the Carlton Club, the social and political heart of the Tory establishment, was a doubly paradoxical act. The Club had long been an exclusively male preserve. Only once in its history had a woman been admitted to its membership: Thatcher herself, who had curiously overcome the disqualifications she suffered on the grounds of her sex by having been unexpectedly elected to the leadership of her party.[7]

The Carlton Club episode captures some of the paradoxes which marked Margaret Thatcher's career in politics and on the platform. From a background of no great privilege she gained entry to the heart of the British establishment: Oxford University, the Bar, the House of Commons, the Cabinet, 10 Downing Street.[8] These centres of power were also specialised sites of discourse where over the centuries distinctive rhetorical practices had been fashioned by and for the men marked out to conduct the nation's business. At Oxford, for instance, the Union, founded in 1823, was greatly valued as a training ground where students ambitious for careers in politics or the law could witness the eloquence of invited speakers and find opportunities to develop their own rhetorical skills. Yet as Thatcher reminds us in her memoirs, when she was an undergraduate in the late 1940s women were excluded from participation in the Oxford Union's debates, though they were permitted to watch them from the gallery.[9] And when subsequently she was able to make her voice public it was typically in long-established arenas and cultures of speech in the shaping of which women had until recently played no part.

Thatcher's prominence as a political speaker in these arenas might seem to make her an appropriate object of attention for a rhetoric with a feminist interest. For fifteen turbulent years (eleven of them as Prime Minister) she led her party in the House of Commons and in the debating chambers of the world. From a historical perspective, she must figure among the most influential and prolific women ever to have practised the traditionally masculine arts of public address. Yet while feminist assessments of Thatcher have asked how far she can be said to have feminised politics and political leadership they have not looked in any detail at the forms and contexts of her oratory or her negotiations with gendered models of speech.[10] Within the field of rhetoric itself feminist initiatives have concentrated on a critique of the rhetorical tradition and its foundational categories.[11] The art of rhetoric was codified in male-dominated speaking cultures: it instructed men in the persuasive skills required for participation in the various spheres of public life (political assemblies, legal tribunals, ceremonial occasions). The exclusion of women from speaking in these domains, and from anything other than a marginal place in the history of rhetoric, has also meant that 'significant kinds of suasory activities have been left out of account', as Molly Wertheimer puts it.[12] With this in mind, feminist rhetoricians have focused less on the classically public utterances of western stateswomen such as Thatcher (novel though these may have been from the point of view of women's history) than on 'suasory activities' which hitherto have been excluded from the rhetorical canon. Questioning the traditional view of rhetoric as an 'agonistic' and publicly staged verbal contest for dominion, they have argued for a revision of the boundaries of the rhetorical, pressing the claims of the more collaborative, consensual, and dialogic activities of private life – conversation, familiar letters, religious reflection, autobiography – to be understood as authentic forms of persuasion, albeit persuasion in a different key.

In this context, as in so many others, Thatcher is a troubling figure, and her rhetorical legacy at best an ambiguous one. She gloried in her reputation for combativeness; she relished the cut and thrust of debate; she loathed consensus and thought of 'détente' as a suspiciously foreign word which served the interests of appeasers and defeatists. More interested in figures from the Treasury than in figures of speech, her oratory celebrates the triumph of fact over imagination. As a self-styled conviction politician, she turned the apparent impediments of her sex and her class to her advantage and practised a rhetoric which by general consent was more vehemently 'agonistic' than any of her rivals could muster.

All this might lead us to conclude that Thatcher was a practitioner of rhetoric in the most patriarchal (not to say rebarbative) of its forms. Yet such reasoning risks reintroducing the essentialist assumptions which have long been employed to justify the exclusion of women from the public stage. Rather than judging Thatcher's oratory by the standards of a 'woman's rhetoric' which is predisposed to seek consensual outcomes, it may be more productive (and more in keeping with rhetoric's spirit of contingency) to examine her self-fashioning in terms of socially and historically specific constructions of the feminine. Cultural and political analysts of her public persona have noted how negation and argumentativeness can function there as signs of a certain kind of femininity. According to Marina Warner, 'Margaret Thatcher has tapped an enormous source of female power: the right of prohibition'.[13] Where James Joyce famously described 'yes' as a 'female word', Thatcher more typically phrases her speeches in a language of negation.[14] It is no accident that the interjected, and eurosceptical, 'No. No. No.' which transfixed the Commons in 1990 has become an embodying catchphrase of her leadership style.[15] While she may have failed to feminise politics she, as Beatrix Campbell acknowledges, 'brought qualities of ruggedness and ruthlessness to femininity which perhaps only men hadn't noticed before in women'.[16] As a gendered outsider in the cockpits of Parliament and the conference hall it is perhaps not surprising that she should have found this unusual assertiveness to be her most persuasive voice.

GENDER AND CHARACTER IN THE COMMONS

When the first woman MP took her seat in 1919, the Commons had been assembling at Westminster, developing its complex procedures and distinctive styles of debate, and creating a collective sense of itself, for nearly six hundred years. For much of its long history women had been denied access to its galleries, let alone to its benches. When Thatcher made her Parliamentary debut in 1959 she was one of only twenty-five women in a House of 630 members. It is not surprising, then, that she should have found it 'a very masculine place', as she puts it in her memoirs. Beyond the Chamber itself she recalls finding 'a bewildering labyrinth of corridors' leading to strange male sanctuaries such as the Smoking Room. Unlike her Labour contemporary Barbara Castle, who claims to have been 'the first woman who dared to invade this traditional male preserve', Thatcher remarks more modestly that 'neither taste nor convention' suggested she should enter it.[17]

The paradoxes and tensions created by the presence of female speakers in this traditionally male space have been theorised from a social anthropological point of view by Silvia Rodgers.[18] By convention invisible to the world outside, and still governed by a highly ritualised code of procedure, the House, she argues, retains the sacred quality of a 'place apart'. Although women are now present in the House, this sense of separateness continues to reflect a presumption of their absence. With this in mind, Rodgers proposes that the Commons 'shares many features with the Men's Houses of certain primitive societies, where the male/female dichotomy is at its sharpest'. Citing Mary Douglas, she suggests that according to the symbolic order of the Commons women must necessarily be regarded as 'matter out of place'. In order for the gendered purity and integrity of the space to be preserved their difference must in some way be resolved or recuperated, for example by reclassifying women symbolically as 'honorary men' or by containing their anomalous status within paradoxical or hybrid categories which Rodgers calls 'supernatural'.[19]

In the course of her career Thatcher was to speak on many platforms but it was in the sealed and regulated rhetorical space of this 'men's house' that her character as a speaker was most intensively defined and tested. When Aristotle identified *ethos*, persuasion effected through the medium of the speaker's character, as one of the three primary means of persuasion, he had no thought that the speaker in question could be anything other than male.[20] When Athenian orators gave proofs of the purity of their characters it was in order to win a kind of trust from the audience which was meaningful only in the civic context of privileges and responsibilities which were denied to women. As the testimony of numerous women MPs attests, these ancient assumptions about the speaker's character did not simply disappear in an era when women had secured an equality of political rights.

In the House of Commons character is immediately apparent both as a medium of argument and as a site of rhetorical contest. Within the limits imposed by the rules of procedure, Parliamentary debate is by convention informal and interactive. The customs of the House, for example, encourage (though they do not require) speakers to give way both to friendly and to potentially hostile interventions. A general theory of Parliamentary character might begin with Aristotle's insight that the speaker's character is created as an effect of discourse, constructed anew on each rhetorical occasion, in and through the medium of speech itself.[21] Rhetorical character (*ethos*) can therefore be seen as a strictly provisional construct, contingent in the House of Commons not so much on the character of an 'external' audience to which it must be adjusted as on the characters of other speakers who may be said to compose an 'internal' audience as well as being equal participants in debate. In this context character emerges from a complex process of identification, anticipation, and counter-construction. The speaking self may declare itself by an affective appeal to values it shares with its audience but in the House of Commons, which is structured by architecture and custom as an adversarial assembly, it is equally likely to define itself in opposition to the character it constructs for an antagonist who may then renew the contest, perhaps by turning the same materials of character against the one who spoke first. In this situation, the characters of self and other, and the rhetorical strategies of *ethos* and what is known as 'ethical digression' (the delineation of the character of an opponent) are dynamically linked.[22] The Parliamentary speaker's character is consequently an insecure possession, potentially made and unmade in the course of a single debate.

In a rhetorical situation such as this, which is premised upon difference, gender, among other differences, may come into play. This was true of the Chamber even when it was an exclusively male space. In the late-eighteenth-century House the Younger Pitt's reputed celibacy and lack of sexual interest in women was sometimes alluded to by his political opponents in support of the charge that he was chilly, austere, and out of touch with the natural temper of the people.[23] Although Thatcher has repeatedly dismissed the importance of gender difference as an element in her public personality, a sense of that difference shapes many of her Parliamentary confrontations. Even the most commanding speakers are unable simply to dictate the terms of Parliamentary debate, and whatever her own intentions and preferences may have been, her public character (like any public character) could always be appropriated as the ground of argument and rhetorical contest. There were to be many occasions during her career in the House when her adversaries attempted to confine her character within gender stereotypes or attempted to discredit her for deviations from stock notions of femininity.

When Thatcher was a junior spokeswoman on pensions for the Opposition, the Labour minister Douglas Houghton was sufficiently impressed by her speech in a debate on National Insurance to figure her as a woman of power, yet he took care immediately to domesticate and deflate his apparent tribute. This 'hon. and battling Lady the Member for Finchley', he remarked, was 'a kind of Parliamentary Boadicea charging around the Chamber stabbing us right and left with a hat pin in one hand and a stiletto in the other'.[24] In the men's house, female articulacy was an incongruous and unaccountable phenomenon, best contained by *meiosis* and the idiom of burlesque. A trace of this mock-heroic tone is discernible in Denis Healey's many exchanges with Thatcher a decade later, but their overall effect is altogether more venomous and confrontational. In January 1975, near the climax of a Tory leadership campaign in which she was a largely unfancied outsider, Healey attacked her opposition to his plans for a capital transfer tax (which was to replace Estate Duty). In what must have seemed at the time a clever piece of ideological inversion, he incongruously cast Thatcher as a Tory replica of Dolores Ibárruri, the great Communist heroine (and most celebrated female orator) of republican Spain. 'The fact is', he told the House, 'that she emerged in this debate as La Pasionaria of privilege. She showed that she has decided, as the *Daily Express* said this morning, to see her party tagged as the party of the rich few.'[25] Uncowed, Thatcher exploited this construction of character to her own rhetorical advantage, demonstrating a genuinely La-Pasionaria-like resilience in her reply, and turning Healey's accusation against his own party. She opposed the tax, she declared, not in defence of privilege but in defence of ordinary families and family businesses which, as a woman from a background in trade, she was especially well placed to represent. The capital transfer tax, she retorted, 'will affect not only the one in a thousand to whom he referred but everyone, including people born like I was with no privilege at all. It will affect us as well as the Socialist millionaires.'[26]

What these Parliamentary constructions show as much as anything is the narrow range of her adversaries' conceptions of femininity and of the subject positions thought to be appropriate for women on the political stage. It was against this limited horizon of expectations, and in the intimidating atmosphere of the 'men's house', that soon after she entered Parliament Thatcher developed a speaking style which played to her considerable intellectual strengths and drew on the skills she had acquired at the Bar. Perhaps acknowledging the need to prove herself to a sceptical House she immediately won respect through a demonstrable command of her brief. Thatcher, it was observed, had always done her homework: she was unusually adept at marshalling arguments in technically complex areas of policy such as national insurance and taxation law. What emerges most clearly from her early performances in the House is an *ethos* of professional competence which she won through her command of statistics, destructive forensic skills, and ability to think on her feet.

This was a period when female speakers were most visible in debates on what were regarded as 'women's issues' or in adopting a consciously woman's perspective on more general aspects of policy.[27] What was distinctive, and historically important, about Thatcher was that she learned how to construct a public personality – and ultimately an instrument of leadership – which both drew on and transcended the discourse of housewifely femininity which she sometimes deployed against her Parliamentary rivals. In 1966, in her first major speech as Opposition spokeswoman on Treasury affairs, she launched a carefully researched attack on the Government's budget proposals, reserving her most stringent criticism for a measure known as the Selective Employment Tax. Briskly dismissing the plan as 'sheer lunacy' and 'absolute nonsense,' she advised the Chancellor of the Exchequer that it would take a woman's grasp of the real to cut through the complex absurdities of his new tax. 'I really think that the right hon. Gentleman needs a woman at the Treasury', she told the House. 'If my chief had come to me and put up a cockeyed scheme like that, I should have asked him if he was feeling all right.'[28]

The womanly common sense to which Thatcher laid claim in this debate was a core element of her Parliamentary persona. A feminised plain speaking was its rhetorical counterpart. The very first words she spoke in the House established a pattern she was to follow throughout her career. Declining to make the maiden speaker's traditional plea for indulgence, she declared that 'This is a maiden speech, but I know that the constituency of Finchley which I have the honour to represent would not wish me to do other than come straight to the point and address myself to the matter before the House.'[29] Both her own example as a speaker and her scattered comments on language use suggest that she had little time for a notion of eloquence characterised by verbal ingenuity, ornamentation, and play. Indeed, if her memoirs are to be believed she was desensitised to the charms of figurative language at an early age. Confessing that as a child she had, in her own words, 'a logical and indeed somewhat literal mind', she recalls having been 'perplexed by the metaphorical element of phrases like "Look before you leap". I thought it would be far better to say "Look before you cross" – a highly practical point given the dangerous road I must traverse on my way to school.'[30] At Oxford, as we have seen, she was denied participation in the displays of eloquence which were staged at the Union but in her memoirs she consoles herself with the thought that 'I would never have excelled in the kind of brilliant, brittle repartee which the Union seemed to encourage. I preferred the more serious forensic style of our discussion in OUCA [the Oxford University Conservative Association] and of the real hustings.'[31] This echoes a remark she made shortly after she had been elected to the leadership of her party. The Oxford Union debates, she told George Gardiner, 'were conducted in a way that would not particularly appeal to women. The approach at that time was very witty, certainly, and "clever", but it lacked gravitas. It was excellent entertainment, and some of the debates were superb, but many of them were rather frothy.'[32] In her mind, it seems, the Oxford Union's favoured verbal facility and practised ease was the rhetorical code of those who lived inside a charmed circle from which lower-middle-class women such as Thatcher herself were excluded. It was thus the code of a Tory establishment which had failed the nation and in a broader sense it was the code of the ever-unreliable British intelligentsia. Most tellingly, it was the code of those who lacked political conviction and had lost touch with the deepest instincts of the people.

In October 1966, knowing that the Labour Minister (and one-time Fellow of New College, Oxford) Richard Crossman would be winding up a debate on prices and incomes, she took the opportunity to discredit her opponent's eloquence in advance. 'We are all used to the right hon. Gentleman's ebullient, effervescent style', she said. 'It is always extremely attractive. It is often something of an Oxford Union style.' Responding to some laughter in the Chamber, she went on: 'I assure hon. Members that I am making no blandishments. The right hon. Gentleman has the kind of style which sounds tremendously impressive and which is most agreeable to listen to, but I find that one never believes a word of what he says because one knows that he is quite capable of making just as attractive an ebullient and effervescent speech tomorrow entirely contradicting all he has said today.'[33] Crossman's oratory was brilliant, but hollow; like the Oxford Union style which had shaped it (for he was reputedly one of the Union's most dazzling debaters) it lacked substance and backbone, and would tack, or break, at times of crisis.

Of course, her own plain speaking is as much a rhetorical construction as the grandest of styles, and it is a relatively simple task to show that, knowingly or not, many of her assertions of plain political sincerity are figuratively produced. 'We say what we mean and mean what we say' is one of many examples of her use of *antimetabole*, where, ironically, the circular and self-validating structure of the figure is asked to create an impression of straight talking.[34] In the crisis years of her rise to power Thatcher's feminised version of plain speaking helped her to seize the political initiative. It offered her a position from which she could undermine a range of political adversaries, from the rump of Tory patricians whose coded dissent she faced down inside her own Cabinet, to the Labour leadership whose 'windy rhetoric' and 'opaque words' she continued to deride even in her final triumphant appearance at the despatch box.[35] In speech, as in the economy, inflation was her sworn enemy, and more often than not the noisiest vessels were men. 'My experience', she observes in her memoirs, wryly inverting the usual stereotypes, 'is that a group of men sitting round a table like little better than their own voices'.[36] In her suspicion of rhetoric, which she conceived of primarily as figurative speech rather than argumentation, she was an instinctive Lockean. But she would have taken issue with Locke's gendering of rhetoric: the comparison he draws between the powers of eloquence and the arts of deception supposedly practised by 'the fair sex'.[37]

In October 1967 Thatcher entered the Shadow Cabinet as Opposition spokeswoman on Fuel and Power, traditionally regarded as one of the most masculine of portfolios. Two debates of this period may serve to illustrate both the rhetorical difficulties she faced in this role and her ability to turn gender difference to her advantage. A month after her appointment she was the only woman to speak at any length in a six-hour debate on the coal industry. In the ideology of the British Labour movement the miner occupied a special place, representing what has been called a working-class 'cult of masculinity' in perhaps its purest form.[38] This was terrain which the Parliamentary Labour Party liked to claim as its own, for it was able to point to the presence of numerous men with practical experience of the coalfields on its benches. Indeed, in the general election of 1966 more ex-miners than women had been elected to the Commons.[39] New to her brief, Thatcher could have been forgiven for viewing the prospect of such a debate with some unease.

The arguments that day focused on problems of overproduction in the coalfields and the best means of managing a reduction in the number of miners and pits. Thatcher's command of statistics and her understanding of the market for coal were predictably secure but she also sought the goodwill of the House by speaking in conciliatory terms of the human costs of unemployment. Replying to her speech in a similar spirit, Harold Neal, who represented the Derbyshire colliery seat of Bolsover, congratulated her on her 'initiation into fuel politics' but warned her that in future she would 'find the ground much rougher than she did this afternoon, and the conflict much more bitter than that to which she has been accustomed in the bipartisan field of social services'.[40] As it turned out, his prediction was to be confirmed before the debate had closed. At one point Thatcher declared, somewhat hypothetically for someone from her background, that she would not send her own son (at the time a fourteen-year-old public schoolboy) down the pit. For this incaution she was courteously but firmly corrected by Alex Eadie who, though he chose not to mention it, had at her son's age already begun work in the Scottish coalfields. These, he reminded her, were not always matters of choice.[41] A more aggressive, and personalised, challenge came later in the debate from Thomas Swain, another former miner. Thatcher had remarked in passing how difficult it was to get hold of the relevant volumes of *Hansard* from the Commons Library. Swain saw this is an opportunity to contest her authority to speak on matters so remote from her life experiences: 'I wish to goodness that my fundamental knowledge of the mining industry had been got out of the Library, like hers. With her fundamental knowledge of the mining industry, with all its ramifications, its dangers, and, above all, its importance to our economy, I am sure she will be worth listening to during the Committee stage', he said, caustically.[42] In a rhetorically constructed clash of opposites Swain claimed to speak the authentic voice of the male industrial worker, hinting at differences of region, gender, and class which would redound to Thatcher's disadvantage.

Six months later, again leading for the Opposition, Thatcher was the only woman to speak in a debate on the Gas and Electricity Bill. This measure was primarily intended to augment the borrowing powers of the Gas Council in order to provide for investment in the gas fields of the North Sea. In her reply to the minister, Ray Gunter, Thatcher skilfully marshalled some deliberative themes, arguing against the expediency of the proposal on the grounds of a deteriorating economic outlook and uncertain prospects for demand. But rhetorically the most interesting moment came when she asked the House to 'look at the matter from the consumers' viewpoint'. She illustrated that viewpoint, and the costs and inconveniences of conversion to natural gas, by introducing a domestic example: 'what happens is that somebody comes to one's house, shakes his head sadly over one's gas cooker and says that it is unconvertible because it is too old, although it is working perfectly well, and shakes his head sadly over the gas fire, which gives perfectly good service, and says "You should have a new one."' When one Labour member, apparently unconvinced by this foray into household economics, indicated dissent, Thatcher upbraided him for his ignorance: 'Perhaps the hon. Gentleman never reads the women's pages in magazines and newspapers. He should. He might then know more about gas and electricity and the public than he does.'[43] Contesting the Government's case, Thatcher offered a reasoned reply which turned on the probabilities of supply and demand but she also exposed her opponents' gendered blindness to the interests and desires of a consumer who later in the speech is casually but significantly represented as female (just as the patronising engineer from the Gas Board had been represented as male).

CONFERENCE ORATORY AND FEMALE LEADERSHIP

While avoiding the ghetto of 'women's issues', as they were narrowly defined at the time, Thatcher opened up a space for argument which none of her rivals in this debate could so convincingly occupy. This half-forgotten speech foreshadows a shift of perspective from the producer to the consumer which was to become one of the hallmarks of Thatcher's mature rhetoric. In political terms her objective was to reduce the power of organised labour but she saw that the gains of such a project could not be secured by legislative means alone. Of equal importance was her rhetorical ambition to bring about a reorientation of the economic self. Addressing a conference of Conservative Trade Unionists in 1979 Thatcher reminded her audience of producers that 'we are all consumers and as consumers we all want a choice. We want to buy the best value for money ... Producers want a protected market for their products. That is the union demand. But the same trade unionists, as consumers, want an open market. They cannot both win. But they can both lose.'[44] Writing in her diary in 1975 the prominent Labour MP Barbara Castle had anticipated Thatcher's reasoning, and explained her rise to power, in strikingly similar terms. The Tories' choice of a woman to lead them signalled a shift in politics, and a lesson from which Labour had to learn. As a female leader, she argued, Thatcher would be unusually well placed to represent and capture the consumer's standpoint:

> I think it will be a good thing for the Labour Party too. There's a male-dominated party for you – not least because the trade unions are male-dominated, even the ones that cater for women. I remember just before the February election last year pleading on the NEC for us not to have a completely producer-oriented policy, because women lose out in the producer-run society ... I believe Margaret Thatcher's election will force our party to think again: and a jolly good thing too. To me, socialism isn't just militant trade unionism. It is the gentle society, in which every producer remembers he is a consumer too.[45]

Thatcherism's typically appetitive and hard-bargaining consumer could hardly be described as 'gentle' but Castle's analysis was none the less astute. As Castle recognised, to speak in the interests of 'the consumer' in the 1970s was to contest the power of a trade union movement which remained largely unreceptive to the economic priorities of women. Implicit in Thatcher's rhetoric of that period is the idea that the Labour movement, and the state-owned monopolies it has created, compose a masculine sphere of the economy, experienced by women in their everyday dealings as oppressive and exploitative. In her 1975 Conference speech she called on the Wilson government to 'stop trying to prove their socialist virility by relentlessly nationalizing one industry after another'.[46] Since we are all, male and female, in some sense consumers, a rhetoric which could appeal persuasively to our interests as consuming selves, and convince those consuming selves that the interests of production stood against them, was likely to prove a powerful weapon, especially at a time of intense industrial conflict.

Thatcher's election to the party leadership gave her an unrivalled authority to present these arguments to the numerous annual assemblies of the Tory faithful, where she could speak directly to an unusually unified and supportive audience while at the same time exploiting the resources of the news media to broadcast her views to the nation at large. The enduring image of Thatcher as a female rhetor is closely associated with these occasions: the lone figure of a woman, illuminated in a great conference hall, voice and body firmly controlled and co-ordinated in the moment of delivery, commanding a platform which only men had ever commanded before. By all accounts Thatcher managed to forge an exceptionally close relationship with her conference audiences. Unlike some of her predecessors, she relished the opportunity to mingle with the rank and file, to observe (and indeed to second) their reactions to debates, and, not least, to reaffirm her ideological bonds with them in her closing speeches. On these occasions, a party renowned as the most patriarchal in British politics found that a female orator could best voice its deepest values and instincts. In considering this paradox, it should be remembered that, while men hold most of the positions of power in the Conservative party hierarchy, women have long played a key role in promoting its political activities and securing its electoral triumphs.[47] This could hardly be described as a feminist party but it is none the less a party shaped by women. Decades before they were admitted to membership women were prized for their industry and persuasiveness as canvassers, a role made the more important by the great expansion of the male electorate in the later nineteenth century. Since 1918, when they were first accepted as members, women have been represented in separate sections within the party structure (currently the Conservative Women's Organization, which convenes an annual conference, and the Conservative Women's National Committee). The party which Thatcher addressed as Prime Minister, numerically dominated by men in the Cabinet and in Parliament, had a preponderance of female members in the constituencies. A beleaguered minority in the Commons Chamber, Tory women are a conspicuous presence in the great halls of Brighton, Blackpool, and Bournemouth, where the annual conference is held.

At the annual Women's Conference the audience is, by definition, exclusively female. According to an observer who attended this event in 1986 Thatcher was regarded by her audience as '"one of us", the proof of the Tory woman's value inside the party'. Admired 'as a tribune of CWO [the Conservative Women's Organization], bravely defying a male-dominated party establishment' she was said to echo 'the concerns and hopes of ordinary CWO members and, by implication ... those of ordinary women voters'.[48] The speech which Thatcher delivered on this occasion, perhaps the most insistently woman-centred of all her public addresses, seems to have been calculated to reinforce these bonds. With a general election in the offing, the speech sets about its task of strengthening the morale of Conservative women with particular urgency: it offers the assembled activists an upbeat review of the government's achievements, calls on them to support its efforts to meet new challenges, and unifies them around a scathing attack on the political opposition. These are the commonplaces of conference oratory, but Thatcher takes care to particularise them, summoning up the life experiences of her audience, and staking out the ground of opinion where Conservative women can meet on equal terms, and where her deliberative themes can take root.

Addressed by a woman to an audience of women, the speech opens with a tribute to female fortitude, personified by the Soviet human-rights campaigner Yelena Bonner, and an affirmation of the enduring value of family and home. A few days earlier Thatcher had met Bonner on the latter's return from a visit to her daughter in the United States. Bonner's admiring impressions of America, cited as proof of the moral and economic superiority of the West, introduce a contrast between political systems which structures the speech:

> What struck her most forcibly was the possibility of actually owning a home of her own, as her children do, and what this meant for human and family life. 'I'm sixty-three,' she wrote, 'and I've never had a house; not only that, I've never had a corner I could call my own.' She went on, 'My dream, my own house, is unattainable for my husband and myself, as unattainable as Heaven on Earth.'[49]

Thatcher cites Bonner's testimony in her exordium in order to remind her audience of women of what Conservatism means for them, and how, as Beatrix Campbell puts it, Conservatism can help them to make sense of their world.[50] The speech *shows* them that this is so, that they may in turn show others. It invites them to enter a pictured scene of the house that Thatcher built, where the party's achievements can be recognised in the tangible form of everyday perceptions and things:

> We should take stock of what we have been able to achieve for family living standards here at home, with pride and gratitude, but without complacency. So, next time you go canvassing, think of Mrs Bonner. When you call on your first owner-occupied home, think of Mrs Bonner. In Britain, there are fourteen million homes like that.

Don't be surprised if the householder who answers your knock on the door is young. In the last seven years, a lot more young people have been able to buy their own homes. That's good news. And you may well see a child in the sitting room using a home computer pretty expertly – probably far better at it than mother or father.[51]

As she completes her inventory, Thatcher takes care to maintain contact with her audience of activists. Her identification with the Tory canvasser is based on more than shared political loyalties. It is also based on a shared sense of women's privileged access to the home, the one place to which their right of entry cannot be questioned. One is reminded that women's effectiveness in their political role as canvassers had been explained, and justified, as a natural expression of the feminine sympathy which they had traditionally shown in their charitable visits to the homes of the poor. Thatcher does not politicise the home in this speech, for that would unhelpfully bring into question the unequal distribution of power between women and men, but she does place women and the home at the centre of her politics. As she was to put it in a later speech to the Women's Conference, the family 'is a nursery, a school, a hospital, a leisure place, a place of refuge and a place of rest. It encompasses the whole of society. It fashions our beliefs. It is the preparation for the rest of our life. And women run it.'[52] In the 1986 speech she returns in her peroration to Bonner and directly addresses her audience of women. The domestic sphere is valued as an enclave and bulwark against the intrusions of the state. As its natural inhabitants and instinctive defenders women, but especially Conservative women, are flattered and urged on as 'the best guardians of our liberties'.[53]

'One of the most revealing things about the rhetoric of the left', Thatcher told the Conservative Conference in 1981, 'is the almost total absence of any reference to the family.'[54] Like all party leaders she necessarily spoke on a wide range of topics but she took care not to cut herself off from traditionally female sites of influence and power. As a female orator she knew where best to pitch her tents and often enough it was in places which her enemies had incautiously left vacant.

CONCLUSION

The Conservative commentator Patrick Cosgrave, who served periodically as one of Thatcher's speechwriters, suggests that much of her rhetoric 'is suffused by appeals, arguments and propositions that could only be uttered by a woman, and to which only a woman could lend authority'.[55] The project of Thatcherism owed a great deal to these modes of speech. As a female orator in a period of deepening economic crisis she was unusually well placed to shift the terms of political debate. Not herself one of the New Right's leading theoreticians, she was none the less better qualified than any of them to represent its doctrines to a national audience. When confidence in the power of public institutions to satisfy wants and to manage change was at a low ebb she was able to personify the moral and economic strengths of the private sphere.

As Barbara Castle foresaw, Thatcher's difference helped her to make a distinctive kind of appeal and in due course to reshape the political land-scape. In her memoirs Thatcher contrasts her own social origins with those of her 'senior colleagues' and concludes that 'They were perhaps too ready to accept the Labour Party and union leaders as authentic interpreters of the wishes of the people. I did not feel I needed an interpreter to address people who spoke the same language.'[56] She seemed able to claim a special understanding of what she called 'the everyday things that families want' and a special access to the instincts – the material needs, drives, and desires – of ordinary people.[57] She seemed to have mastered the deceptively simple rhetorical arts of populism, projecting an image of ordinary people which many ordinary people recognised as a reflection of themselves. She seemed to know how to do what subsequent Tory leaders have despaired of being able to do: 'to make a connection', as the current political vocabulary puts it, or, in other words, to identify rhetorically with her potential supporters. In her first speech as leader to the Conservative Party Conference in 1975, a defining moment in her career to which she was to return repeatedly in later addresses, making a connection was a primary rhetorical objective, for her command of the party was as yet insecure. Her exordium that day was simple but telling:

> The first Conservative Party Conference I ever attended was in 1946 and I came to it as an undergraduate representing Oxford University Conservative Asso-ciation ... That conference was held in this very hall and the platform then seemed a long way away and I had no thought of joining the lofty and distinguished people sitting up there, but our Party is the party of equality of opportunity as you can see.[58]

As she recalls in her memoirs, the 1946 Conference was notable for dissension between the discontented representatives and a faint-hearted leadership which had yet to recover from the shock of electoral defeat.[59] Now herself the leader, she takes her stand rhetorically with the party's rank and file rather than its grandees. As she speaks from the platform, she sees herself through the eyes of those who sit below her in the hall. Of course it was the Parliamentary party which had, quite unexpectedly, elected her, but for the new leader this is the truly empowering moment, when speech dissolves distance, when she connects with her audience and her legitimacy is finally guaranteed. What the party faithful *see* is, evidently, a woman, and it is as a woman, a grocer's *daughter*, that she represents herself as a living proof of the party's creed, as a leader who not only speaks for Tory principles but can claim to embody them.

NOTES

1 For helpful comments on earlier versions of this chapter I am grateful to Michael Edwards, Morag Shiach, and participants at the Thirteenth Biennial Conference of the International Society for the History of Rhetoric (Warsaw, 2001).

2 Margaret Thatcher, *The Collected Speeches of Margaret Thatcher*, ed. R. Harris (London, 1997), pp. 227–35. The most complete and authoritative source for Thatcher's speeches is C. Collins (ed.), *Complete Public Statements, 1945–1990 on CD-ROM* (Oxford, 1999). I refer to printed texts where these exist. See also F. Mikdali, *Margaret Thatcher: A Bibliography* (Westport, Connecticut, 1993).

3 *Parliamentary Debates, House of Lords*, fifth series, 13 November 1984, vol. 457, col. 238.

4 *Parliamentary Debates, House of Lords*, fifth series, 13 November 1984, vol. 457, col. 240.

5 Macmillan's Carlton Lecture is printed in B. Phelps, *Power and the Party: A History of the Carlton Club* (London, 1983), pp. xiii–xxvii. Macmillan's emphasis in the lecture on the need for strong European institutions and détente with the Soviet Union strikes a distinctly non-Thatcherite note.

6 Thatcher, *Collected Speeches*, pp. 235, 233.

7 For different interpretations of this episode see Phelps, *Power and the Party*, p. 81, and W. Webster, *Not a Man to Match Her: The Marketing of the Prime Minister* (London, 1990), pp. 137–42.

8 The best biography of Thatcher is H. Young, *One of Us* (2nd edn, London, 1991). J. Campbell, *Margaret Thatcher: The Grocer's Daughter* (London, 2000), the first of a projected two-volume biography, is especially helpful on Thatcher's Parliamentary activities.

9 Margaret Thatcher, *The Path to Power* (London, 1995), p. 42. Women were not admitted to full membership of the Union until 1963. See B. Harrison (ed.), *The History of the University of Oxford*, vol. 8, *The Twentieth Century* (Oxford, 1994), pp. 355–6 and 381–4.

10 For interpretations of Thatcher and Thatcherism from a feminist perspective see Webster, *Not a Man to Match Her*; M. Warner, *Monuments & Maidens: The Allegory of the Female Form* (London, 1985), pp. 38–60; B. Campbell, *The Iron Ladies: Why Do Women Vote Tory?* (London, 1987); and J. Rose, 'Margaret Thatcher and Ruth Ellis', *New Formations*, 6 (1988), 3–64. For discussion of Thatcher as a speaker see M. Atkinson, *Our Masters' Voices: The Language and Body Language of Politics* (London, 1984); N. Fairclough, *Language and Power* (London, 1989), pp. 169–96; and J. Raban, *God, Man & Mrs Thatcher* (London, 1989).

11 On feminism and rhetoric see especially A. Lunsford (ed.), *Reclaiming Rhetorica: Women in the Rhetorical Tradition* (Pittsburgh, 1995); L. Ede, C. Glenn, and A. Lunsford, 'Border crossings: intersections of rhetoric and feminism', *Rhetorica*, 13:4 (1995), 401–41; M. Billig, *Arguing and Thinking: A Rhetorical Approach to Social Psychology* (2nd edn, Cambridge, 1996), pp. 22–9; M. Wertheimer (ed.), *Listening to Their Voices: The Rhetorical Activities of Historical Women* (Columbia, South Carolina, 1997); and C. Mason Sutherland and R. Sutcliffe (eds), *The Changing Tradition: Women in the History of Rhetoric* (Calgary, 1999).

12 Wertheimer, *Listening to Their Voices*, p. 3.

13 Warner, *Monuments & Maidens*, p. 52.

14 *Selected Letters of James Joyce*, ed. R. Ellmann (London, 1975), p. 285.

15 *Parliamentary Debates, House of Commons*, sixth series, 30 October 1990, vol. 178, col. 873.

16 Campbell, *The Iron Ladies*, p. 256.

17 Thatcher, *The Path to Power*, p. 108; Barbara Castle, *Fighting All the Way* (London, 1993), p. 131. Especially helpful on women in the Commons is B. Harrison, 'Women in a men's house: the women M.P.s, 1919–1945', *The Historical Journal*, 29:3 (1986), 623–54. See also P. Brookes, *Women at Westminster: An Account of Women in the British Parliament 1918–1966* (London, 1967), and E. Vallance, *Women in the House: A Study of Women Members of Parliament* (London, 1979).

18 S. Rodgers, 'Women's space in a men's house: the British House of Commons', in S. Ardener (ed.), *Women and Space: Ground Rules and Social Maps* (rev. edn, Oxford, 1993), pp. 46–69.

19 Rodgers, 'Women's space', pp. 50, 46, 53, 54.

20 Aristotle, *Rhetoric* 1.2.2–4, 2.1.2–4, trans. G.A. Kennedy (New York and Oxford, 1991) pp. 37–8, 120–1.

21 Aristotle, *Rhetoric* 1.2.4, trans. Kennedy, p. 38.

22 On ethical digression see G. A. Kennedy, *A New History of Classical Rhetoric* (Princeton, 1994), p. 67.

23 See J. Morwood, *The Life and Times of Richard Brinsley Sheridan* (Edinburgh, 1985), p. 110; and C. Reid, 'Foiling the rival: argument and identity in Sheridan's speeches', in J. Morwood (ed.), *Sheridan Studies* (Cambridge, 1995), pp. 114–30.

24 *Parliamentary Debates, House of Commons*, fifth series, 25 November 1964, vol. 702, col. 1396.

25 *Parliamentary Debates, House of Commons*, fifth series, 22 January 1975, vol. 884, col. 1553.

26 *Parliamentary Debates, House of Commons*, fifth series, 22 January 1975, vol. 884, col. 1554.

27 As late as 1976 the Labour MP Maureen Colquhoun felt compelled to seek reassurance that 'Mr. Speaker's Department does not think that women members should be restricted in debates to their own areas of understanding as defined by men. I am referring to subjects like social services and mental health.' *Parliamentary Debates, House of Commons*, fifth series, 29 January 1976, vol. 904, col. 787.

28 *Parliamentary Debates, House of Commons*, fifth series, 5 May 1966, vol. 727, col. 1893.

29 *Parliamentary Debates, House of Commons*, fifth series, 5 February 1960, vol. 616, col. 1350.

30 Thatcher, *The Path to Power*, p. 17. As Jonathan Raban observes, 'She distrusts the loose morals of metaphor' (*God, Man & Mrs Thatcher*, p. 4).

31 Thatcher, *The Path to Power*, p. 42.

32 G. Gardiner, *Margaret Thatcher: From Childhood to Leadership* (London, 1975), pp. 32–3.

33 *Parliamentary Debates, House of Commons*, fifth series, 25 October 1966, vol. 734, col. 955.

34 Speech to the Conservative Party Conference, 14 October 1988, *Collected Speeches*, p. 339. Many examples of this kind are likely to have been suggested by Thatcher's speechwriters, with whom she worked in close and sometimes uneasy collaboration. For inside accounts of the speechwriting process see R. Millar, *A View from the Wings: West End, West Coast, Westminster* (London, 1993); G. Urban, *Diplomacy and Disillusion at the Court of Margaret Thatcher: An Insider's View* (London, 1996), pp. 34–62; and J. Hoskyns, *Just in Time: Inside the Thatcher Revolution* (London, 2000).

35 *Parliamentary Debates, House of Commons*, sixth series, 22 November 1990, vol. 181, col. 446.

36 Margaret Thatcher, *The Downing Street Years* (London, 1993), p. 561.

37 John Locke, *An Essay Concerning Human Understanding*, ed. P. H. Nidditch (Oxford, 1975), p. 508.

38 B. Campbell, *Wigan Pier Revisited: Poverty and Politics in the 80s* (London, 1984), pp. 97–115. See also L. Loach, 'We'll be here right to the end ... and after: women in the miners' strike', in H. Benyon, (ed.), *Digging Deeper: Issues in the Miners' Strike* (London, 1985), pp. 169–79.

39 Thirty-two ex-miners and twenty-six women. See D. Butler and A. King, *The British General Election of 1966* (London, 1966).

40 *Parliamentary Debates, House of Commons*, fifth series, 28 November 1967, vol. 755, col. 276.

41 *Parliamentary Debates, House of Commons*, fifth series, 28 November 1967, vol. 755, cols 269, 372.

42 *Parliamentary Debates, House of Commons*, fifth series, 28 November 1967, vol. 755, cols 396–7.

43 *Parliamentary Debates, House of Commons*, fifth series, 22 May 1968, vol. 765, cols 557–8.

44 Thatcher, *Complete Public Statements*, 17 November 1979.

45 Barbara Castle, *The Castle Diaries, 1974–76* (London, 1980), p. 561.

46 Thatcher, *Collected Speeches*, p. 32.

47 On these issues see Campbell, *The Iron Ladies*, and G. E. Maguire, *Conservative Women: A History of Women and the Conservative Party, 1874–1997* (London, 1998).

48 R. N. Kelly, *Conservative Party Conferences: The Hidden System* (Manchester, 1989), pp. 132–4.
49 Margaret Thatcher, *The Revival of Britain: Speeches on Home and European Affairs, 1975–1988*, compiled by A. B. Cooke (London, 1988), pp. 211–12.
50 Campbell, *The Iron Ladies*, p. 2.
51 Thatcher, *The Revival of Britain*, p. 212.
52 Thatcher, *Complete Public Statements*, 25 May 1988.
53 Thatcher, *The Revival of Britain*, p. 221.
54 Thatcher, *Collected Speeches*, p. 145.
55 P. Cosgrave, *Thatcher: The First Term* (London, 1985), p. 5.
56 Thatcher, *The Downing Street Years*, p. 10. On the 'populist idiom' of Thatcherism see Stuart Hall, 'The great moving right show', in Stuart Hall and Martin Jacques (eds), *The Politics of Thatcherism* (London, 1983), pp. 19–39.
57 Thatcher, *The Revival of Britain*, p. 212.
58 Thatcher, *Collected Speeches*, p. 29.
59 Thatcher, *The Path to Power*, p.48.

11

Video Cicero

LYNETTE HUNTER

✳

Margaret Thatcher, the dominant political personality in Britain in the 1980s and the subject of the preceding chapter, figures prominently in Lynette Hunter's wide-ranging discussion of the fate of oratory in a media age. Although the Thatcherites were ridiculed, especially in their early days, as unworldly enthusiasts and members of an esoteric political sect, Thatcher herself never lost sight of the importance of her public personality, of seizing the ground of 'common sense', and of creating an *ethos* which allowed her to assert an identity of interests with 'ordinary people'. In this way oratory in its various modern forms was at the heart of the Thatcherite project: it activated ideology and made it a persuasive political force.

Thatcher's favoured self-image was that of an authentic interpreter of the wishes of the people. But who were (and indeed are) this 'people' to whom orators like Thatcher appeal? In the rhetoric of populism, 'the people', at first sight an unusually inclusive audience, is often defined by what it excludes. In the name of the people populist orators attack what they see as entrenched interests and interest groups (Tory grandees, intellectuals, trades unionists, the public sector), vilify enemies both outside and within, and pour scorn on the defenders of cultural difference. Thatcher's populism thus illustrates (but does not exhaust) Lynette Hunter's thesis that public speech today ignores diversity and assumes common ground rather than arguing for it. In developing this argument in the contemporary context Hunter also returns us to some of rhetoric's enduring issues and themes. How is the orator to win trust without resorting to simple flattery or appealing to a narrow sense of self-interest? How is the orator to unify an audience while respecting differences among those who compose it? How is the orator to persuade without manipulation, and to shape opinion without excluding the audience from the scene of argument?

✳

Our society now has the media for the complete public speaker, the contemporary rhetorician, the modern Cicero on video who tries to speak for us all. Yet if orators in some societies, such as the First Nations of North America, are the source of the social, cultural, political, and religious guidelines for their societies, and are respected if not honoured for this skill, then what has happened to our own politicians? Public speeches, say those of Winston Churchill, have conventionally been part of our valued literary heritage. But as radio and television have opened up, political communication has become more and more a combined verbal and dramatic art for the many, and is often distrusted.

I would like to argue that there is a set of unspoken but widely understood rules of thumb that have habitually been used to assess the value or otherwise of political performance in the media, and that these seem to be contradicted in complex ways by the increasingly diverse make-up of people with access to political power. Because contemporary political rhetoric must be all things to all peoples, it tends to gut the issues of any real debate, to offer to speak for us rather than to us, hence weakening our commitment to political action either by ourselves or by those acting on our behalf.

Classical political rhetoric, from which Parliamentary democracy has got most of its techniques for political oratory, is set up for a circumscribed democracy, in fact an oligarchy. Greece and Rome were slave states, and Rome especially depended on a slave economy. The key element of oratory at the time, and still nowadays, is the ability of the orator to establish common ground with the audience. It must trust the orator. People communicated orally, so if you were listening to a political speech you could nudge your neighbour, interrupt, and make your feelings known by walking out. If today the orator still has to maintain trust, the political constituency is rarely any longer directly present.

A hallmark of Tony Blair's rhetoric in the 1997 election was precisely to establish a trustworthy, recognisable *ethos*. One party political broadcast opens with two slightly more than middle-aged women speaking with a reserved enthusiasm (the slight reticence provides a sense of considered opinion), and moves on to show Blair in his kitchen, in his shirtsleeves, discussing the way that he and his father had had political differences from the beginning, because his father voted Conservative. The sequence closes with Blair saying in an understated and good-humoured way that his father had changed his mind. The absence of triumphalism is key to our approbation. Blair is implying that decent right-thinking people of his father's generation who voted Conservative did so at a time when the Labour Party was not offering them a suitable approach, almost that their influence was responsible for changing the attitude to what Labour thought it should be. Given the urgency of swinging large numbers of voters from Conservative to Labour, the subtle implications were vital. The broadcast is also aiming at another constituency, the middle-class left of centre who traditionally might have identified themselves with Labour but who had been drifting. Again, the persuasion is subtle as Blair is shown playing football with a group of young people, probably around nine or ten years of age, presumably at a community-organised training event; the young people are both boys and girls. In this one sequence around Blair, a vision of possible unity is constructed of a different kind of Labour Party: gender equity, community support, parental responsibility, and, most important, a breakdown in hierarchy as the potential Prime Minister engages in an ordinary activity.

Establishing common ground is not very difficult when you speak to people with the same way of life and similar expectations. In Rome, Cicero was speaking to people with roughly the same income and status, and all of them were men. Just so, at party conferences today, despite a diversity of background there is normally some kind of political consensus. Extracts from the 1992 Conservative Party conference show John Major speaking to the self-selected Conservative core, who stand in for the nation at large who have just voted for a Conservative government yet again. Yet Major speaks not of specific issues but of general themes such as empire and glory, reinforced with music by Elgar, culturally recognisable at the time as Conservative owing to the long association of Elgar with the flag-waving finale to the last night of the Proms at the Royal Albert Hall. Major calls on large themes of patriotism at a time when voters were beginning to get disenchanted with Conservative policies, asking them to look at 'the bigger picture' which is more likely to unite them. Significantly the audience he is addressing is lit to recede into semi-darkness, tinted blue, as the light focuses on him alone, positioning him as the one who will lead them into the light.

In contrast to both these examples, of Blair and Major, think about Labour in the 1980s: a party with a healthy diversity which partially represented the growing diversity of communities in the UK, came head-on up against entrenched strategies of classical political rhetoric which do not admit diversity. Although certainly not the only reason, this lock into an obsolete rhetorical structure contributed to the way Labour became obstinately divisive, and splintered.

WHY IS IT THAT CLASSICAL POLITICAL RHETORIC DOES NOT SEEM TO BE ABLE TO DEAL WITH DIVERSITY? THE ORATOR AND PLAUSIBLE ARGUMENT: ESTABLISHING COMMON GROUND

One of the issues important to rehearse is the difference made in classical rhetoric between probable argument and the plausible rhetoric of opinion. Probable rhetoric works first by suggesting a set of common grounds about which it invites debate, discussion, and finally, in some form, agreement. Only then can it move on to the persuasion proper. In contrast, plausible opinion assumes common ground, assumes that the audience will think in roughly the same way as the speaker, and launches immediately into argument.[1] Aristotle claimed that plausible rhetoric was appropriate only to closed communities such as scientists (seekers after knowledge of different kinds in closed communities), and was not for use in social or political situations where there will be a diverse audience.[2] Plausible rhetoric leaves it all too easy to claim that certain ideas are absolutely true, because they fit inside the taken-for-granted grounds. What the distinction adds up to is one between rhetoric that speaks *to* us (probable) and rhetoric that speaks *for* us (plausible).

Cicero's *De oratore*, which developed a rhetoric for the legal courts, offered an analogy for political rhetoric in a state substantially different from Aristotle's, especially in terms of its size. The population of Rome was much greater than that of fourth-century Athens, the land the Romans ruled was much more far-flung, and a substantial part of the population lived in appalling poverty and extremity.[3] There was much more potential for slave rebellion in Rome, and indeed by the start of Cicero's career there had been two slave uprisings. A number of historians argue that in the aftermath of Sulla's 'reforms', which wiped out many governing families but also expanded the Senate from three hundred to six hundred, the ruling group in Rome became much more diverse. Cicero's particular skill was in the construction of a character, or *ethos*, for the speaker that would appeal to a broader number of people – still only the ruling group, but not just aristocrats. The primary focus of his book *De oratore* is on the creation of a speaking voice that others could trust, believe, and accept as 'one of them'. He says:

> Now nothing in oratory, Catulus, is more important than to win for the orator the favour of his hearer, and to have the latter so affected as to be swayed by something resembling a mental impulse ... For men decide far more problems by hate, or love, or lust, or rage, or sorrow, or joy, or hope, or fear, or illusion ... than by reality, or authority, or any legal standard, or judicial precedent, or statute ... A potent factor in success, then, is for the characters, principles, conduct and course of life, both of those who are to plead cases and of their clients, to be approved, and conversely those of their opponents condemned; and for the feelings of the tribunal to be won over, as far as possible, to goodwill towards the advocate and the advocate's client as well.[4]

All rhetoric has to construct an *ethos* that the audience will trust, but the focus on this construction, so that the audience is manipulated into acceptance rather than considered understanding, is a major step toward a political rhetoric of plausibility that speaks for and not to its audience. Harold Gotoff notes of Cicero with rather overstated relish:

> Every rhetorical stance, every anecdote, every argument, every inflection of a speech, and the manner in which each of these is presented, is calculated to control and direct the attitude of a defined audience in a particular situation ... The arguments Cicero puts forth, whether to elucidate or obfuscate, have the overriding goal of convincing his audience. All is fair in love, war, and oratory ... The voice we hear in the speeches is not that of a teacher or a philosopher. Its goal is not education, but psychological manipulation.[5]

Not that Cicero was the first or only person to do this, by no means. However, his skill, fame, and writing became so influential to classical

Roman culture and later on to Renaissance European society that many people imitated his style and his work became central to an education in rhetoric in both periods. Furthermore Cicero was one of the first in western philosophy to separate the State and the government, and to argue explicitly that the function of the State is to preserve the accumulation of private property.[6] Both elements can be connected with attempts to stabilise the diversity of voices newly come to government, and anxiety about social mobility.

Cicero's focus on the construction of plausible *ethos* is parallel to his concern with the State: both speak for rather than to. Their rhetoric is structured to manipulate into inclusion and assent rather than to persuade through discussion. With this kind of rhetoric there is always an unspoken, silent presence: that of the people who live outside this circle of assumptions. *Ethos* need not be of this cruel inclusionary or exclusionary character, but a focus on *ethos* at the expense of encouraging debate will tend toward the construction of closed circles of argument which accept rather than question common grounds. We can hear and watch him doing this in speech after speech. One of his first legal cases, and the one that brought him to fame, was the *Pro Roscio Amerino* (80 BC). Speaking in the wake of Sulla's killings, Cicero has to defend Roscius from the charge of killing his father, and he was fully expected to fail. In a textbook example of his later prescription, Cicero first sets up his own *ethos*, explaining why he, 'so young, inexperienced, and lacking authority, should have undertaken this case'; he had 'been pressed into service by his friends and under such circumstances could not refuse', that Roscius deserved the truth to be known, and finally that he was 'duty-bound' to defend him despite the heavy burden it would bring. He then moves on to praising the character of the jury, especially that of the presiding officer, and pulling them into his own sense of duty, asking them to lighten his burden because they are men of worth and wisdom. And finally he successfully characterises the prosecution itself as self-serving and criminal.[7] Again, at the centre of his strategy is the construction of a closed circle of assent, which includes himself, the jury and Roscius as just, and excludes the prosecution as criminal. It is perhaps this, more than anything else, that convinces the court to acquit.

It is important that, lacking any personal common ground, or any political position, Cicero draws on the functions of the State and appeals to law and order to create that common ground. The tactic is one that has been fully taken up by contemporary politics. There is a riveting analysis by Justin Lewis of two interviews with Margaret Thatcher in 1979 and in 1981, about riots in London, which demonstrates how this usually works well, but can be a problem.[8] The 1979 interview shows her using the framework of law and order to contain the Southall riots in which Blair Peach was killed. Her prime tactic is to condemn the activities of the National Front not as evidence of racial hatred but as an attack on civilisation, law, and the police. In light of the recent events surrounding the death of Stephen Lawrence, we could have wished for a more searching analysis, but she was successful at the time because she was still able to manipulate the public feeling around the disruptions of the late 1970s, and their issues of law and order, that had brought her to power.

However, only two years later, in an interview with Alistair Burnet about the Brixton riots, she is deprived of this tactic. Lewis details with precision the moves and counter-moves with which Thatcher attempts once again to call on law and order, and those of Burnet who keeps shifting the ground away from the idea that the rioters are criminals and beyond help, to the idea that they may be responding to a complex set of issues to do with racism, and attendant unemployment and discrimination in all areas. He finally points out the lack of trust in the police, which completely undermines her *ethos* of law and order, and she is reduced to emotional rebuttal and the use of tautology (the refuge of those who cannot see outside their own small worlds): that these people are criminals and therefore they will behave in criminal ways – itself a piece of racist comment.

THE ORATOR AND THE NEED FOR A VICE: ESTABLISHING COMMON WEAKNESS

When the humanists of the Renaissance rediscovered the classics, they became fascinated by this idea of *ethos*. Among the Italian city-states, each prince had his rhetor or orator. The power of Machiavelli was in part due to his combining the two activities. Much of his advice book, *The Prince*, is concerned with self-constructed *ethos*: how the Prince must appear to his subjects in order to maintain his rule. Machiavelli points out that no one is perfect, one man may be generous and another greedy, one faithless and one true to his word, and so on. He continues:

> Every one, I know, will admit that it would be most laudable for a Prince to

be endowed with all of the above qualities that are reckoned good; but since it is impossible for him to possess or constantly practise them all, the conditions of human nature not allowing it, he must be discreet enough to know how to avoid the infamy of those vices that would deprive him of his government, and, if possible, be on his guard also against those which might not deprive him of it.[9]

In other words, you shouldn't hesitate to break the social rules of behaviour if you are threatened, but you should make sure that the vices you indulge in will not destroy your plausible *ethos*, and cost you your power.

One of the most obvious examples of this advice has been Bill Clinton, but Clinton's *ethos* as President of the United States always gave evidence of something other than manipulation. The manipulative *ethos* is short term. It is ideal for court cases and for passing political issues, but not for long-term political success. Unlike many high-profile politicians in the United States, or for that matter in England (the focus of this section rather than Britain), Clinton has a specific local base – albeit large – in the southern states of the USA, which he draws on for his *ethos* (where do you geographically place Blair?). He has been called, by an African-American writer (Toni Morrison), 'the first black president of the United States'; he is the southern white man reformed, helping to eradicate the history of race guilt from the country. And for all the questions about his financial dealings and his sexual activities, this local *ethos* held firm. At the same time he did, according to Machiavelli, choose his vice well. Throughout his testimony to Senate on the Monica Lewinsky affair he appears to have refrained from claiming common ground with his accusers. However, this does not say to his audience that he is bad, indeed it implies that he has the sense of decency and decorum to recognise that there is a social code critical of such activity, despite the fact that many in his audience will identify with it. In other words, he presents himself as supportive of that social code, but failing, as all humans do fail from time to time. The effect of this was to encourage the audience to claim common ground with him for itself, which it showed itself keen to do.

Giving an interview directly after the Senate vote on impeachment, Clinton handled his audience in just this way and received rousing applause. The very next day he addressed an even wider audience in his State of the Union address for 1999. In the chamber seated in front of him sat many of the men and women who voted against him the day before, and seated immediately behind him were Vice-President Al Gore and Dennis Hester, the man who led the impeachment proceedings. Clinton's control of his persona was so clear that he was able to use his call to national unity as a not-so-implicit call for renewed support for his presidency and himself personally. The President declares, addressing Hester but with his back toward him, 'At your swearing in you asked us all to work together in a spirit of civility and bipartisanship. Mr Speaker let's do exactly that', and turns to shake Hester's hand. It is a gesture Hester cannot refuse to reciprocate. The look on Al Gore's face says it all; he can barely suppress a smile of astonished admiration. Clinton was a consummate Machiavellian rhetor, and I do not use the term in a derogatory manner.

THE ORATOR AND POLITICAL REPRESENTATION: ESTABLISHING COMMON CAUSE

To return briefly to the Renaissance: English commentators on political behaviour are clearly fascinated by the potential in manipulative *ethos*. There is a distinct shift in advice books from the early part of the sixteenth century, where many still want to maintain the idea of the naturally 'good' man, to the latter, where there is increasing awareness, due not only to Machiavelli but to other European commentators, of the power of rhetoric (written and orated) to sway people whether or not the orator is good or bad. The concern is intimately tied to anxiety about the rise of the merchant class, and even to their assimilation into the aristocracy. Earlier advice books assume that you can behave like a courtly person only if you are born to it. The later books recognise that, in effect, you could learn how to behave as an aristocrat even if you were only a trader: the ultimate example of deceitful *ethos*. George Puttenham, writing in *The Art of English Poesie* (1585), evades the problem by saying that English courtiers are of course good men, and only foreign ones are manipulative.[10] However, the literature abounds with examples of deceitful rhetoric and with advice on how to recognise it.

At the same time, Elizabeth I became more and more remote, to the extent that it has been argued that her government was a strictly limited monarchy.[11] In the latter part of her reign there was enormous attention to the development of the cult of Elizabeth, which should be seen not so much as a cultivation of individual *ethos* but as a solidifying of a representation of the state into a static image: nowhere more obviously found than from the portraits of the Queen painted from a cut-out representation.[12]

When Hobbes describes the state as a Leviathan which represents all the people, he is talking about a political structure that has flipped from the plausible into the absolute, by not only ignoring but also obscuring the fact that there may be alternative grounds for belief and action, depriving the individual or community of any choice of a different way of life. This is a shift of utmost importance to the effects of Ciceronian plausible *ethos*, which was intended to work within a completely different, more flexible and almost mythological, State structure. It is a shift from an *ethos* that speaks *for* us to one that speaks *at* us.

Again it is significant that during this period in England there was great social mobility, exacerbated by Henry VIII's dissolution of the monasteries. From the sixteenth into the seventeenth centuries there were increasing numbers of people gaining access to political power, and, since it was impossible to have a direct democracy because of the geography of the country as well as the sheer number of people eligible, England developed a representative democracy. The voters became 'represented' in Parliament. Central to the idea of representation was the fact that the interests of those representing and those being represented were not far apart, they had similar expectations and lifestyles. Variations in opinion were corralled into the structure of oppositional parties. The idea of a plausible *ethos* remained effective within each party, and continued to be maintained alongside the gradual formation of the absolute *ethos* of the State, or ideology.[13]

However, with the gradual extension of the franchise especially during the latter part of the nineteenth century, culminating in full voting rights in 1928 in England, the structure for this kind of rhetoric changes beyond recognition. More and more people enter the realms of the 'represented' yet those representing them often have little in common with them any more. Various strategies were developed to cope with this diversity of interest, some being rather crude like 'pork-barrel' politics, which works by promising those who vote for you some kind of preferment. But other influential strategies have focused either on the State, and issues of law and order and property, as we saw with the example of Thatcher above, or on the nation, particularly on issues of economic and military war. These two elements are of course intertwined because the definition of a citizen is one who can be called to military action in defence of the nation, and ideology defines many of the ways in which citizens are represented.

War is enormously useful to political *ethos*, and there is a cynical view that war is often maintained as a viable option because it encourages people to coalesce around a common cause and eradicate their differences. Certainly, the *ethos* of a politician such as Winston Churchill revolved around the centrality of war, and had difficulty adjusting to the different demands of the postwar period. Thatcher was commonly accused of pursuing the Falklands war partly because her political credibility was waning; in any event it did have the effect of bringing people together under the Conservative wing once more. Her *ethos* through the preceding several years was also one that exploited the imagery of war in terms of war against the Labour Party. Yet she too became a media victim, destroyed by her *ethos*, from the iron lady of 'the lady's not for turning' to the steel lady of no compassion. John Major's *ethos* was a world away from this aggressive and confrontational stance. Indeed his characterisation of his political voice was so tenuous that for a long time he was exceptionally difficult to satirise, until the cartoonist Steve Bell and some political comedians realised the potential for caricature in the bathetic – Major's apparent tendency to respond to public concern with banal solutions like the 'Cone Phone line' for motorists. Bell reduced Major to someone who always wears their underpants on the outside because they have nothing to hide. This was of course before Edwina Currie told the world of her affair with Major, to which Steve Bell replied by stuffing Major's underpants a little more generously.

THE DIFFICULTY OF THE ABSENCE OF WAR

What each of these party leaders has had to contend with is the absence of war. The issue surfaced rather starkly in the British media in 1998 when Clinton was accused of becoming involved in Iraq in order to deflect interest away from his own actions, and several respected media commentators here seemed implicitly to be suggesting that war might be a good thing to focus people's attention on their relatively high standard of living. Initially, Tony Blair had the same problem, of coalescing public opinion not around war but around peace. At the Nato-Russia summit of 1997 he said, 'Mine is the first generation able to contemplate the possibility that we may live our entire lives without going to war or sending our children to war': conveniently forgetting the Falklands war and the British involvement in the Iraq crisis of 1991, presumably because they were mistakes, wars undertaken on behalf of the British people but not with their wholehearted participation. To forge a different kind of national unity he called, in the time-honoured fashion, on law and order and protection of property. But also, because he is Labour, he had to call on issues of social concern. His response was cautious in all areas except that of the family and of personal morality, which have become central to his *ethos*. Unfortunately, the visible icon of this *ethos* was the disastrous Millennium Dome, a pantheon to the idea of a nation as a culturally unifying expression of people with similar interests in stability and property, and a similar moral agenda.

However, during the Kosovo crisis in 1999 Blair brought this *ethos* into direct combination with a rhetoric of war. In a Public Broadcasting Service interview with Jim Lehrer (23 April 1999) he described Milosevic as a 'dictator' who 'has done some very terrible things', placing his strong condemnation side by side with colloquial understatement. On the complex problems of ethnic cleansing and what he called 'racial genocide', he says directly and simply, 'We either act or we don't'. When he is questioned on his readiness to take up a warlike stance given that he has never been directly involved in war before, he again uses calculated banality, speaking of his 'very very heavy heart', and saying 'we're doing it because it is the right thing to do'. This ability to position himself as 'just another bloke' – someone saying things that your neighbour might say and saying them in a way your neighbour might say them, someone voicing opinions that could be your own – is also perceived as morally truthful. The BBC News on 23 April 1999 (18.05) refers to Blair's response to Kosovo as one expressive of his 'strong Christian convictions'.

Two years later, in the aftermath of the attacks on the World Trade Centre and the Pentagon and the failed attack on Camp David, this ability to bring together the personal with a rhetoric of war becomes more sophisticated. In Blair's address to the Labour Party conference shortly after the attacks on 1 October 2001, he draws on the absence of a specific nationally located 'enemy' and stresses the interrelation among nations all over the globe, saying, 'what has come out of this is a sense of community and international interdependence', and that the 'world community must show as much its capacity for compassion as for force'. He develops this in the speech into a brief commentary on European unity and the need for the euro: as Mark Leonard remarked in the *Observer* (14 April 2002), 11 September paved the way for the euro, with even the eurosceptic *Daily Telegraph* running the headline 'A New Currency for a New World Order'. Words such as 'community' and 'compassion' anchor the *ethos* in the personal and in 'human values'. At the same time they hide the false analogy made between the response of an individual and that of a nation. They imply a direct participation of citizens in global governance, whereas it is necessarily mediated, and not even through an elected 'representative' but through a State-implemented construct known as the 'nation'.

Significantly there is no commentary this time on his Christian perspective, which in the reading of the attacks as motivated by Islamic disenchantment with the power of the United States could have been inflammatory. This loss of an important element in his earlier *ethos* is replaced by even more emphasis on the private individual, and Blair notes, 'For people with work to do, family life to balance, mortgages to pay, careers to further, pensions to provide, the yearning is for order and stability and if it doesn't exist elsewhere, it is unlikely to exist here'. The argument, rather blatantly, suggests that war is necessary in order to maintain the stability necessary to pay one's mortgage. What is interesting is that war is no longer for the glorification of nations which in the past pitted themselves and their citizens against each other. Instead, in this global world with more nebulous 'enemies', war is undertaken by individuals in order to protect their property. The speech cleverly proposes that, far from being reduced to a cultural manifestation, the nation is a military conduit for effective action in maintaining global law and order. This is a substantial and significant development in understanding the relationship between the individual and the nation. For many of us, relations with global power are unthinking and direct, for example, if one buys a coffee from Starbucks. The implication in this speech is that the nation can function as a mediator between the individual and global power, by being the most effective way of maintaining the stability necessary for the protection of property.

The most worrying aspect of Blair's speech to the Labour Party conference in 2001 was his remarks on Africa. Following directly from his commentary on the attacks, and implicitly suggesting a connection, he speaks of the need to 'sort out' Africa. He goes on to describe Africa as a scar, saying that 'if the world as a community focused on it, we could heal it'. Even were there direct connections between the perpetrators of the attacks and 'Africa', Africa is a large and diverse continent with many countries which do not necessarily think of themselves as needing to be 'sorted out', or as being primarily the exploited victims of European imperialism. Blair may of course have been intending to draw parallels between the disaffection of those who have and those who have not in the world, especially with the upcoming summit on Africa held in the summer of 2002 on the horizon. However, the more direct implication is that we have a responsibility to pre-empt instability, if necessary to go to war with countries which 'might' put our mortgages at risk. This position informed the events of the following year during which Blair gradually came round to the support of Bush's aggressive policy toward Iraq.

Quite apart from the conflation of the represented citizen of the nation with the unrepresented member of a global polity, the idea that what defines 'representable' citizens is their ownership of a mortgage, or that this fact of their lives might outweigh moral, social, and political concerns for other people, excludes a large percentage of the populace. What about the ever-increasing number of families housed in bedsits, let alone the move to renting rather than buying? The UK is filled with people of many diverse ways of life and belief. What is intriguing is both how the rhetoric manages to lull a majority of representable people into acceptance, and, in a world of greater and supposedly desirable democratic access to all, how do the unrepresented get heard?

THE MEDIA AND DIVERSITY

While Blair has been somewhat more successful in calling on the moral majority than was Major, he still has a problem with the fact that the UK is a country of difference and diversity; after all he is the man who has *unified* the Labour Party in face of its earlier 'factionalism'. I would argue that in England the problem with difference is largely due to the media, to the position of those who own it, to its pervasiveness and to the techniques that have become common to its development. Anyone who has been interviewed for radio or television, or who has watched a discussion group on television, will know that the speakers are expected to keep what they have to say pre-digested and to the point. The medium is not there to encourage discussion or thoughtful debate. A clear indication of the rhetorical effects of this development is found in the following statement from a most helpful book by Joan Mulholland, *The Language of Negotiation* (p. 99):

> Interviews of such brevity are made understandable to their audiences, because the media utilise society's general stereotypical perceptions of the interviewee and of the interview's form and content as a framework.

This stress on the necessity for the stereotypical runs through all her advice for the interviewee, interviewer, and the interview form and content. I offer an extensive quotation, which is worth reading right the way through, as an example of problems that may occur:

An interviewer might ask such a question as 'Won't that badly affect ordinary families?', expecting everyone to understand that there is something called a family which is everywhere much the same, without questioning the assumption by asking, for example, 'How exactly do you understand the term "family"?', or 'Do you mean the single parent family or the dual parent family?' An interviewee who asked such questions, or who answered the original question with 'It depends what kind of family you mean', would not only confuse the interviewer but could also face problems with audience understanding, until such time as society generally accepts the fact that the 'family' no longer has a single meaning.

Expectations also exist in the audience's minds as to what content the interview will have, what topics will be raised, and what views will be expressed, and any deviations may be resisted as troublesome. For example, people have a standard view of a banker, and every banker is expected to look and sound the part. When confronted by a banker who differs in some way, they could miss much of what is being said while making adjustments to their mental stereotype. Such stereotyping can occur with respect to every element of the interview's content: the matters mentioned, the actions taken, the attitudes expressed, and so on.[14]

This kind of stereotyping is the culmination of plausible *ethos* production but it doesn't answer the needs of an enfranchised population that wants actively to be involved with political change. The lack of detail eviscerates the issue, denies debate, obscures the points of difficulty, and attempts to render all things understandable within the terms of the status quo. When Cicero adopted a similarly plausible *ethos*, he was speaking in a community that had already and by default of the political and legal system selected the terms on which it would argue. It was a small group with common interests, and he was communicating orally and could be responded to orally, indeed he was communicating in order that his audience would act. As he and his group learned to their cost, the exclusion of so many from access to effective government could lead only to violence – a lesson that really should have been learned by the twentieth century but people have an enormous capacity for arrogance. The effect of such plausible *ethos* in our time, where it is mediated far and wide, and where, because of the technology, its content can remain exactly the same no matter in what different arena it is repeated, tends to limit people to saying the stereotypical, the bland, the evasively duplicitous, and weakens the audience's interest in political activity. Politicians speak as though we are all the same. They speak *for* us, not *to* us. But the technology they use turns what they might say *for* us into something spoken *at* us.

What has come to be known as 'grass-roots politics' usually tries to adopt a probable *ethos*, a persuasion or rhetoric that talks to us, engages us in consensus decision-making. And, most importantly, it encourages us to value difference. The problem is, how does this politics mesh with party politics? The Liberal Democrats have attempted to deal with this through proportional representation, which is a clear response to the issue of diversity that other countries have tried. Labour in the 1980s can be seen to be experimenting with having diverse voices within one party. However, the result was a disintegration in the face of the monolithic convention of plausible *ethos* which has dominated politics for centuries. The furore over 'spin-doctors', which reached a peak during 1998 and 1999 and still lingers on, is bewildering: politicians have been 'spinning' opinion since the beginning of recorded history. The main Labour mistake was to allow the spin to become seen in a media world devoted to stereotype that justifies itself by claiming that there is no alternative to the stereotype. Nevertheless, part of the problem was that the spin came from no located place that would make sense of it. Labour had all but moved to the position where it took its own plausible *ethos* for granted: living inside the tautology.

The satirist Rory Bremner, whose work displays extraordinary awareness of rhetorical complexity, played Blair being interviewed by Jon Snow, a real-life news presenter, in the middle of his first term of office. The figure of Blair begins to argue that the British public will have to do a little better to deserve the Labour government he leads, in fact that if they don't improve substantially they'll be lucky if Labour allow them to vote for the Party, 'and then where will they be?' Bremner precisely captures the mindset that locks itself into its own view of the world, and in the process articulates one of the problems the Labour Party had during the subsequent election: they took their support for granted. The arrogance attributed to Blair in that satirical commentary surfaced in a real interview carried out just prior to the 2001 election between the Prime Minister and Jeremy Paxman, an incisive interviewer for a magazine-style television news programme 'Newsnight', which is more concerned to investigate than to present the news. Paxman has a sound rhetorical habit of asking a question in exactly the same way until he gets an answer. Were he to change the wording of the question, say in an attempt to clarify it or lead the interviewee, it would be an invitation to compare the two versions of the question and jump through the inevitable gaps. However, having already established this reputation in an interview with Michael Howard, in which Paxman asked him the same question fourteen times, he proceeds in one section of the interview with Blair to ask him the same question seven times or at least ten with variation, as Blair attempts to rephrase the question in a manner that would more appropriately suit his recent policies.[15]

The interview (part of which is transcribed as an appendix to this essay) contains many workmanlike displays of debate technique. There is evidence that Blair may be more used to open debate, and not as familiar with tight timing. He gives himself time to think by repeating phrases, and tries to control the direction of the interview by sending the question back again with variation and a smile. But these are both also helpful colloquial techniques that contribute to his genial persona. It is always easy to spot his weaknesses because his syntax collapses, with for example 'I don't really – it's not – it's it's not no it's not . . .', or 'the gap between those who, the person who earns the most . . .' This latter example is also interesting for a fluid confusion between the sounds of 'earns', 'owes', and 'owns' that trips up the repetition of what one assumes is 'earns' in the second half of the sentence.

But both Paxman and Blair are experienced in the genre, and fairly well-matched. If Paxman repeats a question, Blair keeps repeating his answer – in this sequence to the surreal end that he shifts the ground by finally suggesting that he is answering in 'the way I choose to answer'. Paxman catches up and accuses him, 'Prime Minister with respect people see you asked an absolutely straightforward question and they see you not answering it', to which Blair replies, equivocating, 'Yeah because I choose to answer it in the way I am answering it'. The casual 'Yeah' in the reply admits the problem, but the rest slides away into tautology. Paxman finally says, 'You're answering another question', and this change of tactic allows Blair to re-structure the framework. He takes charge of the debate by implying that he is clarifying previous evasion, 'Well, answering actually in the way that I want to answer it, and I'll tell you why I want to answer it in this way . . .', merely to go on to restate his previous answer. Paxman draws the topic to a close shortly after with the tart comment, 'Prime Minister I assume you want to be Prime Minister

I just want to be an interviewer [Blair: OK all right] so can we stick to that arrangement? ...'

What is interesting is that Rory Bremner subsequently did a satire on this interview, again with Jon Snow, again with a perceptive stripping away and exposure of rhetorical strategy. He has the actor playing Alistair Campbell, Blair's assistant, say, 'If he keeps on asking you the same question, keep giving him the same answer'. This time, however, he sustained a new tack on the character of Blair, underlining his propensity for naivety.[16] To date naivety, or perhaps 'transparent honesty', is Blair's well-chosen 'vice', one with which his public can empathise and one that is always on the cusp of moral simplicity. He will not only be able to get away with this vice unless he falls into egregious error, but it works to his advantage.

Not only does the media stereotype, but it is also pervasive. I have watched a kind of political strategy which I imagine was in effect until the twentieth century in the UK, within the context of First Nations politics in Canada. The signal difference is that nineteenth-century political communities excluded up to 95 per cent of the population, and the First Nations communities exclude few of their members. First Nations people, particularly those with strong band organisations and in non-urban areas such as the Yukon Territories, often actively agree to be represented. Sometimes they select an advocate, usually at community level where the political interchanges are varied and where story is frequently a medium for persuasion. If story is used to persuade, then the audience will construct what they need from it, and should, if educated in their own culture, recognise the limitations and extents of that story. In other words the rhetoric of story is more likely, but not necessarily, going to invite a probable *ethos*. When those selected people go to district, provincial, or national assemblies, they will interpret the story depending on what is needed by that grouping, probably rephrasing into the structure of agonistic debate expected within the political discourse of western nation-states.[17] And if they speak in smaller groups, in the small circles of government, they will speak differently again.

What is intriguing here is that the recording media are not necessarily present at many of these gatherings, so there is no way that the speakers can be called to account for inconsistency. The politicians can be all things to all people by being different things to different people, and with no loss of credibility. Indeed inconsistency is an inappropriate term to bring to credibility here, for the whole point of probable *ethos* is to work on probably-the-best outcome rather than to prescribe an outcome from the beginning that will inevitably hit snags and resistances. That work can be learned from, and the lessons taken back into other groupings. A remarkably similar description was made by Edwina Currie of Major's political style within the party itself. She noted that

> It dawned on us later that he managed to impress each of us that he agreed with whoever he was talking to. That's where the slipperiness comes in. Teddy Taylor told me [Major] had said to him, 'I think I ought to tell you in confidence that I'm the biggest Eurosceptic in the cabinet'. And I tell you what, [Major] told us pro-Europeans how glad he was that we'd formed our group to help, and he was really pleased about it. It was absolutely breathtaking. (*Guardian*, 2:7, 4 October 2002)

In her analysis he did this kind of politicking precisely because he had no policies, and was therefore not accountable. The distinction here is that, although credibility is not an issue, accountability is. It is significant however, that this rhetorical technique only works in particularised locations. One of the essential ethical functions of the media is to insist on accountability. However, in England, the media also capitalise on the fact of political representation which implies similarity rather than difference. They record and replay the politician to the whole country, even though politicians have to respond to the needs of different communities. The media turn what they say into truths rather than probabilities, and all absolute truths are only the reverse face of the plausible.

But there is a third and more invidious problem with the media: that the business of mediation is effectively in the hands of people outside the community, the government, even the nation. Look at the sparring in 1999 of Rupert Murdoch and Tony Blair over the euro: Blair is said to have asked privately for Murdoch to temper the response of the *Sun* newspaper, which Murdoch owns, but Murdoch, who was and is well known for his anti-European feelings, refused to do so. Murdoch's *ethos* was exceptionally powerful, particularly because it was unseen and mediated through the press, that fourth estate of a State whose *ethos* obliterates the possibility of being aware of the sources of power and the potential for alternatives. The implication is that a rhetoric of difference would have enormous impact on a State ideology and its interconnections with the transnational, particularly on the accumulation of private property.

PROBLEMS WITH CONTEMPORARY
POLITICAL RHETORIC

First, how do we connect the politics of community, using a rhetoric of difference, to government which uses a rhetoric of sameness? What strategies could bridge the gap?

Second, how do we accommodate a politics of diversity with different voices? And how do we choose from among those different voices when developing government strategy, so that we remain responsive and responsible to that difference?

Third, how do we connect politics with global finance, the rhetoric of government which is at least visible if stereotypical, to the rhetoric of the transnational corporation, which is frequently invisible? How do we relate the one which is responsible to its people to the other which is responsible to no one? [18]

The rhetoric of the government and of the State used to be quite close, largely for economic reasons. These days they have separated somewhat, partly again for economic reasons. Whereas post-Renaissance representations of citizens within a nation and the representations for subjects of the State were interconnected, now it's difficult to say how far representation of citizens carries weight when individuals are affected by changes in the State due to transnational rather than national issues. This may be the reason that the rhetoric of government has moved into the private: the private always used to be separate from public government, but increasingly it's become an issue. Maybe western nations recognise that the family is the basic unit of economy and of social stability in the nation, and therefore need to maintain it. Maybe States, both national and global, affirm this on one hand but subtly disrupt it on the other.

What we need is a new rhetor for our age. Perhaps the term 'advocacy' [19] will be to the twenty-first century what 'inclusion' was for Cicero, or what 'representation' was for Hobbes. At the moment the Ciceronian *ethos* that speaks for us rather than to us is being overtaken by a Hobbesian *ethos* that speaks at us – and this at a time when we have moved on and need rhetorical strategies for dialogue, people speaking to each other, to make difference an active agent in the political world.

APPENDIX: BBC INTERVIEW BETWEEN JEREMY PAXMAN AND TONY BLAIR, APRIL 2001

P: Do you think that a company can make, er, too much in profits?

B: In what sense do you mean?

P: Do you think profits can ever be unjustifiably large?

B: I think they can be if they are monopoly profits which is why we for example taxed the privatised utilities, got the excess profits and put that to work in the new deal, but I don't believe for example that if you're acting in a competitive market it's the job of government to come along and tell a company that they're making too much profit.

P: Do you believe that an individual can earn too much money?

B: I don't really – it's not – it's it's not no it's not a view that I have, what do you mean that we should sort of cap someone's income?

P: Umm ...

B: Not really no why what's the point. We could spend ages trying to stop the the sort of highest paid earners earning the money and actually in an international market today you'd probably just drive them abroad. What does that matter? The important thing is to level up those people who don't have opportunity in our society.

P: But where is the justice in taxing someone who earns £34,000 a year which is about enough to cover a mortgage on a one-bedroom flat in outer London at the same rate as you tax someone who earns £34 million?

B: Because ... Well the person who earns £34 million is they are paying the top rate of tax on £34 million will pay far more tax than the person on 34,000.

P: I'm asking you about the rate of tax.

B: Yeah I know, but what I'm saying to you is that the rate is less important in this instance than the overall amount of tax that people would pay but you know what would happen, if you go back to the times [cut in transcript] ... you know what would happen [cut in transcript] ...

P: Where's the justice in it?

B: Well ... The justice, you see, when you say to me 'where's the justice in that', the justice for me is concentrated on lifting the incomes of those who don't have a decent income. I don't see, it's not a burning ambition for me to make sure that David Beckham earns less money.

P: But Prime Minister the gap between rich and poor has widened since you while you've been in office.

B: Well actually a lot of those figures incidentally are based on a couple of years ago before many of the measures we took came into effect. But the lowest-income families in this country are benefiting from the government their incomes are rising up. Now the fact that you have some people at the top end who [P: benefit more] well fine if they're earning more well fine they pay their taxes.

P: Is it acceptable for the gap between rich and poor to widen?

B: It is acceptable for those people on lower incomes to have their incomes raised. It is unacceptable that they're not given the chances. To me the key thing is not whether the gap between those who, the person who earns the most in the country and the person who owes/earns the least ... whether that gap is different, or not ...

P: So it *is* acceptable for the gap to widen between rich and poor?

B: It is not acceptable for poor people not to be given the changes they need in life. My task ...

P: That's not my question.

B: I know it's not, it's the way I choose to answer it. Because if you end up going after those people who are the most wealthy in society what you actually end up doing is in fact not even helping those at the bottom end. Now ...

P: So the straight qu ... So in fact the answer to the straight question is it acceptable for the gap between rich and poor to get wider, the answer you're saying is yes.

B: No it's not what I'm saying, what I'm saying is I'm saying that my task is ...

P: Well you're not saying no.

B: But I don't think that is the issue. I think the issue ...

P: You may not think it's the issue, but it is the question, with the greatest of respect.

B: It may be the question ...

P: It is OK for the gap to get wider?

B: It may be the question but it's not the way I choose to answer it. The way I choose to answer it is to say the job of government is to make sure those at the bottom end get the chances they don't have.

P: Prime Minister with respect people see you asked an absolutely straight-forward question and they see you not answering it.

B: Yeah because I choose to answer it in the way I am answering it.

P: But you're not answering ...

B: I am answering it. What I'm saying is that the most important thing [P: the question is] is to level up and not level down.

P: The question is, is it acceptable for the gap between rich and poor to get bigger?

B: What I'm saying to you is that in fact whether the very richest person ends up becoming richer, the issue is actually whether the poorest person is given the chance they ... they don't have.

P: I understand what you're saying but the question is about the gap ...

B: Yes I know what the question is, I'm choosing to answer it in my way rather than yours.

P: But you're not answering it.

B: I am, I'm answering the way that I believe it's the role of government ...

P: You're answering another question.

B: Well, answering actually in the way that I want to answer it, and I'll tell you why I want to answer it in this way, because if you end up saying no ... actually my task is to stop the person earning a lot of money, earning a lot of money, you waste all your time and energy taking some money off the people who are very wealthy, in actual fact in today's world they'll probably simply move elsewhere and make their money. And what you're not asking me about but which would be a far more fruitful line of endeavour, is what are you doing for the poorest people in our society to give them a boost.

P: OK well let's talk a little bit about tax. You have promised ...

B: Well why don't we talk about the poorest in society and what we're actually doing for them?

P: Prime Minister I assume you want to be Prime Minister I just want to be an interviewer [B: OK all right] so can we stick to that arrangement? ...

NOTES

1 The differentiation between plausible and probable rhetoric occurs throughout the history of recorded rhetorics. The specific words used in this essay have been chosen because they are the keywords used during the Renaissance period, a time when many of our current political structures in the West were being formed. For more detail on the strategies see L. Hunter, *Critiques of Knowing: Situated Textuality in Science, Computing and the Arts* (London, 1999), especially chapters 3 and 4.

2 Aristotle elaborates on this in *Topica*; for a discussion see L. Hunter, *Critiques of Knowing*, chapter 1; see also L. Hunter, 'Ideology as the ethos of the nation state', *Rhetorica*, 14 (1996), 197–229.

3 N. Wood, *Cicero's Social and Political Thought* (London, 1988), pp. 33–5.

4 Cicero, *De oratore* 2.42.178, 43.182, trans E.W. Sutton and H. Rackham (Cambridge, Mass., and London, 1942), I.325, 327.

5 H. Gotoff, *Cicero's Caesarian Speeches* (London, 1993), p. xii.

6 See in particular the chapter on the 'Art of Politics' in Wood, *Cicero's Social and Political Thought*.

7 P. Prill, 'Cicero in theory and practice', *Rhetorica*, 4 (1986), 94–5.

8 J. Lewis, 'The framework of political television', in J. Hawthorn (ed.), *Propaganda, Persuasion and Polemic* (London, 1987), pp. 157–71.

9 N. Machiavelli, *The Prince* (New York, 1992), p. 40.

10 For a general discussion of these issues see L. Hunter, 'Civic rhetoric in England 1560–1630', in F. Ames Lewes (ed.), *Sir Thomas Gresham and Gresham College: Studies in the Intellectual History of London in the Sixteenth and Seventeenth Centuries* (Aldershot, 1999), pp. 88–104.

11 P. Collinson, quoted in D. Norbrook, 'Rhetoric, ideology and the Elizabethan world picture', in P. Mack (ed.), *Renaissance Rhetoric* (London, 1994), pp. 140–64 (p. 147).

12 See the Gallery Guide to 'Images of Women', Leeds City Art Galleries (1991) and associated commentary by G. Pollock.

13 See Hunter, *Critiques of Knowing*, chapter 1.

14 J. Mulholland, *The Language of Negotiation* (London, 1991), p. 100.

15 BBC interview, April 2001, transcription the author's own.

16 'Bremner, Bird and Fortune', Channel Four, Election Special, May 2001.

17 See L. Hunter, 'Difference as equality: stories in/of Nunavut', plenary lecture to the London conference on Canadian Studies (forthcoming in *Canadian Studies*).

18 See L. Hunter, 'Listening to situated textuality: working on differentiated public voices', *Feminist Theory*, special issue on 'Gendering Ethics/The Ethics of Gender', ed. L. Hogan and S. Roseneil, 2 (2001), 205–18.

19 For one discussion of this see N. Yuval Davis, *Gender and Nation* (London, 1997).

Glossary

Amplificatio: expansive use of words and phrases, frequently by pairing synonyms and antonyms.

Antimetabole: repetition of words in successive clauses, with the order reversed, e.g. 'ask not what your country can do for you; ask what you can do for your country' (J. F. Kennedy).

Antitheton: proof of a proposition or a composition constructed of opposites.

Apostrophe: interruption of the speech to address a person or thing either present or absent.

Assembly: see *Ecclesia*

Boule (Council): at Athens, an executive body of five hundred male citizens over the age of thirty, selected by lot, which prepared business for the Assembly and carried out its decisions.

Dispositio: organisation of the material in a speech; in classical rhetoric, the second of the five 'faculties' of the orator (usually translated as 'arrangement').

Ecclesia (Assembly): the Athenian legislative body, made up of adult male citizens.

Elocutio: style; in classical rhetoric, the third of the five 'faculties' of the orator, regularly divided into three kinds (plain, middle, and grand).

Ethos: the portrayal of the orator's character through the medium of the speech; in classical rhetoric, one of the three primary means of persuasion or rhetorical proof (*entechnos pistis*).

Exordium, proemium: the first (introductory) part of an oration, which seeks to make the audience attentive and well-disposed towards the speaker (*captatio benevolentiae*).

Fasces: in ancient Rome, bunches of rods and axes, carried by lictors (*q. v.*). The *fasces* were symbolic of the magistrates' power of corporal punishment.

Inventio: the discovery and treatment of appropriate arguments; in classical rhetoric, the first of the five 'faculties' of the orator.

Lictors: in ancient Rome, attendants on magistrates who carried their symbols of power, the *fasces* (*q. v.*).

Meiosis: a form of detraction or belittling, often achieved by means of a single word or adjective (e.g. 'the little woman').

Memoria: memory, especially the training of memory by means of mnemonic systems and techniques; in classical rhetoric, the fourth of the five 'faculties' of the orator.

Peroration: the concluding part of an oration which in classical rhetoric was thought especially appropriate for strong emotional appeal (*pathos*).

Proemium: see *Exordium*.

Pronuntiatio: the use of voice and gesture in the practice of speaking; in classical rhetoric, the last of the five 'faculties' of the orator (usually translated as 'delivery').

Sophist: a teacher of wisdom in the arts of public life, especially rhetoric.

Thesmothetai (sing. *Thesmothetes*): the six junior archons (magistrates) at Athens, who had a primarily judicial role.

Topos: literally a 'place', the word *topos* carries a range of meanings, including strategies of argument useful in all genres of speech and, as aids to composition, commonplace passages that can be used in a variety of contexts.